PROTECTING
YOUR ORGANIZATION'S
TAX-EXEMPT
STATUS

Mark Bookman

PROTECTING
YOUR ORGANIZATION'S
TAX-EXEMPT
STATUS

A Guide for
Nonprofit
Managers

Jossey-Bass Publishers · San Francisco

GRACE COLLEGE LIBRARY
WINONA LAKE, INDIANA

Copyright © 1992 by Jossey-Bass Inc., Publishers, 350 Sansome Street, San Francisco, California 94104. Copyright under International, Pan American, and Universal Copyright Conventions. All rights reserved. No part of this book may be reproduced in any form—except for brief quotation (not to exceed 1,000 words) in a review or professional work—without permission in writing from the publishers.

For sales outside the United States contact Maxwell Macmillan International Publishing Group, 866 Third Avenue, New York, New York 10022

Printed on acid-free paper and manufactured in the United States of America

 The paper used in this book meets the State of California require-
ments for recycled paper (50 percent recycled waste, including 10 percent post-consumer waste), which are the strictest guidelines for recycled paper currently in use in the United States.

Library of Congress Cataloging-in-Publication Data

Bookman, Mark, date
    Protecting your organization's tax-exempt status : a guide for nonprofit managers / Mark Bookman.
      p.   cm.—(A Joint publication of the Jossey-Bass nonprofit sector series and the Jossey-Bass higher and adult education series)
    Includes bibliographical references and index.
    ISBN 1-55542-432-5
    1. Corporations, Nonprofit—United States. 2. Taxation, Exemption from—United States.   I. Title.   II. Series: Jossey-Bass nonprofit sector series.   III. Series: Jossey-Bass higher and adult education series.
HD2769.2.U6B66   1992
658.15'3—dc 20   91-36572
                                                              CIP

FIRST EDITION
HB Printing   10 9 8 7 6 5 4 3 2 1   *Code 9230*

A joint publication in

The Jossey-Bass
Nonprofit Sector Series

and

The Jossey-Bass
Higher and Adult Education Series

Contents

Contents

Part Four: Guidelines for Action

Preface

Government policy for nonprofit organizations is in flux. The past decade has seen all levels of government engage in unprecedented questioning of the tax exemptions and other privileges that are extended to the nonprofit sector. Many factors contribute to the perpetuation of this questioning environment. Among the most significant are the growth of the service sector as a major element of our nation's changing economy; the growth of the nonprofit sector; the continuing evolution of the nonprofit sector in terms of organizational form, service goals, and income sources; the increased competition between the for-profit and nonprofit sectors; government officials' more questioning attitude toward the government's historical policy for nonprofit organizations; and the need for all levels of government to find new funding sources. Two major economic changes underlay these factors: the need to reduce the federal deficit and, since 1980, the reemergence of free-market concepts as the approach that drives much of the federal government's policies.

Since the mid 1980s, the questioning of tax-exempt organizations has set the stage for major changes in government policy toward nonprofit organizations. This questioning is seen in the Subcommittee on Oversight hearings, increasing state legislative interest in the concept of unfair competition, increasing activism in the courts on issues of unfair competition and property tax exemption litigation, as well as a far more aggressive attitude by many administrative entities in questioning the actions, rights, and privileges of exempt organizations. This activity has clearly made the role of a manager or board member of a nonprofit organization far more complex than in the past. Although there is an extensive literature available to individuals who need to gain a better grasp of the legal and economic issues underlying these government actions, its form makes it difficult to use. Much of the literature is either very technical or written from too narrow a perspective for general use. Thus many persons involved with nonprofit organizations, as well as elected and appointed officials working to determine government policy, have found it essentially impossible to gain a comprehensive understanding of the laws that generally have an impact on nonprofits as they are now written, let alone what would occur if existing policy were altered. It is this difficulty that prompted the writing of this book.

Based upon my personal experience, it is clear that most nonprofit managers do not understand the current law and have no game plan for either complying with it or dealing with calls for change to the special tax treatment now enjoyed by nonprofits. Yet more and more managers are beginning to recognize they can no longer avoid these matters. Professional associations that represent various segments of the nonprofit community are paying increasing attention to such issues. If nothing else motivates individual managers and boards to address these questions, the intention of the federal government to markedly increase the auditing of these organizations, as well as the growing "war stories" shared by colleagues who have had to deal with audits, state unfair competition legislation, and litigation, will put taxation issues on the agenda of most nonprofit organizations.

For more than two decades I have been associated with a diverse set of nonprofit organizations as a board member, a chief executive officer, a midlevel manager, and a volunteer. Because of my training in the law, my inclination has been to track legal issues that have an impact on nonprofit organizations. During my career I have been a defendant in an unfair competition suit (which was dismissed at the pleading stage), successfully responded to claims of unfair competition from local merchants, presented written testimony on behalf of an international association to the Subcommittee on Oversight, and made numerous presentations and written extensively on these topics.

At the urging of Michael Olivas, the director of the Institute for Higher Education Law and Governance at the University of Houston, I spent much of the 1989–1990 academic year engaged in further research on taxation issues. My position as a visiting scholar at the institute allowed me to correspond with close to 100 organizations and individuals. Those contacted represent the full spectrum of opinion on this subject area. My research initially led to the development of a successful short course and coursebook taught at Rice University in the spring of 1990. Since joining the faculty at Lee College, the University of Judaism, I have continued this research.

The Purpose and Uniqueness of This Book

The literature that currently exists tends to be written from a strong advocacy perspective. This allows one to make strong philosophical statements, but it does little to assist in either developing sound government policy or helping those who run nonprofit organizations to develop a means to meld these issues into what most managers and board members believe is an already overcrowded agenda. Although I am an advocate for the nonprofit sector, my viewpoint as a manager and an attorney has never been that this sector is infallible. For example, in previous writings I have strongly advocated the need for this sector to strengthen its efforts at self-policing and to ensure that all reasonable steps are taken to assist all nonprofit organizations to act in full compliance with the law.

To preserve the tax-exempt status of legitimate nonprofit organizations is the underlying goal of this book. To accomplish this, there is an extensive review of the arguments that support the current structure of government policy, as well as the arguments that are being presented by advocates for change. Managers and directors of nonprofits must gain a clear understanding of current law at the federal, state, and local levels, including existing statutes, administrative interpretations, and judicial decisions. Because of the unique role voluntary organizations have played in our nation since colonial times, it is important that those involved with nonprofit organizations, as well as those involved in the current debate, fully understand the rationales for government policy as it now stands. This is a second goal of *Protecting Your Organization's Tax-Exempt Status.*

Many of the existing statutory and regulatory schemes for nonprofit organizations are based on actions taken near the turn of this century. Although there have been some changes in government policy in response to the evolution of the nonprofit sector, this policy has not kept pace with the changes in the nonprofit community. It is clear that change in the current legal scheme is in the process of happening, due either to legislative action or to the judiciary's needs to develop usable standards for responding to increasing litigation on unfair competition and the awarding of tax exemptions.

It is imperative that those involved in the nonprofit sector fully understand what may occur. To develop this understanding, examples of statutory changes that have recently occurred or are currently under serious consideration, as well as recent judicial decisions, government audits, and successful action plans by a variety of nonprofit organizations, will be reviewed. This information is presented in order to assist each organization in developing its own action plan.

The uniqueness of *Protecting Your Organization's Tax-Exempt Status* is that it addresses all three levels of government: federal, state, and local. Additionally, it provides a compendium of successful strategies used by a diverse set of nonprofits. The book provides sufficient detail to give someone who advises a nonprofit organization a quality overview, while also providing board members and managers with comprehensive information that will enable them to understand current legal requirements and potential ramifications of proposed changes in the current legal scheme. Additionally, the book provides extensive information on how to prepare and respond to an audit, and how to develop and implement a successful plan to address political and legal challenges.

This book also forthrightly reviews areas that the nonprofit sector must address if it is to avoid external regulation. Specifically, the book discusses the need to develop standards and self-regulation for individual segments of the sector, such as higher education, voluntary hospitals, and recreation/community centers. In the same vein, it addresses the possible need to reconsider, and perhaps curtail, certain income-producing ventures.

To assist the reader in understanding judicial decisions, there is a set of resources on federal and state cases. Resource D lists IRS advisory opinions by topic. Within the body of the book, Chapters Five and Nine are devoted to applying the substantive materials to specific settings. These discussions are intended to show the reader how each level and branch of government may act toward specific types of nonprofit organizations. Finally, an extensive bibliography is provided so that the reader can pursue items of particular interest.

Audience

The primary audience for *Protecting Your Organization's Tax-Exempt Status* includes current managers of nonprofit organizations and those who desire to assume these positions. As an attorney, I engage in possible malpractice when I am not fully prepared on issues that have an impact on my client. Similarly, if a manager of a nonprofit organization does not fully grasp the current legal tax scheme, the potential risks of substantive change in this scheme and the immediate need to implement an aggressive action plan amounts to "malpractice." Those who sit on governing boards and those who provide professional advice to these boards should have a full command of the information, strategies, and concepts presented in the following pages.

Those elected officials, staff, and appointed officials who have the responsibility of developing and enforcing government policy will also find this book useful because it presents a full overview of government policy at all levels of government today, as well as the historical rationale for and development of these policies.

A third set of readers includes the leadership of our nation's for-profit community. All too often, its members tend to oversimplify the other sectors of the economy. There is much misinformation regarding what organizations current laws do tax, as well as on limits on other privileges of nonprofits. Much of this sector has sat on the sidelines in the recent debate, and yet all for-profits will be affected if those advocating change are fully successful. Changes currently being proposed by some parts of the for-profit sector would significantly alter our nation's service delivery system. How this may affect the economy, access to services, and the potential need to increase government's role in providing domestic services needs to be fully evaluated by the entire for-profit community.

I have reviewed business and economics textbooks as well as the writings of a wide range of theorists on the topic of taxation of nonprofit organizations, and I rarely find comprehensive consideration of the many issues involved in multilevel government policy for nonprofits. In this book, my aim has been to merge my practical experience as a manager with my legal training and academic research efforts. These multiple perspectives allow for a very different review of how current law actually works, the practical effect that proposed changes may have, and the actions nonprofits can reasonably engage in to challenge current government policy and increased government audit activities. It is my view that fellow researchers, theorists, and instructors in areas affected by the taxation of nonprofit organizations will find my perspective to be of assistance in their own analysis of these increasingly complex public policy issues. Similarly, those teaching in disciplines affected by nonprofits' tax treatment should seriously consider the use of this book in their courses in order to present a more holistic analysis of the issues. The growth of the service sector and the concomitant growth of the nonprofit sector means that appropriate courses in business, political science, public administration, economics, and law can no longer ignore the issues that arise from increased competition between the nonprofit and for-profit sectors of our economy.

Organization of the Book

Protecting Your Organization's Tax-Exempt Status is divided into four parts. Part One places the taxation and unfair competition issues in context. The reader is given some background on the impact of the federal deficit, the embracing of privatization theories by many government officials, and the changing attitude of government officials toward the nonprofit sector. There is also a discussion on the multiple economic and sociological factors that emerged in the 1980s and forever altered the role of the nonprofit sector within the economy as a whole.

Chapter One offers an overview of the arguments articulated by both the advocates for substantive change and those supporting the continuation of our nation's present approach to nonprofit groups. This chapter concludes with a general review of how current tax law applies to the nonprofit sector, the lack of agreement on the meaning of key concepts (for example, what is "unfair competition"?), and the need to develop interdisciplinary models based on quality data to determine what our nation's future policy direction should be.

Chapter Two gives the reader a historical perspective on government policy toward nonprofit organizations. The chapter focuses on the federal level, since this is where much of the underlying policy thrust for all levels of government has occurred, and it shows how periodic changes have been made to our federal tax codes in order to address changes in the nonprofit sector and attempts by some to misuse the sector's tax advantages. Equally important, Chapter Two discusses the reasons why tax privileges have been granted to certain organizations. It then gives information on the range of organizations that are granted exempt status. The last segment of Chapter Two introduces the unrelated business income tax.

Part Two provides an in-depth look at the Internal Revenue Code sections that apply to the taxation of nonprofits and the behaviors of the branches of the federal government. Chapter Three begins with a review of the elements required to gain exempt status initially and the actions required of exempt organizations to maintain this status. Specific examples from a broad range of nonprofit organizations are used to illuminate the behaviors that will ensure the denial of tax exemption, the need for exactness in all organization documents and actions, and how the Internal Revenue Service (IRS) and courts have developed definitions and tests for the many ambiguous terms in the Internal Revenue Code.

The process for determining which income generated by an exempt organization is not taxable and which income is unrelated and therefore taxable comes next in Chapter Three. This review first provides a comprehensive discussion of what constitutes unrelated business income, and then it discusses the major factors that exclude certain income from being taxed. Here, too, many examples that look at both specific behavior forms (political activity) and generic income-generating actions (leasing space) are used. The remainder of Chapter Three examines the fragmentation test, convenience exception, and political activity. These topics are reviewed here because of their major impact on federal taxation of potentially exempt organizations.

In looking at the many specific rules contained in the Internal Revenue Code, the goal is to provide the reader with as clear an understanding as possible of how the courts and the IRS resolve a given issue. Some of the examples in this and subsequent chapters show that as exempt organizations develop new behaviors, there may well be disagreement within the courts, between the courts and the IRS, between Congress and these other government entities, and within the IRS itself as to what government policy should be.

In Chapter Four we move into a discussion of the many technical and philosophical exceptions to the general unrelated business income tax provisions. I have made no attempt to present all of the details of these rules; instead, my aim is to provide readers with enough information so that they have a general understanding of the issues and their applicability to individual organizations. Therefore, in Chapter Four, I discuss the leasing rules, income from advertising, joint ventures, dual use facilities, and a number of other areas.

To assist the reader in applying the information provided in Chapters Two to Four, Chapter Five approaches the Internal Revenue Code from the perspective of particular types of organizations. The areas of education and voluntary hospitals are covered in the greatest detail. Among the other types of organizations reviewed are religious organizations, museums, recreational associations, trade associations, and the Underwriters' Laboratory, Inc.

Since the Congressional hearings in 1987 and 1988 there has been much speculation on possible changes to the unrelated business income tax. Chapter Six reviews those items that have gained the most serious attention.

In Part Three, the book shifts its focus to state and local issues. Chapter Seven discusses unfair competition and activity at the state level, beginning with a comprehensive review of the unfair competition debate. The chapter also includes extensive information on the aims of the Business Coalition for Fair Competition and a discussion of the coalition's proposed model bill on unfair competition. Much of this chapter is dedicated to the various types of activity now occurring at the state level: legislative, judicial, and political pressure. The chapter concludes by first discussing the proactive responses of some parts of the nonprofit community and then presenting what the future may bring.

Chapter Eight looks at local government, with most of the focus on property tax exemptions. The chapter begins with a review of litigation in this area, as well as litigation on exemptions from other local taxes. This information sets the stage for a discussion on the types of property tax exemption statutes that have been developed by the various states. Recognizing the desperate need of local government entities to find new income sources, this chapter offers information on options other than altering current tax exemptions that nonprofits and local government might pursue in concert. Specific examples are given of joint efforts in a variety of states, as well as the growth of the concept of fees in lieu of taxes.

Litigation in the area of property tax exemption has occurred almost since the first state exemption was granted. The remainder of Chapter Eight focuses on the most recent litigation and the emergence of judicially created multipart tests. The latter has happened because judges need to have some type of clear yardstick to use in this type of litigation. In many ways, these tests are being developed because the nonprofit sector has failed to develop its own standards and state legislatures have failed to modernize property tax exemption statutes.

Chapter Nine contains a set of case studies that look at dif-

ferent components of the nonprofit sector. It includes both exam-
inations of specific large segments of the sector (higher education,
YMCAs, and voluntary hospitals) and a detailed review of a typical
controversy between a single, large nonprofit organization and its
host community. These case studies meld statutory law, litigation,
judicially created tests, the use of political pressure, and the con-
frontational behaviors of various parties to discuss what is currently
occurring.

The two chapters of Part Four provide practical information
and make a few suggestions for the future. Chapter Ten addresses
the issue of having each nonprofit organization develop an action
plan to ensure compliance with all existing laws and regulations,
as well as to meet any challenges to tax exemption. There is extensive discussion of how an organization should prepare for, and
behave during, a government audit. There is also detailed advice on
how an organization can proceed to develop and implement a comprehensive action plan. Recognizing the diversity in the size and
nature of exempt organizations, this chapter concludes with the
rationale of the suggestions' applicability to all organizations.

Chapter Eleven concludes the book with a brief discussion of
how all segments of the economy should proceed in the future. Here
we again address the need for the nonprofit sector to examine the
development of standards and self-regulation, as well as for the for-
profit sector to more fully analyze the total outcomes of what some
of its members are proposing. The chapter also looks at what futurists predict will be the growing role of an even more diverse
nonprofit community in the next century.

The resources and references of this book are also of importance to the reader. The resources were developed to allow readers
to quickly identify case law and IRS opinions that are of interest
to them, as well as to assist readers in pursuing research on specific
items. Similarly, the references are intentionally quite extensive and
include writings from all perspectives. Readers are encouraged to
use them to pursue specific areas of interest.

A Note of Caution

Many of the legal issues covered in *Protecting Your Organization's
Tax-Exempt Status* are in the "gray" area. In some situations, different courts have come to opposite decisions on the same issue.

Some of the areas discussed are currently under review by legislative and regulatory bodies. It is very difficult to generalize, particularly at state and local levels, so the reader is urged to use the information provided in this book as a guide. But on matters of specific legal interpretation, the reader must gain advice from competent legal counsel and tax consultants.

Does Nonprofit Equal Tax Exempt?

Technically speaking, a nonprofit organization need not also be a tax-exempt organization. As will be reviewed in the chapters that discuss the federal level, the Internal Revenue Code provides specific conditions that must be met for an organization to gain an exemption from federal income tax. Not all nonprofit organizations meet these requirements.

"Nonprofit" is a state-level legal concept. Each state government has established its definition of a nonprofit organization. Although there is a set of generic requirements for nonprofit status that applies in most jurisdictions, the exact application of these requirements differs in individual states. Similarly, each state may have additional requirements for an organization to meet to attain nonprofit status. This same individuality of approach by jurisdiction applies to local property tax exemptions.

For ease of writing, the term *nonprofit organization* is used throughout this book in a broad, generic way. The determination of whether a specific nonprofit organization is exempt from a particular tax or covered by an unfair competition statute is based on the laws applicable to that single issue.

Acknowledgments

This book would not have been possible without the many people and organizations who have responded to my requests for advice and assistance. In the initial stages of my research, letters requesting information were sent to close to 100 individuals and organizations. The advice, encouragement, and assistance of persons involved with nonprofit organizations and small businesses have greatly contributed to my aims. As you read the book and review the references, some of these contributors will become obvious. A few individuals and organizations went beyond simply responding to my letter of inquiry and were particularly helpful. In no particular order, these persons and organizations were John Francis; the Catholic Health Association; Dan R. Mastromarco, assistant chief counsel for tax policy of the U.S. Small Business Administration; J. David Seay, vice president and counsel for the United Hospital Fund; the YMCA of the United States; the National Association of College Stores; Larry L. Mathis, president of the Methodist Hospital system; the National Association of Retail Druggists; Harvey Goodfriend; and the Business Coalition for Fair Competition.

A number of people have been of particular assistance in this book's production. But for the urging of Michael Olivas it is likely I would not have attempted this project. His moral support, as well as the access to legal materials and to the parties involved in these issues gained by my status as a visiting scholar, was indispensable. For the materials copied and many letters typed on my behalf, as well as prompt response to my need for case citations, I am indebted to Debra Easter, the office manager at the Institute for Higher Education Law and Government. Additionally, the staff at the Rice University Office of Continuing Studies and Special Programs provided critical assistance in my efforts to complete the coursebook (which served as the initial draft of this book) for my short course offered on their campus.

I am also indebted to the support given me by the University of Judaism. Even though I have only recently joined the staff, both the senior administration and my faculty colleagues have given me strong support and encouragement as I struggled to find the time to complete the many last details needed to bring this book to publication.

Finally, I would like to thank my close friend Fred Henderson and my wife, Dena, who assisted by proofreading various drafts, by typing the initial draft, and by carrying out the many mundane tasks needed to complete publication.

This book itself is dedicated to my parents, Barbara and Milford "Bud" Bookman, who raised me to have a commitment to all of humankind.

Agoura Hills, California   Mark Bookman
January 1992

The Author

Mark Bookman is the Zarem Professor of Business at Lee College, the University of Judaism. He received both his B.A. degree (1970) in history and his J.D. degree (1973) from the University of California at Los Angeles. Since 1973 he has been a member of the California Bar Association.

Prior to joining the faculty ranks, Bookman spent nearly two decades in senior administrative positions within higher education and nonprofit organizations. His positions on the executive committee of the Association of College Unions-International and as president of the Auxiliary Organization Associations of the California State Universities have involved him in the issues of unfair competition and unrelated business income tax throughout the 1980s.

While serving as an administrator, Bookman made numerous presentations to both regional and national associations on taxation and unfair competition issues. For the past few years, his major research focuses have been in the areas of privatization and government tax policy toward the nonprofit sector. His first book, *Contracting Collegiate Auxiliary Services* (1989), has been well re-

ceived throughout the United States and among the British Commonwealth nations. His 1990 article in the *Chronicle of Higher
Education,* entitled "Colleges Must Report and Pay Taxes on Their
Unrelated Business Income," was partially based on research completed for this book.

PROTECTING
YOUR ORGANIZATION'S
TAX-EXEMPT
STATUS

Part One

Tax Exemption
Under Challenge:
The Context

Chapter 1

The Current Debate
Over Tax Exemption

This book addresses the unrelated business income tax, unfair competition, and local government taxation of nonprofit organizations. This introductory chapter gives readers the general background of the current debate on these issues, the relative perspectives of the parties, and the conflicting messages to which the nonprofit sector has been attempting to respond.

The Current Environment and Debate

During the 1970s and 1980s, government and business leaders increasingly called upon nonprofit organizations to become more self-supporting. These calls for increased self-sufficiency came at the same time that government officials made explicit their expectation that tax-exempt organizations should assume the responsibility of meeting an expanding set of societal needs. For example, even as our political leaders called upon higher education to generate more income, these institutions were urged to be one of the significant forces in improving the nation's economy. A report from a National

Governor's Association meeting entitled "America in Transition: Report of the Task Force on Science and Technology" urged higher education to aim more of its research at commercial needs, and the governors called upon higher education to provide "entrepreneurship training and to assist through the state university systems" with economic development ("Governors Ask Universities . . . ," May 24, 1989, p. 25).

Colleges and universities found support from business and elected officials when they responded to these requests: "Those institutions that are responding to the challenge of meeting state needs are finding . . . that they are able to obtain 'new' money for such efforts" (Hines, 1988, p. 71). Newspaper headlines, articles, and books extolled the virtues of specific colleges and universities that had increased their income from research discoveries via patent and copyright fees (Schrage, 1989; Goldstein, 1988). Others spoke of the increased faculty awareness of "real-world" problems as a significant benefit of joint higher education and industry entrepreneurial effort (Fairweather, 1988). Similar expectations were placed upon other segments of the nonprofit community.

Yet even as the nonprofit sector was not only urged to become more self-supporting but often rewarded for doing so, forces began to build to attack it for its success in these efforts. The growth of the service sector of the economy, which placed a greater number of for-profit organizations in competition with nonprofits, as well as expanded entrepreneurial efforts by the nonprofit community, began to generate claims of "unfair competition" from some parts of the for-profit sector. Thus, while higher education's efforts to assist an area's economic development through the establishment of research parks were praised by many elected officials and businesses, those businesses that perceived competition from these efforts, as well as some elected officials (including some who had recently praised them), argued that various tax exemptions available to higher education gave it an unfair competitive edge in developing income-generating facilities.

During this same time period, due to the federal deficit, all levels of government have needed to find new revenue sources. In the past few years, the underlying question has been whether the concerns of elected officials about the income-generating activities of nonprofit organizations is revenue driven or policy driven.

It must be recognized that during the past twenty years there has been a major increase in the revenue-generating activities of the nonprofit sector. Among the reasons cited for this are (1) the major drop in government funding to nonprofit organizations in general, (2) the major decrease in funding to government social service agencies, (3) changes in government tax policy toward charitable donations that have made this an uncertain income source, (4) increased competition within the nonprofit sector for gifts and donations, and (5) the ability to generate income from some programs to "cross–subsidize" non–income-producing activities, which has become a more generally accepted principle (Fairweather, 1988; Hines, 1988).

In addition to these factors unique to the nonprofit sector, two major changes in our nation's economy also altered the relationship between the nonprofit and for-profit sectors. The rapid growth of the service sector has dramatically altered the level and nature of competition. It is now a generally recognized fact that the service sector is the fastest-growing sector in the United States. Studies have shown that the growth in competition between the for-profit and nonprofit sector is a two-way concern. That is, "we have found as much concern within the nonprofit sector over the 'flip-side' of the coin—for-profit entry into traditional nonprofit arenas" (Copeland and Rudney, 1986, p. 755).

Yet the pressure about "unfair competition" has been directed only toward the nonprofit sector, which brings us to the second major change in our nation's economic outlook. The Reagan administration heralded the unabashed embracing of free-market economic theories as the resolution of our financial problems. In this environment, the small business person is in the role of the "good guy." Any forces that diminish the ability of small businesses to succeed became automatically suspect. This created the right political time for those who wanted to advocate changes in our nation's approach to nonprofit organizations to be heard.

Activities in the nonprofit sector, often at the behest of political and business leaders, have aided the cause of advocates for changing the tax treatment of nonprofit organizations. In some instances, segments of the nonprofit sector were too successful in their efforts to become "more businesslike." The use of business terminology to describe actions and the increasing use of the "bottom line" in making service and resource allocation decisions has tended to undermine the public's confidence in nonprofit organizations.

A 1988 survey by Arthur D. Little, Inc. showed that the public perception of our nation's hospitals was that they are primarily business enterprises. The survey asked: "Are hospitals business enterprises or social service organizations?" Some 67 percent of the national sample responded that they are business enterprises, while only 26 percent stated that they are social service (Catholic Health Association of the United States, 1989a, p. 61).

A second major segment of the nonprofit sector, higher education, finds a similar attitude. In a recent study the Higher Education Research Program stated, "The caricature that has emerged of higher education is one of an industry that, having been put through the ringer in the 1970s, recovered in the early 1980s and then began to grow rich and even greedy as the decade wore on" (Klinger, 1989, p. 10).

Tax-exempt organizations have further weakened their position by their noncompliance with income tax reporting and the actions of some to manipulate the law in their zeal to generate new income. The increased use of parent corporations with both nonprofit and for-profit subsidiaries, sophisticated funding schemes, and the movement into questionable income-producing activities by a small percentage of nonprofit organizations have raised questions about this entire economic segment.

It must also be recognized that a very large amount of income is involved in these issues. If one simply looks at one small part of the nonprofit sector, college and university bookstores, to the common person, the dollars involved are astronomical. The National Association of College Stores estimates that in the 1987–1988 school year its members grossed approximately $4.5 billion. (Note: This organization represents approximately 2,500 college and university stores.) When you add to this the income from museum gift shops, hospitals, fees-for-service-supported social service agencies, fees-for-service-supported organizations offering recreational and other services, and other income-producing activities of the nonprofit sector, the total dollars involved compel a second look.

The very strength of nonprofit organizations, their diversity and independent capacity to be responsive to local community needs, has also become a weakness. To maintain this diversity has required giving individual organizations almost total freedom of operation by national associations. Thus there is little internal regulation within this segment of the economy, a lack of self-regulation that fosters an environment in which government becomes the sole vehicle through which correcting action can occur. When government acts, it tends to develop policy aimed at the "lowest common denominator": That is, policies tend to attempt to protect against the most grievous types of action. Where this occurs, policies often punish legitimate activities as well as questionable ones.

The Views of the Protagonists

The literature and the testimony before legislative bodies on these taxation issues clearly present two distinct views. Although this is not terribly surprising in terms of the advocacy testimony, this posture also pervades the literature and the testimony of "experts." Perhaps it is this lack of areas of common agreement that has made this debate a relatively bitter and divisive one.

Advocates of the small business community, generally speaking through either the Small Business Administration or the Business Coalition for Fair Competition, have enunciated a broad set of proposed statutory changes at the federal and state levels of government. The underlying thrust of this advocacy group is the need for a major overhaul of the tax structure as it applies to nonprofit organizations.

Speaking on behalf of the Business Coalition for Fair Competition, Joseph O'Neil told the Subcommittee on Oversight: "At the outset, let me affirm that the manifold abuses from unfair competitive activities by tax exempt organizations . . . still continues" (U.S. Congress, 1987, p. 258). He goes on to assert that these abuses are clear grounds for immediate and substantive changes in the Internal Revenue Code. The position of the Small Business Administration is that nonprofit organizations supported by gifts, grants, and contributions should continue to be exempt from taxation. But if an organization is relatively self-supporting, that is, it gains significant income from fees for services or goods, this is unfair competition and it should be treated as a for-profit organization.

The nonprofit sector sees things quite differently. Their advocates assert that the anecdotal testimony of small businesses is often incomplete and misleading. Furthermore, even where improprieties may exist, this is the exception and not the rule. In this light they have urged Congress and other legislative bodies to proceed prudently and not overturn a structure that has proven viable since the inception of our nation.

Nonprofits like to discuss the many virtues of their entrepreneurial activities. Among the benefits they note are (1) the creation of jobs, and job training, for specific underemployed segments of society not served by for-profit organizations; (2) meeting service needs not responded to by the for-profit sector; (3) the support of non–income-producing programs whose costs cannot be covered through government funds or donations; (4) meeting demands that they become more self-supporting; and (5) the development of operating systems and employee behaviors that improve their overall efficiency. Nonprofits also disagree that the presence of fees for services equates to a commercial program. They note that fees for services, particularly for social services, rarely cover direct costs and while "nonprofits are doing more 'income-generating' . . . activities . . . the motive is rarely to create profit" (Wellford and Gallagher, 1988, p. 2). Mississippi State's Charles H. White comments on this issue: "We're able to run a first class teaching operation and expose students to real production methods without any state or federal funds" ("Colleges Are Reviewing . . . ," 1988, p. 25). (This was stated in reference to a university-operated dairy facility.)

The for-profit sector tends to step around the assertions of positive service of the nonprofit sector. Instead, advocates for the for-profit sector focus on what they term a "level playing field." That is, they do not object to competition; they simply want all of the competitors to be under the same rules. The for-profit community wants to describe the nonprofit sector as consisting of two groups: those that are supported by donations and those that are self-supporting. Nonprofits bristle at the "simplistic understanding of the nonprofit sector" by the Small Business Administration and others (Wellford and Gallagher, 1988, p. 3). Advocates for the nonprofit community argue for the need to recognize their tremendous diversity in terms of size, funding, funding sources, structure, purpose, and economic and social impact. It is this diversity, they believe, that makes the need for very careful review and only well-crafted legislative changes appropriate.

The parties can agree that competition exists, but they disagree about whether this is inappropriate and whether, and to whom, it is unfair. As one association states, "The issue is not whether competition exists, but rather, whether either sector—nonprofit or for-profit—has an unfair competitive advantage" (Wellford and Gallagher, 1988, p. 3).

The Current Approach to Tax Laws

Nonprofit organizations play a critical role in our nation. They are major providers of social services, innovators in identifying service needs and responding to these needs, an ensurance of consistency of service to communities and population groups regardless of financial return, and providers of a significant impact on the economy—as employers and as purchasers of goods and services. Additionally, these organizations are important in maintaining society's moral standards (through the individual's commitment of service to the community) by providing volunteer opportunities and by addressing issues that, due to their political sensitivity, our government attempts to avoid.

The diversity and independence of these organizations present the opportunity for abuse. Because there are more than one million nonprofit organizations in the United States, only loosely aligned through national and regional associations, it has been very difficult to develop meaningful standards. This in turn has allowed a minority of these organizations to attempt to stretch the bounds of the privileges granted to them.

Our legislative bodies and courts have developed an increasingly muddled set of rules with which these organizations need to comply. At the federal level we find some courts developing a "commerciality standard," which is not clearly established in the law and is rejected by other federal courts. On the issues of unfair competition and exemption from property taxes, the picture state by state, and even within a single state, is equally uncertain.

It must also be recognized that small businesses, and the owners of small businesses, also make critical contributions to the economy and service delivery. These organizations and people deserve to be able to understand the rules of competition and should be assured that tax-supported entities cannot unfairly use "the people's" money to compete.

Defining what constitutes unfair competition is no trivial matter. Although a particular set of small businesses may feel it is "unfair" for nonprofit organizations to provide a service similar to theirs, it may be in the best interest of society as a whole, as well as others in the for-profit sector. It is only by weighing all economic, service, and moral issues that this can be resolved. Much of the current statutory law on the taxation of nonprofit organizations is based upon a balancing of society's needs and the potential value of government-provided competitive advantages.

The most pressing need in this debate is for the development of a coherent and consistent government approach toward nonprofit organizations, which must begin at the federal level. For this to occur, Congress needs to make a declarative statement on this topic, which in turn must be translated into appropriate tax code and perhaps other statutory modifications. Such a review must be driven by policy and not revenue issues. It is also far too important to be left to special interest groups from either camp.

Efforts like the Taxpayer Compliance Measurement Program now being completed by the Internal Revenue Service and the revision of the tax information and reporting forms used by exempt organizations is the type of government research that needs to occur. But these efforts only address limited issues and are at least partially dependent on the quality of the effort of the exempt community to respond to these federal initiatives. There is still much information that needs to be compiled on issues such as the potential effect on service delivery if changes are made in the tax laws. Will these changes materially help or hurt the for-profit community? Will they affect all of the for-profit community or only particular segments? What are the long-term implications for the need for additional government spending to provide services if nonprofit organizations have their scope of permissible services or income levels altered? These are a smattering of the issues for which answers need to be known before the best policy decisions can be made.

The current debate is structured on the view that there are a set of "good guys" and a set of "bad guys." Which groups fall into each category is dependent on who is doing the categorizing. Debates structured in this way put government policy makers in a no-win situation; that is, whatever decisions they make will anger a significant partisan group. Typically, when this occurs, policy resolves tend to be inconclusive compromises, often motivated by factors having little to do with the issue initially being addressed.

The nonprofit sector bears a large part of the blame for the superficial and incomplete level of the current debate. Through interdisciplinary efforts, comprehensive models can be developed that could be the foundation for a coherent national policy toward the nonprofit community. Yet there seems to be little interest or concern within the higher education community to allocate resources to assist in this way.

The best paper I have found on the need for improved research and how it can be applied was written by senior staff in the Small Business Administration for a colloquium held a few years ago (Swain and Mastromarco, 1988). In this article the authors speak to the need not only to gather additional data but first to develop usable methodologies. They note that in many ways the forces propelling the debate today are the same as those that generated government action in 1950 and 1969, yet there has been no improvement in the quality of the information on which the debate is based. Instead, they believe, "the complaints . . . have merely become audible enough again for policy makers to take notice" (Swain and Mastromarco, 1988, p. 2).

This approach would also provide a process in which the treatment of the nonprofit sector by government could have a more defined evolution. The capacity to develop predictable outcomes to changes in behavior and societal conditions would be of benefit to everyone.

The Evolution
of Government Policy
Toward Nonprofit Organizations

A Brief History of Federal Law and Tax-Exempt Status

In comparison to all other nations, the role of nonprofit organizations in the United States is unique. Chapter Two presents the history of government policy toward nonprofits in the United States. The first section of this chapter focuses on the philosophical and policy rationales that have underlined the development of this sector of the economy. In order to develop future government policy about the role of nonprofit organizations, it is imperative that one first understands why the United States has consciously and consistently given special policy treatment to nonprofit organizations.

After a full analysis of this history, this chapter proceeds with a review of those organizations that are granted exempt status under the Federal Income Tax Code. This book examines the federal level of government first, since it is this level that has developed the basic approach to nonprofit organizations for all levels of government in the United States. This discussion concludes with perhaps the most significant change in government policy in this century: the implementation of the unrelated business income tax. The latter tax applies to certain income-generating activities of tax-exempt organizations. As the last section of this chapter explains, this tax was developed by Congress to remove any unfair competitive edge that an exempt organization might have if it should compete in the market place with a for-profit organization.

The renowned Chief Justice Marshall of the United States Supreme Court observed in *McCulloch v. Maryland*, 4 L. Ed. 579 (1819), that "the power to tax involves the power to destroy." The reverse is also true: The decision not to tax involves the power to create. The history of tax-exempt organizations and the laws surrounding them in the United States are founded on this principle. The Tariff Act of 1894 imposed the first general corporate income tax: a flat tax of 2 percent on all corporate income. In passing this legislation, Congress specified which organizations would be taxed. Section 32 of the Tariff Act of 1894 carried forward English common law and exempted nonprofit charitable organizations, religious and educational organizations, fraternal societies, certain mutual savings banks, and certain mutual insurance companies. Although this act was found to be unconstitutional, it set the basis that the federal government has followed in exempting a broad set of nonprofit organizations from income tax.

After the passage of the Sixteenth Amendment, the Revenue Act of 1913 adopted essentially the same approach. This statute exempted "any corporation, or association organized and operated exclusively for religious, charitable, scientific or educational purpose." The current Internal Revenue Code has adapted this approach to the increased complexity of our current economy and service delivery system. Thus, through a series of amendments, additional organizations have been added to those that may gain tax exemption: Groups that prevent cruelty to animals and children (1918), community chest, fund or foundations, and literary groups (1921), testing for public safety (1954), and sports competition organizations that foster national and international athletics (1976) are some of the groups that have been specifically enumerated. Today there are approximately twenty-five categories of exempt organizations.

Since World War II, a number of important modifications to the exemption have been extended to these organizations. Perhaps the most significant were actions taken in 1950 that changed the test to determine exempt status and created the concept of the unrelated business income tax.

In the precedent-setting case of *Trinidad v. Sagrada Orden de Predicadore*, 263 U.S. 578 (1924), the destination of income test was developed. Under this test, the decision as to whether an organization's income was tax exempt was determined by how the net income was used. Thus, in the infamous N.Y.U. Macaroni Company case, the income derived by an otherwise commercial company was found to be exempt from taxes because it was used to support an educational institution. Recognizing that this concept would allow tax-exempt organizations to engage in almost any type of retail enterprise without incurring any federal income tax, Congress amended the Internal Revenue Code and created the concept of the unrelated business income. As reflected in congressional debate, it was the intent of Congress to rectify the unfair competitions problems which existed in the law (House Rep. No. 2319, 1950, pp. 36–37). Since 1950, with various modifications, if an otherwise tax-exempt organization engages in activity that is not "substantially related" to its tax-exempt purpose, income derived therefrom is taxable irrespective of the purpose to which it is put.

The problems of individuals manipulating tax-exempt structures for personal economic advantage generated a major review of tax-exempt organizations by Congress. In the Tax Reform Act of 1969, the concept of private foundations was created. Under this concept all Section 501(c)(3) organizations were presumed to be private foundations unless they could meet a donation test. It is important to note that "traditional" tax-exempt organizations were exempt from this test: churches, educational institutions, hospitals and medical facilities, research organizations, and government units. The full enumeration of these traditional exempt organizations is found in Section 509(a). If an organization was found to be a private foundation, this generated a set of negative consequences: (1) created a 2 percent excise tax on all net profits, (2) created special reporting requirements aimed at determining if self-dealing was occurring, (3) denied the deductibility from their income tax of donations to these organizations by donors, and (4) created a set of stiff excise taxes on these activities if self-dealing occurred.

The 1969 act also made a few other important changes. It

specifically authorized audit cooperation between state and federal agencies. Congress also extended the unrelated business income tax to churches and almost every other organization that could gain tax-exempt status. Additionally, this act developed special rules for a number of sophisticated arrangements intended to circumvent the unrelated business income tax (for example, debt-financed acquisition of property and issues relating to controlled organizations).

As early as 1934, Congress legislated to limit the involvement of tax-exempt organizations in political activity. At that time the wording "no substantial part" of an exempt organization's activity may be "propaganda or attempting to influence legislation" was added to the Internal Revenue Code. In the Revenue Acts of 1976 and 1978, Congress again acted to limit the political activities of tax-exempt organizations, creating a set of regulations that organizations must follow when engaging in the political arena. This included Section 501(h), which created a "safe harbor" provision for measuring permissible legislative activity that could be elected by tax-exempt organizations. The latter was felt to be needed because, as with many other sections of the Internal Revenue Code, key tests are not defined. Few large exempt organizations have chosen to include themselves under this standard. The standard is based on a percentage of gross income, which does function well for an organization with a relatively small level of annual income (under $1 million).

Congress last addressed this area by legislating that for tax years beginning after December 22, 1987, all Section 501(c)(3) organizations would incur an excise tax on expenditures opposing or supporting a candidate for political office. It is important to note that legislative activity does not include "efforts to influence the executive branch in connection with existing legislation" (Rapp, 1989, p. 44) and "that a legitimate basis exists to distinguish between the appropriation of funds with respect to legislation already authorized and all other legislation" (Rapp, 1989, p. 44). Similarly, the Internal Revenue Code does not bar or limit nonpartisan analysis or communication with an exempt organization's "natural constituencies." At the same time, the Internal Revenue Code was amended to bring all tax-exempt organizations within the sections prohibiting political activity.

Tax acts in the last two decades also saw Congress alter the rules applicable to unrelated business activity. As with most of the changes since this concept was originally created, these were technical in nature and focused on a particular set of organizations (for instance, the tax treatment of trade shows and state fairs). In the second half of the 1980s, Congress showed renewed interest in this area. In 1986 four actions were taken by Congress to alter judicial decisions and to respond to concerns from the Internal Revenue Service. Of a more technical nature, specific rules were created as to the income derived from the exchange or rental of membership lists and the distribution of low-cost items incidental to soliciting charitable contributions.

Actions of a philosophical nature, which may foreshadow future congressional activity, also occurred. Great visibility has been given to the changes made by Congress as to the deductibility of gifts to tax-exempt organizations. A trend of the decade prior to this action was substantial annual increases in donations, but in terms of both actual and inflationary dollars, this was reversed in the late 1980s. Many believe this has occurred due to the new limits placed on deductible gifts by the Tax Reform Act of 1986. Of less immediate visibility, but possibly of greater policy consequence, was the enactment of Section 501(m), which states that income from certain "commercial" insurance sold by exempt organizations is unrelated business income. Thus we see for the first time a commerciality standard being used by Congress to determine the taxability of specified income. Shortly thereafter, in 1987, Congress amended Section 512(c)(2) to restrict exemptions from the debt-financed property rules and tax an exempt organization's share of income from a publicly traded partnership. This act also added new reporting requirements as to relationships between exempt organizations and requires public disclosure as to the amount of a solicited gift that is not deductible.

The Rationale for Tax Exemption

The past few years have seen increased activity within federal agencies and Congress in regard to tax-exempt organizations. It is felt by most observers that this is the beginning of extended activity at the federal level to determine public policy. These actions will be reviewed in depth in subsequent chapters.

Charitable nontaxed organizations have been a unique part of our nation's heritage since the colonial period. The renowned historian Alexis de Tocqueville found it necessary to comment on this in his work *Democracy in America:* "Americans of all ages and all dispositions constantly form associations . . . , religious, moral, serious, general or restricted. . . . The Americans make associations to give entertainment, to found seminaries, to build inns, to construct churches, to diffuse books, to send seminaries to antipodes, in this manner they found hospitals, prisons and schools. . . . Wherever at the head of an undertaking you see the government in France, or a man of rank in England, in America you will be sure to find an association" (Hopkins, 1987, p. 11). The concept of these organizations was so imbued in the social fiber of our nation that one can find little in the Congressional Record discussing the legislation that Congress initially passed to exempt such organizations from taxation.

There is general agreement as to the reasons given historically for creating tax exemption for charitable organizations. The former director of the Employee Plan and Tax Exempt Organizations Division, Office of Chief Counsel of the Internal Revenue Service, James McGovern, noted three reasons: (1) our heritage in founding this country of supporting religious and charitable organizations, (2) the morality of not taxing organizations whose purpose is to provide mutual benefits for their members and who are funded by their members, and (3) the policy that organizations that help the "poor" should not be taxed (McGovern, 1976). To these reasons one can add the desire to advance education and science, to foster volunteerism within our society, and to lessen the need for government to provide a range of services. Former Secretary of the Treasury George P. Schultz, speaking to the House Ways and Means Committee in 1973, stated: "These organizations are an important influence for diversity and a bulwark against over-reliance on big government" (Hopkins, 1987, p. 7).

The Congressional Record yields support for the "lessening the burdens of government" rationale: "Government is compensated for the loss of tax revenue because it does not have to 'foot the

bill' for services and benefits for the 'general welfare' of the nation"
(House Rep. No. 1860, 1939, p. 19).

Some theorists view tax exemptions and deductions as revenue losses. They argue that if policy makers want to gain more
direct control over all allocations, such revenue "losses" must be
eliminated. To some extent both Congress and the United States
Supreme Court have endorsed this concept. In the Budget Act of
1974, Congress attempted to coordinate tax exemption with appro-
priations. In upholding the government's right to restrict the political activities of exempt organizations, the Supreme Court stated
in *Regan v. Taxation with Representation of Washington,* 461 U.S.
540, 544 (1983): "Both tax exemption and deductibility are a form
of subsidy that is administered through the tax system. A tax exemption has much the same effect as a cash grant . . . deductible contributions are similar. . . . " Other theorists find fault with this
reasoning. Looking at our heritage, they argue that there are fundamental sociopolitical concepts which foster the third (nonprofit)
sector of our economy and "advance the quality of the American
social order" (Hopkins, 1987, p. 28) in that "the heritage and political philosophy of this country strongly emphasizes individual
and private institutions working for public ends. Pluralism and
volunteerism is what the charitable deduction is all about" (Hopkins, 1987, pp. 49–50).

The latter approach was endorsed by Congress in 1987 in the
Findings and Recommendations of the House Ways and Means
Oversight Committee on Federal Tax Rules Governing Lobbying
and Political Activities: "Charitable and other tax exempt organizations are an essential part of society. Nonprofit organizations have
promoted the general welfare, stimulated scientific and technolog-
ical progress, cultivated education, cultural and artistic endeavors,
fostered religion and provided a wealth of independent thought and
innovative ideas" (Treusch, 1987).

Some theorists believe that the rationales that have historically supported the concept of tax-exempt organizations are no
longer applicable. They argue that the for-profit sector is now prepared to meet those needs historically provided by the nonprofit
sector. These theorists also believe that exemption from corporate

income tax provides organizations with an unfair edge when they compete with for-profits.

Although the debate on unfair competition defies a simple response, the argument that tax exemption in total should be repealed brings widespread opposition. Bruce Hopkins argues: "The policy of exempting certain organizations from taxation furthers many national policies . . . tax reform and tax equity will become empty and counter-productive 'accomplishments' if achieved at the expense of innumerable worthwhile institutions" (Hopkins, 1987, p. vii). It is Hopkins's belief that "the tax exemption system exists basically as a reflection of the affirmative policy of the American government to not inhibit by taxation the beneficial activities of qualified exempt organizations acting in community and other interests" (Hopkins, 1987, p. 14).

Instead of eliminating all tax-exempt organizations, Henry Hansmann argues that today we should divide nonprofits into two groups: "donative" and "commercial." The former gain much of their support from voluntary contributions and would continue to be exempt. The latter are essentially funded by fees for services and would be denied exemption. Citing the action by Congress to tax commercial-type insurance offered by otherwise tax-exempt organizations, Hansmann argued in a speech to INDEPENDENT SECTOR in 1987: "If that line of reasoning prevails how does one defend tax exemption for hospitals, nursing homes, day-care centers, health maintenance organizations, publishers and all other types of nonprofits that provide services to and in competition with ordinary businesses" ("New Threats to Commercial Nonprofits," 1987, p. 4).

While recognizing Hansmann's rationale, many supporters of tax exemption for all organizations now covered in the Internal Revenue Code argue that the approach of looking solely at the source of income ignores most of the rationale for the existence of this exemption. Those holding this view also believe that this approach ignores other realities of the natural behavior of the for-profit sector that make the need for tax exemption a critical societal need. A summary of their arguments includes the following.

1. Organizations that actualize and support society's values of giving, volunteerism, self-help, and community involvement
2. Organizations that provide service stability, irrespective of profitability
3. Organizations that minimize social problems, develop new markets and technology, and fill voids, particularly in emergency situations
4. Organizations that lessen the burden on government to provide services
5. Organizations that have governance structure that makes them accountable to the entire service community
6. Organizations that have a bottom line of service, not profit
7. Organizations that service the most vulnerable populations
8. Organizations that respond to a greater range of values, particularly those generated by minority populations in our society

[See, for example, the testimony of Bradford H. Grey of the National Academy of Sciences and Susan Rose Ackerman to the Subcommittee on Oversight (U.S. Congress, 1987, pp. 995 and 1930).]

Organizations That Are Covered

Today there are numerous categories of tax-exempt organizations, yet the root of this concept lies in "charitable, educational, scientific and religious organizations." The regulations to the Internal Revenue Code state that charitable includes "relief of the poor and distressed or the underprivileged. . . . " [Regs. S1.0501(c)(3)-1(d)(2)].

Providing assistance to the poor is most often the laypersons' concept of charitable. In the twentieth century we have seen "the trend away from providing direct financial assistance (more and more the province of government) to the provision of services" (Hopkins, 1987, p. 2). Thus we have seen exempt status given to organizations that assist with securing employment (for example, vocational training, establishing a market for goods produced by the impoverished and physically limited, and employment for the elderly), provide assistive services (for example, legal aid societies and bail for the poor), provide assistance to maintain employment (for example, day care centers, rights of public housing tenants, and subsidized medical care), or provide information and counseling services (for health, housing, finances, and education). Similarly, groups that provide low-income housing, as well as money management and home meals and transportation services for the elderly and handicapped, have been granted tax-exempt status, as have groups that provide rescue and emergency services. In practice the definition of charity is far broader than the traditional concept embodied in the English common law. Today the focus is on organizations that assist the general welfare of the nation.

Historically much of the activity around tax-exempt status has been in defining an educational, religious, or scientific organization. This analysis can often become quite complex and technical, and it is not the purpose of this book to fully explore this issue. The materials that now follow are intended to give some idea as to the boundaries of the current law.

Few tax-exempt groups today give service solely to the poor. In *Eastern Kentucky Welfare Rights Organization v. Simon*, 506 F.2d 1278 (D.C. cir. 1974), the court of appeals stated that "charitable is capable of definition far broader than merely relief of the poor." Looking at how health care is now funded (Medicare and private insurance), the court determined that the need to provide services to the poor is no longer an essential element of tax-exempt status. This decision supports the rationale used by the service in granting tax-exempt status to a medical facility simply for providing emergency room service to anyone regardless of the ability to pay (R.R. 69-545, 1969-2, C.B. 117).

The advancement of education and science has been broadly defined by the courts and the executive branch. Exempt status has been granted to organizations that establish or maintain nonprofit educational institutions, finance scholarships and other forms of student assistance, establish or maintain public libraries and museums, or advance knowledge through research, publications, seminars, and lectures. The latter category includes the teaching of industrial skills, conducting work experience programs or apprenticeship programs, operating an international student exchange program or an honor society, and evaluating the service obligations of broadcasters.

Satellite activities of educational institutions are also granted exempt status. In this group are found publication of student journals, a training table for athletes, operation of an international student center, an alumni association, the operation of interscholastic athletics, student volunteerism, and financial assistance programs. University-affiliated organizations also frequently gain tax-exempt status. The organizations most typically covered are bookstores, food service, housing, and intercollegiate athletic organizations. As a general rule fraternities and sororities are denied exempt status as auxiliary organizations of exempt colleges and universities, but they can gain federal income tax exemption under other sections of the Code.

The current Internal Revenue Code also provides tax exemption for a variety of other organizations. The list is relatively long and quite specific; for instance, in 1954 groups that test for public safety were added. It is important to note that the Code uses the disjunctive "or" between types of exempt organizations; thus it is only necessary to qualify under one of the enumerated categories.

The Internal Revenue Service had over 820,000 Section 503(c)(3) and (4) tax-exempt organizations registered in 1986. As we enter the 1990s, there are clearly more than one million tax-exempt organizations, if one includes all categories, the many churches that are not required to apply for exempt status, and the many small organizations that fail to file formally. However one wants to measure the size of this sector of our economy, it has seen rapid growth in the last half of this century. It is the growth of the tax-exempt sector, and particularly its increased reliance on self-generated income, that has caused many of the concerns of small businesses. A U.S. General Accounting Office briefing report to the Joint Committee on Taxation, entitled "Competition Between Taxable Businesses and Tax-Exempt Organizations," shows that in 1946 exempt organizations generated 43 percent of their income from noncommercial sources and 57 percent from other activities. By 1978 noncommercial income had fallen to 25 percent and by 1982 it had fallen to 19 percent (Nichols, Naves, and Olswang, 1989, p. 249). "Other activities" was defined as income from business receipts, interest, dividends, rents, royalties, and the sale of goods and services.

As Congress looks at these data, it has one other set of statistics at its disposal. The General Accounting Office, in its report entitled "The Availability and Completeness of Returns of Tax-Exempt Organizations," found that of those organizations that filed a Form 990 in 1986 some 48 percent were missing one or more support schedules (Klinger, 1988). The General Accounting Office has advised Congress that well under 50 percent of all tax-exempt organizations required to file the mandatory Form 990 did so and less than 10 percent filed Form 990T. (The latter is required if an organization has more than $1,000 of unrelated business income.)

Although these data provide a great deal of information, they also leave many questions unanswered. This information provides little guidance to policy makers as to where there is competition between sectors, what effect recent and proposed Internal Revenue Code changes have had or may have on income sources or service delivery, and what the net impact is on the federal budget. For those at the federal level who develop our income tax laws, these data create a concern that many tax-exempt organizations are either ignoring the law or are ignorant of it. A considerable group believes that if tax-exempt organizations properly followed existing statutes, the taxes collected would be far greater. This belief is buttressed by the dramatic increase in taxes paid by tax-exempt organizations the year following the beginning of the current inquiry by Congress.

The Unrelated Business Income Tax

As previously discussed, the unrelated business concept was codified in 1950. Prior to that time an organization was either totally taxable or totally tax exempt. With this code change, a tax-exempt organization was allowed to engage in activities that could give rise to taxable income, activities that were to be "unrelated" to the exempt purpose of the organization. This concept will be more fully reviewed in subsequent chapters. As with other areas of tax-exempt organizations, there are few data on the unrelated business income tax. A 1985 General Accounting Office study estimated noncompliance in terms of dollars of tax as 25 percent for social welfare organizations, 58 percent for charitable and education organizations, and 61 percent for business leagues (Weisbold, 1988).

As discussed in the previous subsection, Congress has also been advised that far fewer than half of all tax-exempt organizations seem to file the required annual information return and that less than half of those organizations that file the unrelated business income return do so properly. Finally, Congress is aware that in 1986 $55 million of unrelated business income taxes were paid. Yet just one year later, after the Subcommittee on Oversight began its well-publicized review of tax-exempt organizations, some $119 million were paid. This doubling of unrelated business income tax payments in one year suggests that there may be far more in taxes that should be paid.

Tax-exempt organizations have seemingly exerted very little effort to develop data on this topic. A 1986 study by the National Association of College and University Business Officers (NACUBO) suggested that those concerns raised by small businesses based on anecdotal information may not have general applicability. (Note: This survey was mailed to approximately one-sixth of the 2,641 members of NACUBO. Of these some 195, 7.5 percent, responded.) Some of the results of the survey are:

1. Only six of the respondents provided noninstitutional travel service.
2. Seventy-six engaged in some type of computer sales, with only nine allowing sales to the general public.
3. The services that started after 1975 were responses to new technologies, not efforts to move into markets that had been created previously by for-profits.
4. Twenty percent of the respondents had been audited by the Internal Revenue Service and in only three occasions did the respondents report exceptions or disallowances by the IRS.
5. Only six schools reported being involved in an unfair competition suit (U.S. Congress, 1987, p. 457).

These data, although not entirely conclusive, remind us that all institutions of postsecondary education are not made from the same mold. In the unfair competition debate, the headline makers have been predominantly the large, public, comprehensive universities, which make up a relatively small percentage of all institutions involved in higher education. As one looks at the various statistics that are available, it is important to recognize the diversity of tax-exempt organizations. All too often conclusions are drawn based on the actions of a narrow slice of the picture, yet the policy actions promulgated from these conclusions affect all organizations.

As the section on the history of tax-exempt organizations discussed, the unrelated business income tax is a relatively recent concept intended to remove potential unfair competition between this sector and the for-profit sector. Much of the debate in recent years has focused on whether these code sections are accomplishing their intended goal. Unfortunately, there are insufficient data for anyone to do more than theorize on this. The prevailing view of theorists, both pro tax exempts and pro small business, is that the unrelated business income concept is needed. One of the leading pro–small-business theorists, Hansmann, has told the Subcommittee on Oversight that there are "very strong economic arguments for retaining UBIT in roughly its current form" (U.S. Congress, 1987, p. 1832). He argues that the unrelated business income concept forces operating efficiency by nonprofits when they compete with for-profits, it encourages nonprofits to properly diversify investments, and, since in his view a tax exemption equates to a government subsidy, it is inappropriate to give these organizations a financial advantage in unrelated activities. It must be noted that many theorists believe that this view has no basis whatsoever. John G. Simon, for example, believes that nonprofits are simply not part of the tax base at all. Their belief is that without a profit and private inurement motive, there is nothing to tax. If something cannot be included in the tax base, logic dictates that it cannot be subsidized.

Review of statements by members of Congress in the past few years and discussions with staff of those on the Subcommittee on Oversight clearly show that the prevailing view among policy makers is that expressed by Hansmann. Our policy makers are concerned that tax-exempt groups not be allowed to compete, with advantages similar to those found in the operation of a commercial enterprise by New York University, which gave rise to the 1950 legislation. There is general agreement in Congress on the need to be certain that these code sections are modernized to our current setting. Other than this, however, there does not seem to be consensus on any other policy issues.

Part Two

Federal Law
and the
Internal Revenue Code

Federal Law
on Tax-Exempt Status and
Unrelated Business Income

With Chapter Three we begin the discussion of how exempt status for an organization, as well as the taxability of income generated by exempt organizations, is determined at the federal level of government. Our starting point is the review of how an organization gains exempt status and the basic actions in which an organization must engage to maintain this status. This chapter proceeds with an explanation of what constitutes unrelated business income. As will be seen in this and subsequent discussions, due to vagueness in the Internal Revenue Code and the constant changes occurring in both the nonprofit and for-profit sectors, the courts and the Internal Revenue Service exercise significant influence on how these Code sections are interpreted.

The remaining sections of Chapter Three address the major issues in determining whether income generated by an exempt organization is taxable. We thus begin the discussion of the most complex materials in this book. Complexity occurs due to the ambiguities in the Internal Revenue Code and the increasing sophistication of the business practices of exempt organizations. These factors have compelled the administrative and judicial branches of government to review their interpretations of Code sections and to modify their previous interpretations as needed. As the reader will learn, the unrelated business income sections of the Code contain numerous tests, exceptions, and exemptions. In this chapter we begin the process of determining whether specific income is taxable or not.

Gaining Tax-Exempt Status

To gain tax-exempt status, an organization must file the appropriate form and supporting documents with the Internal Revenue Service. The legal structure of the organization is not determinative. An organization may be incorporated, a trust, or an unincorporated association. To gain exempt status an organization must file the Application for Recognition of Exemption (Form 1023).

If a tax-exempt organization wants to create a legally separate entity, it must allow this entity to be truly separate. Among the factors that are reviewed are that there is an appropriate apportionment of expenses and no comingling of funds. The former should be done via a written agreement. Not to do this could cost an organization the ability to achieve or maintain tax exemption.

To consider filing for tax-exempt status, a group must be able to match its purpose with one of the exempt functions enumerated in the Code. Although they are beyond the purpose of this book, there are critical practical effects as to which exemption an organization seeks. Once exempt status is granted, it is difficult to change the type of exemption, and even if the change is granted, it may not be retroactive. The nature of the exemption granted may determine whether one can receive tax deductible gifts, whether the organization is under the restrictive rules of private foundations, and other important factors.

As discussed previously, Congress has amended many times the types of organizations that qualify for tax exemption. These amendments most often occur to meet the changing nature of our society. Thus in 1974 Congress passed legislation that granted tax-exempt status to consortia controlled by tax-exempt organizations formed to make cooperative investments. This allowed an entity like the Common Fund to be tax exempt.

State and local government are not included in the list of groups that may gain tax-exempt status. Federal income tax exemption is not needed for most of their functions, yet in some instances these tiers of government have found it advantageous to create tax-exempt subsidiaries. An example of this is the formation of a local library district. The key question in terms of gaining exempt status for these types of organizations is the extent to which they exercise government powers. For example, if they have regulatory powers (normally referred to as police powers), they will be denied an exemption. To be exempt, such a district may have the power to set a tax rate, but it must rely on local government to levy and collect the tax. Finally, the power of eminent domain is sufficient to make an organization a government subdivision.

The IRS generally takes the position that public colleges and universities are not political subdivisions of the state, because they do not directly possess the power to tax, eminent domain, police powers, and other sovereign powers. Also, an organization established to support a tax-exempt organization is itself tax exempt. It is this concept that grants exempt status to university foundations and auxiliary organizations (see Rev. Rul. 67-149, 1967-1 C.B. 133, IRS Private Letter Ruling 8424001, Rev. Rul. 81-19, 1981-1 C.B. 353, IRS Private Letter Ruling 8419085).

In some instances subdivisions of state and local government find it advantageous to gain tax-exempt status. This is particularly true for some public colleges and universities. Because some public institutions of higher education have the power to tax (for example, California community colleges) or the power of eminent domain (for example, the University of California), they are considered political subdivisions of the state. For these types of organizations, the ability to form quasi-independent foundations and other auxiliary organizations that can gain exempt status can be quite important.

Assuming that an organization can match itself with a listed exempt function, it must then show that it will serve a sufficient class, that is, a sufficient segment of the community. As with many other sections of the Internal Revenue Code, this test is constantly evolving. For instance, prior to the 1970s it was the position of the IRS that the "elderly" did not constitute a sufficient class. Today the elderly are considered a sufficient class; the economic means of the class being served is not the determinative factor. Thus community recreation facilities, if available to the general public of a given community, do constitute a sufficient class (see Rev. Rul. 67-325, 1967-2 C.B. 113). Similarly, the number of individuals directly served may be relatively small, as long as the primary effect is to benefit the community and not the individual.

The Internal Revenue Service will next apply the "organization test" and the "operation test." Here the IRS attempts to determine if the group is intended to be organized and operated for an exempt purpose. The practice of the IRS has been to examine the creating legal documents (such as the charter, articles of incorporation, and by-laws) for the organization test. If these documents show that all assets are dedicated to an exclusive tax-exempt purpose, this test has been passed. Included in the items that the IRS looks for is a disillusionment clause, which ensures that should an organization cease to exist the assets will be used for an exempt purpose. A very recent Tax Court decision differs with the approach used by the Internal Revenue Service. The Tax Court has ruled that this is a factual test; thus the IRS should look beyond simply the written documents if the applying organization can present evidence to show that it meets this test [see *Colorado State Chiropractic Society v. Commissioner*, U.S.T.C. V.93 #4 (filed October 19, 1989), Docket No. 17702-88X].

The operation test is passed if an organization shows that its actual activity is intended to accomplish the exempt purpose enumerated in its creating documents. Here the IRS usually has some actual behavior on which to base its conclusion. This occurs because most organizations begin operation long before they have filed the requisite documents and before the Internal Revenue Service has reviewed and ruled on them.

The tests reviewed to this point can generally be met by attention to the drafting of the originating documents. The remaining initial tests are far more substantive in nature. The next issue is whether an organization has as its base a tax-exempt "exclusive purpose." The regulations define exclusive as "primary, but not solely." The test is failed "if more than an insubstantial part of its activities is not in furtherance of an exempt purpose" [Reg. Sec. 1.501 (cl(3)-1(c)]. The IRS bases its initial determination on the organization's attestation as to why it exists. Over time the IRS may challenge an organization's exempt status if it feels that actual behavior has not matched the initially stated intentions. There are extensive case law and administrative rulings on exclusive purpose. The few examples that follow are intended to present some of the issues that are of current concern.

It is clear that if an organization's purpose is to provide guidance on tax avoidance, tax-exempt status will be denied [see *Christian Fellowship v. Commissioner,* 70 T.C. 1037 (1978) and *National Association of American Churches v. Commissioner,* 82 T.C. 18 (1978)]. One also finds the emergence of a commerciality test within some courts; if it is felt that the organization is operated like a business, it is in fact a business [see *Presbyterian and Reformed Publishing Company v. Commissioner,* 79 T.C. 1070 (1983) and *The Incorporated Trustees of the Gospel Workers Society, Inc. v. United States,* 510 F. Supp. 374 (D.D.C. 1981) aff'd 672 F.2d 894 (D.C. Cir. 1981) cert. den. 456 U.S. 944 (1982)]. Here too exempt status was denied.

In determining primary purpose, the IRS examines who actually receives the benefit. Thus it has found that the construction and operation of a downtown parking garage by a business association is exempt because the real benefit accrues to the city. If the primary purpose appears to be service to nonmembers of the organization, tax exemption is denied (see Rev. Rul 78-51, 1978-1 C.B. 165).

Specificity of purpose can determine the outcome of this test. In a series of rulings on child care, the court has looked at whether the primary purpose is education or custodial care. The former is specifically exempt under Section 501(c)(3). The latter is not enumerated in the Internal Revenue Code and is not exempt. [See *San Francisco Infant School, Inc. v. Commissioner,* 69 T.C. 957 (1978) and *Michigan Earlychildhood Center, Inc. v. Commissioner,* 37 T.C.M. 808 (1978)].

The courts early defined the term "charitable" in a flexible way [see *United States v. Properties of Social Law Library* (1st Cir. 1939)]. This has helped to allow for a continuing evolution of the key terms in Section 501(c)(3). At one point, to gain an exemption for providing medical services an organization needed to exhibit substantive service to the poor and needy, but now an organization need only show the provision of medical services per se to an appropriate class [see *Eastern Kentucky Welfare Rights Organization v. Simon*, 506 F.2d 1278 (D.C. Cir. 1974)].

The courts have shown the ability to look past the written purpose of an organization to its actual behavior to determine if an exemption is warranted. A few years ago the Tax Court reviewed a situation in which the stated purpose of the organization was the rehabilitation of young people. Upon examining the facts, the court concluded that the real organizational goal was its survival [see *Shiloh Youth Revival Centers*, 85 T.C. 565 (1987)] and denied a tax exemption.

If the primary purpose of an organization is to generate profits, it will be denied a tax exemption. It is the practice of the Internal Revenue Service to deny or revoke an organization's exempt status if over half of the group's income is unrelated to its exempt purpose (see General Counsel Memorandum 39108). Even where an organization performs a function that could be exempt, if there is a substantial commercial purpose, exemption will be denied. The courts are particularly skeptical of franchise operations for private gain [see *est of Hawaii v. Commissioner*, 71 T.C. 1067 (1979)].

An exception to this posture occurs where a trade or business is in furtherance of an organization's exempt purpose and where the exempt organization is not organized or operated for the primary purpose of conducting said trade or business. In one case an organization had as its exempt purpose the employment of the blind. The court found that the organization's purchase and sale of products made by the blind, even though this is how the organization generated the majority of its income, did not threaten its exempt status [see *Industrial Aid for the Blind v. Commissioner*, 73 T.C. 96 (1979)].

If an organization is operated for private gain or purposes, it will be denied exempt status (see Rev. Rul. 66-104, 1966-1 C.B. 135). Private gain can come in many forms. Overly generous compensation, below-market or no-interest loans, lease arrangements, gifts, and other forms of remuneration to "insiders" have been found to be private inurement [see *Birmingham Business College, Inc. v. Commissioner*, 276 F.2d 476 (5th Cir. 1960); *Founding*

Church of Christian Scientology v. U.S., 412 F. 2d 1197 (Ct. Cl. 1969) cert. den. 397 U.S. 1009 (1970); and *John Marshall Law School v. United States*, 81-2 U.S.T.C. 9514 (Ct. Cl. 1981)]. If the private gain is considered to be incidental, the organization's right to exempt status is not threatened. The IRS has ruled this way on many occasions. One example is where an education accreditation association accredited "very few" proprietary schools among the many institutions that it reviewed. The private inurement gained by a few individuals was incidental to the gains to education by the development of standards (see Rev. Rul. 74-16, 1974-1 C.B. 126). In another situation a for-profit provided most of the support for an exempt nineteenth-century village. The for-profit had its name included in all advertising and on all publications and used this in its own advertising. Here too the IRS felt that the actual private gain was incidental to the benefit to the general public (see Rev. Rul. 77-367, 1977-2 C.B. 193).

The fact that "insiders" receive substantial private gain does not automatically deny exempt status. In one fact situation, a group of physicians formed an organization to provide services to a hospital. The activity of this group assisted in the clinical training of medical students. The fees paid for these physicians' services were distributed to the member physicians. The court held that the private gain of the physicians was incidental to the public benefit from the training of the students [see *University of Massachusetts Medical School Group Practice*, 74 T.C. 1299 (1980)]. In a somewhat different situation, the court denied the request for an exemption. A book-publishing venture was found to have a substantial purpose to generate net income that was allocated in the form of grants to the authors of the published books. The court found that the private inurement outweighed the public benefit of the publications [see *Christian Manner International, Inc. v. Commissioner*, 71 T.C. 661 (1979)]. The Internal Revenue Code does allow an exempt organization to have a qualified profit-sharing plan, as found in Section 401(a). Further elaboration can be found in General Counsel Memorandum 38283 and IRS Private Letter Ruling 8442064. The Internal Revenue Service has also found that properly constructed employee incentive plans do not give rise to private inurement. The IRS examines whether the plan is simply a device to distribute profits to principals, creates what amounts to a joint venture, is the result of arms-length negotiations, and has reasonable actual results. To rule on this last condition requires the service to review the actual levels of compensation given to employees to render a final ruling (see Rev. Rul. 69-383, 1969, and IRS Private Letter Ruling 8808070).

It is public policy that exempt organizations cannot engage in political activities. If an organization's main or primary purpose(s) may be attained only by gaining the passage or defeat of legislation and it advocates for this objective, it is an action organization. In this sense, "legislation" includes initiatives, referendums, and the election of individuals, as well as the passage of a statute. As an action organization, exempt status will be denied. If the organization provides only nonpartisan analysis, study, or research, it may be granted exempt status.

The IRS has provided some guidance as to what constitutes impermissible political activity through its rulings. One ruling aids in determining when an activity is editorial and permissible or propaganda and impermissible (see Rev. Rul. 86-43, 1986-2 C.B. 729). For educational organizations, the service has defined when a class project requiring participation in a political campaign does not endanger tax-exempt status (see Rev. Rul. 72-512, 1972-2 C.B. 246).

In the Internal Revenue Code, a charitable purpose cannot be illegal or contrary to public policy. This concept was reaffirmed in a case involving Bob Jones University, which acted discriminatively on the basis of race. The United States Supreme Court found such activity clearly contrary to public policy and upheld the revocation of an education exemption.

Maintaining Tax-Exempt Status

After an organization has attained exempt status, it must engage in certain actions to retain this status. The Code requires that the organization notify the Internal Revenue Service of any "material" change, which could occur either by a change in structure (organization) or the actual activities and behavior of the organization (operation).

Most exempt organizations are required to file an information report on an annual basis by completing Form 990. The Internal Revenue Code provides three exceptions to this requirement:

1. Churches, their associations, and certain related groups
2. Section 501(c)(3) and (4) organizations, as well as other specified groups, whose gross receipts are less than $5,000
3. State and local government entities as defined by Section 115

A state college or university must determine if it meets the conditions of Section 115. In most instances these institutions do fall within this exception (see IRS Private Letter Ruling 8419007). Also, exempt organizations with gross unrelated business income greater than $1,000 must file Form 990T, even if the Code exempts the group from filing Form 990. Section 511(a)(2)(B) specifically states that all unrelated business income requirements apply to state colleges and universities. These forms are due on the fifteenth day of the fifth month after the close of an organization's tax year. If an organization files Form 990 after its due date, it may be fined $10 per day, but the fine may not exceed the lesser of $5,000 or 5 percent of its gross receipts. A penalty may be assessed for an incomplete form and schedules at the same rate. Failure to properly file Form 990T also carries a penalty. The group may be fined 5 percent per month up to 25 percent of the taxes owed for a late filing and all applicable interest.

The Omnibus Budget Reconciliation Act of 1987 specified a set of public disclosure requirements for most exempt organizations. Under this act (1) all Section 501(c)(3) groups must make an exact copy of their information returns available to the public; all attachments to the report must also be available but the names and addresses of contributors may be omitted; (2) the forms must be available for three years after they are filed; (3) the forms must be available at the group's main office and "any other office that has 3 or more employees"; (4) an organization may not question the identification or purpose of the requestor; and (5) the exempt organization is not required to make copies but it must allow the taking of notes and photocopies.

Form 990 requires the listing of the five highest-paid employees, the compensation of the five highest-paid persons provid-

ing professional services and statements on specified activities (for
example, lobbying, business with a trustee or director, and the
granting of certain scholarships, loans, and fellowships). Tax-
exempt organizations are now also required to disclose relationships with Section 501(c) and Section 527 (political) organizations.
Failure to comply with these requirements may result in fines of $10
per day up to $5,000, and willful violators may be fined an addi-
tional $1,000. In addition to the penalties already mentioned, Con-
gress has provided additional penalties for willful violators. Those
who willfully do not file, or who file fraudulent returns, or who
willfully fail to comply with public disclosure requirements or intentionally underpay estimated taxes face fines and possible im-
prisonment.

There is one other note of caution. In a rare action, the IRS
posted a formal announcement in its *Bulletin* (November 11, 1989)
expressing concern that exempt organizations are not properly reporting income from games of chance and bingo. In this announcement the Internal Revenue Service carefully restated the current law:
As of November 11, 1986, income for games of chance is unrelated
business income for all organizations except those located in North
Dakota. The sole exception to this is those organizations that can
meet the rules found in Section 513(f). This announcement parallels
the IRS's stated concern that exempt organizations are not complying with disclosure requirements as to the portion of contributions
to special events and the like that are not deductible. Announce-
ments of this nature indicate a growing concern within the federal
bureaucracy that exempt organizations are not willing to comply
with the law.

Unrelated Business Income

This section begins the review of determining whether income
generated by an exempt organization is taxable or not. The information in the remainder of Chapter Three and all of Chapter Four
can be quite complex. The goal is to give the reader a basic understanding about how the determination of taxability is made. It is
not intended that you become a legal expert on the many nuances
that will be touched on.

A key factor to understand is that for income generated by an exempt organization to be taxable it must (1) not be substantially related income, (2) be from a trade or business that is regularly carried on, and (3) not meet any of the exceptions or exemptions. Unless each of the conditions is met, the income is not taxable. The remainder of Part Two strives to give as clear a set of definitions as possible to these concepts. Extensive use of court decisions and service advisory opinions is made because this is where much of the current interpretation of federal tax law is found.

As discussed in the section on the history of these Code sections, the concept of unrelated business income was codified in 1950 in Section 511. The Code (Section 512) defines unrelated business income as the gross income from an unrelated trade or business, less deductions for "directly" connected expenses, but there are a number of exceptions to this definition. Unrelated business income does not apply to any trade or business conducted largely by volunteers, to the sale of any goods or services meeting the "convenience" exception, or to the sale of donated goods. Education has also been granted a special exemption for any activity in which students perform 50 percent or more of the service as part of the educational curriculum.

The Code also exempts subdivisions of a state from unrelated business income. The IRS has stated that this tax immunity only extends to "governmental functions." The service has found that when an organization provides unemployment insurance to a group of exempt organizations, it falls within Section 115 (see IRS Private Letter Ruling 8836003). Many other functions performed by a state (for example, utility service or operating a hotel for the general public) are not exempt (see IRS Private Letter Ruling 7904006). As previously mentioned, the Code specifically applies unrelated business income to all state colleges and universities.

Since 1969 legislation, unrelated business income applies to essentially all exempt organizations. An organization's exempt classification (that is, which type of exemption the organization is granted) can affect the calculation of this tax [*Zeta Beta Tau Fraternity, Inc.*, 87 T.C. 421 (1986)]. Similarly, see the cases and service rulings on social clubs, where the unrelated business section has somewhat different wording and the service and some courts have differing views on how to apply it [see IRS Private Letter Ruling 8551003, *North Ridge Country Club*, 89 T.C. 563 (1987), and *Portland Golf Club v. Commissioner*, 110 S.Ct. 2780 (1990)].

In most instances organizations will use the corporate tax rates to determine their unrelated business income tax. Charitable trusts use the individual tax rates. The gross income or loss from all unrelated activities of an organization is combined to determine its tax obligation [see *North Ridge Country Club*, 89 T.C. 563 (1987)].

The Internal Revenue Code requires that (1) for income to be unrelated it must be generated by a trade or business, (2) this activity must be regularly carried on, and (3) the trade or business must not be substantially related to the organization's performance of its exempt purpose. Note that profit motive per se is not a requirement of unrelated business income. A trade or business is defined as any activity carried on for the production of income from the sale of goods or services and possessing within the meaning of general federal income tax principles the characteristics of a trade or business (see I.R.C. Section 162).

The legislative record indicates that the main purpose of imposing an unrelated business income tax was to eliminate unfair competition: "The problem at which the tax on UBI is directed is primarily that of unfair competition. The tax free status of . . . (IRC Sec. 501) organizations enables them to use their profits tax-free to expand operations, which their competitors can only expand with the profits remaining after taxes (House Report No. 2319, 1950, pp. 36–37). Yet the judicial record on this is mixed.

In a case involving income from bingo games, the court found that unfair competition is not a technical requirement to incurring tax [see *Clarence La Belle Post No. 217 v. U.S.*, 46 U.S.C.L.W. 2684 (8th Cir., June 12, 1978)]. Other courts have held that unfair competition is a critical element [see *Hope School v. U.S.*, 612 F.2d 298 (7th Cir. 1980) and *American Bar Endowment v. U.S.*, 761 F.2d 1573 (Fed. Cir. 1985) rev'd 477 U.S. 105, 106 S.Ct. 2426 (1986)].

Congress has seen fit to address a number of specific income vehicles to ensure that this concept of fairness as to the dollars available to invest in business activities is maintained. One example of this is the tax on debt-financed income: "A number of examples have arisen where these organizations have, in effect, used their tax exemption to buy an ordinary business. That is, they acquired the business with no investment on their own part and paid installments out of subsequent earning—a procedure which usually could not be followed if the business was taxable" (House Report No. 2319, 1950, pp. 36-37). In these instances Congress has developed special rules, some of which are discussed in Chapter Five.

As with taxable businesses, tax-exempt organizations may deduct appropriate expenditures. The difficulty is apportioning expenses between related and unrelated activities. To be deductible an expenditure must have a proximate and primary relationship to the income-producing activity. The IRS will normally allow a division of expenses that has a reasonable basis, but this does not mean that exempt organizations will be granted carte blanche in making these determinations. In one case the courts supported the IRS's denial of an organization's division of expenses. The organization in question was found to have maintained inadequate records and to have followed insufficient accounting procedures [see *CORE Special Purpose Fund v. Commissioner*, 49 T.C.M. 626 (1985)].

Separating Taxable and Nontaxable Income

The prior section discusses the basic rules for unrelated business income. Many key phrases in these code sections as well as various tests and exceptions have been developed by Congress in an attempt to further this tax's original intent. It is the combination of these factors, as well as the numerous special rules reviewed later in Part Two, that make the application of the unrelated business income tax quite complex.

To determine if income is taxable, an exempt organization should first examine a series of threshold tests that remove most income generated by exempt organizations from taxation. This will include the trade or business regularly carried on and substantially related tests. If these tests do not exclude a source of income from taxation, an organization will next need to look at a set of major exceptions that remove income from taxation. Should there still be uncertainty as to whether certain income is taxable, the organization must then examine a set of specific exceptions and tests. The remainder of this chapter will discuss this process.

In 1969 the Code section discussing trade or business was amended by Congress. Trade or business for unrelated business income tax purposes is now defined as any activity carried on for the production of income (not profit) from the sale of goods or services and that possesses within the meaning of general federal income tax principles the characteristics of a trade or business (Section 162). An activity does not lose its trade or business status because it is carried on within a larger complex of activities that are themselves exempt.

The term *trade* or *business* is not defined in the Code, although one federal court did define it in a 1983 case. This court found that it is an activity (1) earning a profit from the sale of goods or services, (2) generating benefit to the individual members and not the profession itself, or (3) engaging in unfair competition with a taxable enterprise, or (4) not traditionally engaged in by exempt organizations or constituting an intrusion into traditional commercial areas, or (5) conducted in a competitive or commercial manner [*Carolina Farm and Power Equipment Dealers Association, Inc. v. United States,* 699 F.2d 167 (4th Cir. 1983)]. This court included in its definition the earning of profit, although the Code itself does not seem to require this. Most courts do not require the generation of profits per se but the reasonable expectation that a profit will be generated. Both the IRS and the courts regularly find no such expectation where an activity has consistently generated a net loss. Other factors reviewed are the manner in which the activity is conducted, the expertise of the taxpayer or advisers, the time and effort expended, and the taxpayer's success in other ventures [see *Cleveland Athletic Club, Inc. v. United States,* 588 F.Supp. 1305 (N.D. Ohio 1984) rev'd 779 F.2d 1160 (6th Cir. 1985)].

Because an activity has had a loss, there are times when the exempt organization wants the activity to be declared an unrelated trade or business. The Internal Revenue Service regularly rules that where there is an absence of a profit motive there can be no trade or business. This position has been upheld by many courts [see *West Virginia State Medical Association v. Commissioner,* T.C. No. 41 (Sept. 20, 1988)].

The Internal Revenue Service has consistently taken the position that a social club, a Section 501(c)(7) organization, cannot offset unrelated business income with losses from the sale of food and beverages to nonmembers unless the requisite profit motive is present (see IRS Private Letter Ruling 8551003). This issue arises because the unrelated business income wording applicable to social clubs is somewhat less complete than that which applies to Section 501(c)(3) organizations. The wording for these groups has no reference to a trade or business test. The lower federal courts have been split on this issue [see *Cleveland Athletic Club, Inc. v. United States*, 588 F.Supp. 1305 (N.D. Ohio 1984) rev'd 779 F.2d 1160 (6th Cir. 1985) and *North Ridge Country Club*, 89 T.C. 563 (1987)]. In a 1990 ruling the Supreme Court resolved this matter in the case of *Portland Golf Club v. Commissioner*, 110 S.Ct. 2780 (1990), when it endorsed the position of the IRS. Here the Supreme Court ruled that three consecutive years of losses create a presumption of a lack of profit motive. Thus the profit motive test for social service organizations is now identical to that for Section 501(c)(3) organizations.

The court in *Carolina Farm* typifies the attitude of the IRS and a growing number of jurisdictions in "aggressively pursuing the view that certain characteristics of an activity unavoidably lead to a conclusion that the activity is a trade or business" (Hopkins, 1987, p. 716). Essentially the attitude is that if an activity is "run like a business" it must be one [see *Presbyterian and Reformed Publishing Company v. Commissioner*, 79 T.C. 1070 (1983) and *The Incorporated Trustees of the Gospel Workers Society v. United States*, 510 F.Supp. 374 (D.D.C. 1981) aff'd 672 F.2d 894 (D.C. Cir. 1981) cert. den. 456 U.S. 944 (1982)]. In these cases the Tax Court and the United States district court for the District of Columbia looked at the presence of a profit motive, whether the activity was conducted in a commercial or competitive manner, and whether the management of the activity was efficient and effective. It should be noted that these two courts have historically had a disproportionate impact on tax law for exempt organizations.

Court rulings do not provide clear direction as to whether finding competition with a for-profit entity is a requirement to the existence of a trade or business. Although all circuit courts have not yet addressed this issue, those that have are clearly divided. Thus we see that the fourth and sixth circuits endorse this requirement, while the fifth and eighth circuits do not.

The nature of an activity does not necessarily determine whether it is a trade or business. The issue most often is how the organization goes about performing the activity. Thus the Supreme Court has found that if an activity is pursued essentially full time with regularity to the production of income, it is a trade or business and not a hobby. This is true even where the goods and services component of the test is not met [*Commissioner v. Groetzinger*, 107 S.Ct. 980 (1987)].

The determination as to whether an activity is a trade or business is based on the specific fact situation. Although normally a single transaction will not be a trade or business, if the transaction is large enough it may be found to be one [see *Cooper Tire and Rubber Company Employee's Retirement Fund v. Commissioner*, 306 F.2d 20 (6th Cir. 1962)]. On the other hand, the annual trade show was not found to be a trade or business [see *Orange County Builders' Association v. United States*, 65-2 U.S. Tax Cas. 9679 (D. Cal. 1965)]. Similarly, the IRS has determined that if the preponderance of an organization's income comes from one event, this event is a trade or business (see Rev. Rul. 57-13, 1957—2 C.B. 316). The IRS has also found that where a possibly related function is conducted on a very large scale it can be a trade or business (see Rev. Rul. 60-86, 1960—1 C.B. 198). This concept of scale, as well as the concept of commerciality, has been endorsed by the Supreme Court in applying this test [see *American Bar Endowment v. United States*, 106 S.Ct. 2426 (1986)].

Not all income-producing activities are found to be a trade or business. For example, a court has ruled that the mere management of investments does not constitute a trade or business [see *Continental Trading, Inc. v. Commissioner*, 265 F.2d 40, 43 (9th Cir. 1959) cert. den. 361 U.S. 827 (1959) and *Whipple v. Commissioner*, 373 U.S. 215 (1963)]. Similarly, the service has determined that income from the collection of installment payments and income from the lending of securities is not a trade or business (Rev. Rul. 69-547, 1969-2 C.B. 130 and Rev. Rul. 78-88, 1979-1 C.B. 163).

The IRS has also ruled that the source of the product being sold can determine whether an activity is a trade or business. It has found that "when a bloodbank is merely disposing of products which result from the performance of its exempt function, it will not be engaging in a trade or business" but the sale of plasma purchased from other bloodbanks does constitute a trade or business (see Rev. Rul. 78-145, 1978-1 C.B. 169).

The IRS regularly asserts, and the courts at times agree, that an activity is a trade or business and not educational. This has occurred with the operation of quasi-retail auxiliary services, a broadcast station, an endowment fund's management service, and other activities. In most instances specific exceptions in the Code mean that the activity is not taxable (for instance, the convenience exception and the substantially related test) even though the income-producing activity is found to be a trade or business. But if the income is from commercial sources and competes with commercial stations, a university broadcast station, for example, will be found to generate unrelated business income [*Iowa State University of Science and Technology v. United States*, 500 F.2d 508 (1974)].

Membership organizations often find that services provided to their members will be a taxable trade or business. The issue is whether the service provided is of benefit to the profession or to the individual members. Activities such as an agricultural organization's sale of supplies to members, a labor organization's semiweekly bingo game, an agricultural organization's commission from selling member livestock, and fees to labor organizations from performing accounting and legal services were found to be primarily of benefit to the individual members. As such, these activities are a trade or business.

The fact that an activity is found to be a trade or business is only the first step in determining if it generates unrelated business income. Next the Code asks if the activity is "regularly carried on." To determine this, one looks at the frequency and continuity with which the exempt organization engages in the activity, compared to similar activities by for-profit organizations. This means that in some fact situations an activity engaged in once a year may be taxable while another type engaged in once a year may not be.

The IRS has found that in some instances advertising sold for a school yearbook may generate unrelated business income. This occurred where the advertising was sold by a commercial firm (see

Rev. Rul. 73-124, 1973—2 C.B. 190). The IRS will also find that advertising sold for sporting and cultural events conducted by exempt organizations is taxable if engaged in a systematic way and consistently promoted. If the sales are conducted in a "casual way," the income so generated will not be regularly carried on. Courts have agreed with the approach taken by the IRS on this issue. An ancillary issue for the courts is whether there is extensive effort and planning, as one would expect to find in a commercial venture [see *Parkland Residential School, Inc.*, 45 T.C.M. (CCH) 988].

At the Tax Court level, once a commercial advertising firm is used to conduct the advertising sales, the determination as to the regularly carried on test is now based on the activity of the entity selling the advertising and not the activity of the exempt organization [see *NCAA*, 92 T.C. No. 27 (1989)]. Yet in hearing the appeal of this case, the tenth circuit court of appeals came to a different conclusion [see *NCAA v. Commissioner*, 90-2, U.S.T.C., par. 50,513 (10th Cir. 1990)]. The latter court chose to focus on the time span used to generate the advertising income. In this case the exempt organization (the NCAA) contracted with a for-profit company to sell advertising for game programs, sold in conjunction with basketball tournaments. This court felt that since the selling of the advertising occurred over a few weeks, unlike most advertising sales, which occur on a year-around basis, it did not constitute a regularly carried on activity. Thus the income generated by this activity for the exempt organization was not taxable. This ruling seems to overturn the service's long-term position, which included "preparatory time" in determining the length-of-time issue for the regularly carried on test.

The Internal Revenue Service has indicated that it will indirectly contest this decision by using its position in other federal circuits. The IRS hopes to gain a contra ruling in another circuit. This means that the Supreme Court will address the issue only when the IRS has a circuit court ruling that supports its position.

It should be noted that both the courts and the IRS are developing a commerciality approach in applying the regularly carried on test. That is, the more an organization conducting an activity behaves like a commercial firm, the greater the probability that it will be found to be regularly carried on.

The regulations state that an annual fund-raising dance conducted by an exempt organization is not regularly carried on [Reg. Sec. 1.513-1(c)(2)(iii)]. The courts have interpreted this to be true even where the annual event has extensive planning and uses professional entertainers to execute the event [see *Suffolk County Patrolmen's Benevolent Association, Inc.*, 77 T.C. 134 (1981)]. Similarly, if an activity is engaged in only one time by an exempt organization, the IRS will find that it is not regularly carried on. This has been true where one tax-exempt organization developed computerized administrative programs and sold them to three other exempt organizations and where a university sold a set of apartments in a single bulk sale (see IRS Private Letter Rulings 7905129 and 8017016).

The fact that an activity does not occur on a twelve-month basis does not mean that it is not regularly carried on. Since nonexempt organizations typically sell Christmas cards on a seasonal basis, when an exempt organization sells Christmas cards in a similar way this activity is regularly carried on (see IRS Private Letter Ruling 8203134). Thus the analysis process used by the Internal Revenue Service compares the behavior of the exempt organization to that of a for-profit organization that engages in the same activity.

Assuming that an activity has been found to be a trade or business and that it meets the regularly carried on test, it will not be considered taxable if it is found to be substantially related. The "substantially related test" attempts to determine if the means by which the income is generated contributes importantly to the accomplishment of the organization's exempt purpose. The IRS and the courts will base their determination on the facts and circumstances presented by a particular activity [see *Commissioner v. Groetzinger*, 107 S.Ct. 980 (1987)].

There are a number of exceptions to the facts and circumstances approach. If substantially all work is done by volunteers, if the convenience exception is applicable, or if practically all of the goods are donated, the income generated will not be taxable. Similarly, the Internal Revenue Service Code exempts qualified public entertainment at fairs and expositions, qualified conventions and trade shows, certain bingo games (those legal under state law and conducted by Section 501(c)(3) organizations), the trading or renting of mailing lists between two exempt organizations, and unrestricted donations even though the donor receives a premium with a value not to exceed $5.

In terms of trade shows sponsored by Section 501(c)(3)–(6) organizations, they must meet a specified standard to fall outside of the facts and circumstances approach: (1) The trade show must be conducted regularly, (2) it must stimulate interest and demand for products and services or new rules and regulations for the industry, and (3) the show may not be aimed at selling a particular exhibitor's goods.

In looking at the facts and circumstances, the adjudicating party will examine issues such as who actually receives the benefit and the size and extent of the activity in relation to the nature of the exempt function it purports to fulfill. Thus an activity that may be substantially related in one setting may not be in another.

Looking at the development of parking garages and shuttle services to stimulate trade in a city's downtown, the IRS has found that where the service is performed without favoritism to any merchant or group of merchants it is substantially related. If the program is a typical park-and-shop validation program, where for a minimum purchase some merchants will validate a customer's parking coupon, the facts and circumstances now present show an unrelated activity (see Rev. Rul. 79-31, 1979-2 C.B. 206).

Where it is found that the benefit of an activity is for the individual members and not an organization itself, the activity may not be substantially related. An exempt association that promotes auto racing was found to be engaged in a substantially related activity when conducting a certification program. The Internal Revenue Service found that this activity was designed to protect against trade abuses within the industry, which was part of the group's exempt purpose (see IRS Private Letter Ruling 7922001). Yet where an association of credit unions published and sold to its members a consumer information magazine, the activity was determined to be unrelated because it served the individual consumer and not the credit unions (see Rev. Rul. 78-52, 1978-1 C.B. 166).

The cost and nature of an activity is another item that may be reviewed. In instances where the purpose of an organization is to promote youth physical fitness, the fact that fees were at so high a level as to limit membership, or where the exempt purpose was to provide for the social welfare of young people but the activity was operated in a commercial manner, the activity was found by the IRS not to be substantially related (see Rev. Rul. 79-360, 1979-2 C.B. 237 and Rev. Rul. 79-361, 1979-2 C.B. 237). But where the income-producing activity so furthered the exempt purpose of the organization, the size and the extent of the activity was not controlling [*Edward Horton, Jr.*, 56 T.C. 147 (1971)].

As in other areas, the IRS and the courts do not always agree on an issue. The IRS has found that a state bar association's sale of forms to attorneys is an unrelated activity because it "does not contribute importantly" to accomplishing the organization's exempt purpose; yet in a similar fact situation a court has found such an activity to be substantially related [see Rev. Rul. 78-51, 1978-1 C.B. 165 and *San Antonio Bar Association v. U.S.*, 80-2 U.S.T.C. 9594 (W.D. Tex. 1980)].

The rental by a college or university of its facilities to a third party has been found to be both related and unrelated. For instance, sports camps, if they provide instruction for the participants, are substantially related (see Rev. Rul. 77-365, 1977-2 C.B. 192, Rev. Rul. 80-297, 1980-2 C.B. 196, and IRS Private Letter Rulings 8151005, 7908009, and 7826003). The determination as to whether leasing a campus's facilities to another organization is substantially related is based on the content of the program of the leasing group. Yet it must be remembered that the determination that a facility rental is not substantially related is not the final determination. If such income is found to be "passive income," it will not be taxable. (This concept will be discussed in more detail in the next section.) In many instances, an exempt organization's leasing of its facilities will generate taxable income (see Rev. Rul. 76-402, 1976-2 C.B. 177).

The substantially related test is one of the most contested issues in determining whether an exempt organization's income is taxable. This issue often arises after an affirmative determination is made that an activity is a trade or business. An illustrative set of these rulings indicates that the IRS and the courts often find that an activity that is a trade or business is still not taxable because it is substantially related. Among trade or business activities that have been found to be substantially related are the operation of a laundry service, residence hall, travel service, pro shop, bar, concessions, and a campus dining program by a university; the operation of a lawyer referral service by a bar association; the sale of products in connection with educational programs; the sale of computer software by an organization whose purpose is to make new technology widely available to the public; the sale of posters and other promotional material carrying an organization's program message; a college-operated professional repertory theater open to the general public; a university's operation of an international student center; and a journal published by law students (see Rev. Rul. 81-18, 1981-3 C.B. 353, Rev. Rul. 76-33, 1976-1 C.B. 167 and IRS Private Letter Ruling 8138075, Rev. Rul. 67-327, 1967-2 C.B. 187 and IRS Private Letter Ruling 8115025, IRS Private Letter Ruling 8340102, Rev. Rul. 58-194, 1958-1 C.B. 240, IRS Private Letter Ruling 8542001, IRS Private Letter Ruling 8518090, IRS Private Letter Ruling 8512084, IRS Private Letter Ruling 8633034, Rev. Rul. 69-400, 1969-2 C.B. 114, IRS Private Letter Ruling 7840072, and Rev. Rul. 63-235, 1963-2 C.B. 110).

The tax treatment of university travel programs has been questioned by for-profit competitors for years. To date these small businesses have been frustrated in their attempts at litigation [see *American Society of Travel Agents v. Blumenthall*, 46 U.S.L.W. 2195 (U.S. Court of Appeals for the District of Columbia, 1977) and *American Society of Travel Agents v. Simon*, 566 F.2d 145 (D.C. Cir. 1977) cert. den 435 U.S. 947 (1978)]. Nevertheless, the IRS has reviewed the scope of permissible activities a number of times and developed reasonably narrow guidelines as to which travel activities will be considered substantially related. In 1990 the service issued an updated test for travel tours, which makes it very difficult for most travel programs to be educational and therefore substantially related. To be educational a tour must now (1) have a "bona fide educational methodology" exhibited by "organized study groups, reports, lectures, library access, reading lists and mandatory participation"; (2) be done in a "highly professional manner as exhibited by daily lectures and the like"; (3) focus on the study of a subject, with appropriate academic credit awarded; and (4) be "selected for its educational value and the qualifications of the tour leader" (see

IRS Tech. Adv. Mem. 9027003, Rev. Rul. 67-327, 1967-2 C.B. 189, and Rev. Rul 70-534, 1970-2 C.B. 113).

The issue of whether intercollegiate all-star and "bowl" games are substantially related has been reviewed by both the IRS and the courts. This type of fact situation is an excellent example of where the service initially ruled one way and then, in the face of court rulings and the nature of the issue vis-à-vis society, changed its position. Initially the IRS found these athletic contests to be unrelated yet upon reconsideration determined that these activities furthered the purpose of promoting sports activities among young people, which is related to the organization's exempt purpose. This means that income from broadcasts, ticket sales, and the like is not taxable [see *Mobile Arts and Sports Association v. United States,* 148 F.Supp. 31 (D. Ala. 1957) and Rev. Rul. 80-296, 1980-2 C.B. 195].

The Internal Revenue Service has reversed itself on other matters when the exempt organization has used the administrative appeals process and mustered a substantial case. In the mid 1970s, the IRS initially ruled that Stanford University owed $8.4 million in taxes on income from real property, a golf course, and broadcast rights. In 1978 the IRS issued a regional conferees administrative decision that Stanford had no tax liability for these activities. [See *Board of Trustees of the Leland Stanford Junior University v. County of Santa Clara,* No. 337067, Sup.Ct. Santa Clara Cty. (1978) for a related property tax case also won by Stanford, and Rev. Rul. 78-98, 1978-1 C.B. 167.]

The tax status of hospital activities has been heavily debated. In most instances courts have found that services provided to non-patients of a hospital are not substantially related [see *Carle Foundation v. United States,* 611 F.2d 192 (8th Cir. 1979)]. But in a rural setting where it was difficult to attract and retain doctors, the court found that servicing patients of the hospital's medical staff who were not hospital patients furthered the hospital's primary purpose of providing health care [*Hi-Plains Hospital v. United States,* 670 F.2d 528 (5th Cir. 1982)].

The IRS takes the position that medical tests for a hospital's physicians at teaching and research hospitals are substantially related (Rev. Rul. 85-109, 1985-2 C.B. 165). In a companion ruling, the service found that similar tests conducted at nonteaching hos-

pitals are not substantially related unless they contribute importantly to that type of hospital's exempt purpose. The latter may
occur where the hospital is conducting community service testing
or where the hospital specializes in drug overdose testing (see Rev.
Rul. 85-110, 1985-2 C.B. 166).

Another area of heavy debate in recent years has been the tax
status of the broadening scope of materials that are sold by museums. The service has issued a litany of revenue ruling and private
letter rulings on this subject. Among them are the decision that the
sale of city souvenirs and scientific books is not substantively related, the fact that an item has a utilitarian purpose does not foreclose the question of substantial purpose, food service for staff and
patrons is substantially related, the sale of reproductions of works
on display is substantially related, articles of an "institutional or
artistic nature" are substantially related, and the sale of T-shirts and
stuffed animals is not substantially related (see Rev. Rul. 73-105,
1973-1 C.B. 264; IRS Private Letter Rulings 8814001, 8034022,
8303013, 8328009, 8032028, and 8432004; Rev. Rul. 74-399, 1974-2
C.B. 172; and Rev. Rul. 73-105, 1973-1 C.B. 204). In rulings of this
nature, the IRS is careful to point out that with a different set of
facts the same activity might be ruled on differently.

This concept can be seen where the service was asked to review the sale of stationery items, serving items, desk accessories,
nature gift items, emblem toys, and wearing apparel by a national
conservation group. Because this organization's exempt function
included educating the public, the Internal Revenue Service found
that each of these items was substantially related because it stimulated the public's interest in wildlife conservation (see IRS Private
Letter Ruling 8107006). Using similar reasoning, a court found that
the sale of artwork was substantially related because it increased
public awareness of the organization's exempt activity [*Cleveland
Creative Arts Guild v. Commissioner*, 50 T.C.M. 272 (1985)]. Similarly, the sale of public books was found to be substantially related
by the IRS where an organization's exempt purpose was to dissem-
inate public knowledge (IRS Private Letter Ruling 8404045). Using
the dissemination of knowledge concept, the IRS has also found
that there is no unrelated business income when a college licenses

copyrighted curriculum to other schools (IRS Private Letter Ruling 8824018).

Relatedness can turn on who uses a service. In looking at the use of university recreation facilities and travel programs, for example, this is often the pivotal issue (see IRS Private Letter Ruling 8115015, Rev. Rul. 79-98, 1979-1 C.B. 167, and Rev. Rul. 70534, 1970-2 C.B. 113). Where the users are the organization's service population, the activity is substantially related.

In the area of products and materials testing, the pivotal issue is the purpose and the product being tested. Where the product is being tested for a commercial entity to determine its marketability, even if the testing is for safety standards, the income generated by doing the tests is taxable (see Rev. Rul. 68-373, 1968-2 C.B. 206 and Rev. Rul. 78-426, 1978-2 C.B. 1751).

Relatedness may turn on how the goods that are sold are acquired. Where the goods were produced by the exempt organization's students, the IRS has found the activity to be substantially related (see Rev. Rul. 68-581, 1968-2 C.B. 250). The issue may also be the service that is being provided. When an exempt organization dedicated to preventing cruelty to animals engaged in grooming and boarding animals, the IRS found the fees that were collected were not substantially related (Rev. Rul. 73-587. 1973-2 C.B. 192).

Some colleges and universities operate a campus farm as part of the academic program. In a setting where the campus operates a dairy farm, the sale of milk and cream has been considered to be related, but it is not related to process these products into other goods.

In examining an activity that is often found to be substantially related, courts may determine it taxable if the facts and circumstances warrant. Thus a magazine produced by an exempt organization and sold to its members, where the magazine's content was found to focus on internal news and the activities of the members instead of to provide educational information, was found not to be substantially related. [See *Phi Delta Fraternity v. Commissioner*, 90 T.C.B. (May 16, 1988).]

The diversity of the issues that can arise in determining if an activity is substantially related are enormous. This section gives an overview of some of the more typical and policy-setting incidents.

Resource A on Unrelated Business Income Tax Cases gives additional examples and further explains some of the fact situations that have been used.

Using the Fragmentation Test

In determining whether an activity is unrelated to an exempt purpose, the Internal Revenue Service and the courts look at each individual activity separately. The fact that an activity occurs within the context of an exempt activity does not automatically mean that it cannot be found to be unrelated. This is called the fragmentation test.

An example of this test will be seen in the discussion in the next chapter of the rules to determine whether advertising within an exempt magazine is related or not. In many settings such advertising will incur the unrelated business income tax while the income from the sale of the magazine will not be taxable [see *American College of Physicians v. United States*, 106 S.Ct. 1591 (1986)].

The fragmentation test also comes into play in determining whether losses from an unrelated activity can be used to offset gains from other unrelated activities by the same exempt organization. As was discussed in the review of the trade or business test, if an activity has a history of generating a loss, it will not meet the standards of this test. In one case a university operated a radio and a television station. The latter generated net income while the former consistently generated a loss. The university was not allowed to diminish the tax generated from the television station by the losses from the radio station. Both activities were unrelated because they were operated in a commercial manner [see *Iowa State University of Science and Technology v. United States*, 500 F.2d 508 (1974)].

Taxing Passive Income

Irrespective of the nature of the activity, the Internal Revenue Code states that passive income to an exempt organization will not be taxed. The Code defines the basic forms of such income as dividends, interest payments, payments with respect to securities loans, annuities, royalties, certain rents, and gain from the sale of real property [see I.R.C. Section 512(c)(1)(2)(3) and (5)]. Most of the adjudication on these Code sections has determined whether the income is truly passive or whether the exempt organization's actions have converted the income into an active form. Where the latter is found, the income is now taxable unless it meets one of the other exceptions.

One major form of passive income for many exempt organizations is the collection of rent. Rental income is passive if the payment is only for space and normal maintenance services (heating or cooling, lights, trash removal, cleaning of shared public areas). If there are services for the convenience of the occupants, this income will become active income [custodial and cleaning services, food, laundry, security, grounds maintenance (see IRS Private Letter Ruling 7740072)].

The name given by the recipient organization to a source of income is not determinative as to how it will be treated under the Code. An organization cannot call income from a trade or business "rent" and thereby escape taxation. Similarly, to the extent that "rental" payments are based on a percentage of the net income of an occupant, the income is active.

If the rental agreement covers personal property as well as real property, all or part of the income may move into the active form. The rules on this state: (1) If less than 10 percent of the payment is for personal property, the entire amount is passive; (2) if between 10 and 50 percent of the payment is for personal property, the percentage of payment attributed to personal property is active; and (3) if more than 50 percent of the payment is for personal property, the entire payment is active.

Artificial division of a lease into two agreements, one for real property and a second for personal property, will not avoid converting some or all of the income into the active form. The taxability of rental income is determined on the first day of the lease unless the rent attributable to personal property increases by 100 percent or more or the lease terms are modified, resulting in a rent increase. The latter might occur where additional space was included in the agreement; it does not include a rent increase due to inflation.

The leasing of facilities by colleges and universities to professional teams has resulted in a number of administrative rulings by the IRS. In its determinations, the IRS has treated these rental agreements just like any other lease. Where the agreement only covers the use of playing fields, locker rooms, and the like, the income is passive (see IRS Private Letter Ruling 8024001); but where services such as meals, grounds maintenance, and security are included, the income becomes active (see Rev. Rul. 80-298, 1980-2 C.B. 197).

The lease of other facilities by an exempt organization is treated in the same way. There is no active income where the organization leases tennis courts, dressing rooms, and the like to another party. As with the leasing of space to professional teams, if other services such as coaches, trainers, and administrative assistance are included in the agreement, the income becomes active (see Rev. Rul. 80-297, 1980-2 C.B. 196).

Royalty income is another major source of passive income for exempt organizations. The historical reason for this exemption is that there is no competition with for-profits in generating this form of income. In the past decade, we have seen a marked expansion in the efforts by exempt organizations to generate royalty income from patents or copyrights, the licensing of their name and logo, and other related forms. As long as the only obligation of the exempt organization is to allow the use of its name and logo, the income so generated is consistently found to be passive. The IRS has ruled that income to an exempt organization for allowing the use of its name and logo in association with group insurance, an exempt museum's name and logo used with a commercial product, a trade association's name and logo used with traveler's checks, or an amateur sport's association with a commercial product are all forms of passive income (see I.R.S. Private Letter Rulings 8828011, 8511079, 8352090, and 8006005 and IRS General Counsel Memorandum 3997).

In a 1990 ruling the IRS exhibited its intent to closely scrutinize licensing agreements. A tax-exempt organization had appointed another entity to develop a "licensed" insurance program for its members. The service found the second organization to be an agent of the exempt organization. In this case the exempt organization did much more than allow the use of its name. It also endorsed the insurance program, had advance approval of the content of all mailings, could select the insurance company to be used, and could approve all plan modifications (IRS Private Letter Ruling 9029047). Thus this income was active and taxable.

All attempts to describe income as royalty income have not passed the inspection of the IRS or the courts. Two areas of particular concern in the past decade were advertising income and the use of mailing lists. Because of the complexity of the rules affecting these activities and the widespread use of them by exempt organizations, they will be given special treatment in Chapter Four. All comments on these activities will be deferred at this point.

Some exempt organizations receive appreciable income from mineral rights. Generally speaking, such income is considered a royalty and is passive. The IRS has stated that where a nonprofit's income from its mineral rights is based on the gross profit reduced by all expenses of development and operation, it is receiving an exempt dividend (IRS Private Letter Ruling 7741004), but where an exempt organization's income is based on a "working interest," the income becomes active.

Fixed-sum payments for the right to use an asset are royalty income; thus payments for the use of copyrights and patents are normally passive income. For this to be true, the exempt organization must have both beneficial and legal title (see Rev. Rul. 76-297, 1976-2 C.B. 178). If the patent or copyright returns to another party after some specified period, there is no legal title and the income is no longer passive.

If a tax-exempt organization forms a nonprofit corporation to market its patents and gives legal title to the patents to the new organization, and as consideration for this the new organization agrees to give all net profit to the exempt organization, the income to the exempt organization is passive (IRS Private Letter Ruling 8827017). But if the exempt organization retains control over the enterprise it has supposedly licensed, the income is active [see *Fraternal Order of Police, Illinois State Trooper Lodge No. 41 v. Commissioner*, 833 F.2d 717 (7th Cir. 1987)].

An amount deducted by an exempt organization from royalty payments collected from licenses for distribution to the beneficial owners as patent development and license fees is not royalty income to the exempt organization. Since fees for development and management are active income, this income is taxable [see Rev. Rul. 73-193, 1973-1 C.B. 262, *Service Bolt and Nut Company Profit-Sharing Trust,* 78 T.C. 812 (1982) aff'd 724 F.2d 519 (6th Cir. 1984)].

As with dividends, interest income is passive income, even if the form of the loan is not the normal savings account or purchase of a bond. Thus the lending of securities has been found to generate passive income (see Rev. Rul 72-521, 1972-2 C.B. 178).

Affinity cards are an example of an income-generating vehicle that was not conceived of when the Internal Revenue Code sections on passive income were under review by Congress. This income activity is an excellent example of the IRS's ability both to respond quickly to a new issue and to alter its position based on perceived public policy. Initially the IRS ruled that payments for the use of an exempt organization's name and logo in relation to an affinity card was a royalty (IRS Private Letter Ruling 8747066). Shortly thereafter the Office of General Counsel for the IRS issued an opposite ruling (IRS General Counsel Memorandum 39727). The General Counsel determined that the rules on mailing lists controlled this income source. Since affinity cards were not specifically mentioned in this code section [Section 513(h)], the income must be active; the IRS then released a new ruling and advised that income from affinity cards would be considered active income (IRS Private Letter Ruling 8823109). In the Subcommittee on Oversight's review of the unrelated business income tax, there was unanimous agreement among committee members that income from affinity cards should be subject to taxation. Thus it seems certain that the position of the IRS will be eventually codified into the Internal Revenue Code.

The fragmentation test has been used in examining an exempt organization's income from a limited partnership. To the extent that the income is from the exempt organization's role as a limited partner, the income is active. If the exempt group has made an arms-length loan to the partnership, the income so derived is passive interest income (see *Service Bolt and Nut Company Profit-Sharing Trust* and Rev. Rul. 79-222, 1979-2 C.B. 236).

Convenience Exception

Generally, income generated by higher education, hospitals, museums, and other Section 501(c)(3) organizations from the provision of goods or services for the convenience of their staff and members is exempt from taxation. This exemption diminishes the need for the IRS and the courts to determine which activities are substantially related and facilitates the ability of these organizations to accomplish their exempt purpose.

In relation to colleges and universities, if a service is provided for the convenience of faculty, students, and staff it is exempt. Note that this listing does not include alumni or "friends of the university." Under this exemption, sales from the campus bookstore, food service, recreation center, social and recreational programs, laundry facilities, dormitories, and a variety of other activities are easily found to be exempt from unrelated business taxes without needing to get into the more complex issues of trade or business, substantiality, and the like.

The diversity of activities by these institutions has compelled them to periodically ask the IRS for guidance as to a specific activity. Particularly in the area of college bookstores, we have seen many such advisory opinions. The IRS has easily found that the sale of required classroom materials; trade books; items with campus logos, marks, or name on them; school supplies; low-cost novelty items; high-demand convenience items; records; tapes; and the like are exempt from taxation. As items take on a useful life of more than one year and seem to have no relation to higher education per se, the advice is that they will be taxable. In this group one finds watches, higher-priced gift items and apparel, appliances (such as televisions and refrigerators), plants, and similar tangential goods. [But note that the leasing of appliances was found not to be taxable (see Rev. Rul. 1981-8 I.R.B. 45 and IRS Private Letter Rulings 8004010, 8025222, and 8605002).]

The convenience exception has allowed hospitals and museums to provide food service programs for their staff and their patients. Similarly, the typical hospital convenience store selling flowers, get-well cards, books, writing materials, convenience items, and similar goods is covered by the convenience exception, as is a hospital's operation of a laundry for its patients and staff.

This exception does not give these exempt organizations license to sell anything to these classes of persons. In the earlier discussion on the substantially related test, a range of activities by colleges, museums, and hospitals was reviewed, which is included neither in the substantially related or the convenience exemption. Thus a hospital's sale of pharmaceuticals to patients or staff physicians who are not also hospital patients is taxable, as is a broad range of items sold in a museum gift shop.

As with other exempt organization activities, the IRS and the courts utilize the fragmentation test in examining convenience exception requests. In looking at a university's ski facility, the IRS stated that although the use of the facility for recreational purposes by the university's students is exempt under the convenience exemption, use by the general public and students from other colleges is not (see Rev. Rul. 79-98, 1979-1 C.B. 167). Similar treatment occurs where other campus services are used by persons other than faculty, students, and staff.

As with the other tests and exemptions, the fact that an activity is not covered by the convenience exception does not mean that it is a taxable unrelated activity. The reviewer must now look at the other exemptions, exceptions, and special rules to determine taxability.

Political Activity

The Internal Revenue Service Code has placed limits on the allowed political activities of an organization to gain and maintain the privilege of exempt status. Initially the goal was to bar involvement in partisan activity, which included efforts to influence how the electorate might vote on a proposition, initiative, or referendum as well as candidates for office. Over time this prohibition has extended to lobbying activities on matters before legislative officials.

Determining how much political activity will threaten an organization's exempt status has been quite difficult because of a lack of specificity in the Code. In an attempt to clarify this issue, Congress passed Section 501(h) of the Internal Revenue Code, which bars an organization from having a "substantial part of (its) activity" as prohibited political action. The new Code section developed an economic test for this, stating that an organization may be involved in political activities to the extent that it spends no more than

> 20 percent of its first $500,000 or a maximum of $100,000
> 15 percent of its next $500,000 or a maximum of $75,000
> 10 percent of its next $500,000 or a maximum of $50,000
> 5 percent up to $2,000,000 or a maximum of $25,000

If an organization's income exceeds $2,000,000, it may not spend any additional funds. The amount that an organization may spend is cumulative for that tax year. As an example, an organization with gross revenues of $1,500,000 may spend up to $225,000 without risking its exempt status.

This means of measuring political activity is elective. It has been found to be quite useful for smaller exempt organizations. Most of higher education has not elected to use this test, however, and churches and private foundations are barred from doing so.

As was discussed previously, not all political activity is barred. Testifying on proposed legislation, making available comparative, nonpartisan studies, providing technical advice in response to questions, and working with staff in the administrative branch on the interpretation and implementation of legislation are all permissible activities.

In 1990 the Internal Revenue Service released a comprehensive set of regulations implementing Section 501(h). Those organizations that have chosen to place themselves within this section, and those considering this election, should study these regulations in detail. The new procedures are found in the Internal Revenue Code Regulations Section 56.4911. An excellent review of these new regulations can be found in *The Nonprofit Counsel* newsletter, beginning with the October 1990 issue.

In the early 1980s, a coalition of elected officials and exempt organizations filed suit against the Code sections barring lobbying activities. It was their feeling that the current Code and its interpretation by the federal administration had gone so far in barring activities that it was a breach of free-speech rights. The United States Supreme Court found that the plaintiffs' arguments were without merit. In doing so the Court again noted that exempt status was a privilege on which Congress could place reasonable restrictions [see *Regan v. Taxation with Representation of Washington*, 461 U.S. 540 (1983)].

Other Exemptions

The Internal Revenue Code sections addressing tax-exempt organizations and the unrelated business income tax contain many other exemptions. Some are based on our nation's desire to support volunteerism and charitable contributions. Thus, where substantially all of the labor associated with a particular activity is donated, or substantially all of the goods are donated, there is no tax liability. This is true even where the underlying activity is not substantially related, is a trade or business, and is regularly carried on (see IRS Private Letter Ruling 8820061). Similarly, income from research by a university or college, whether basic or applied, is exempt unless it is conducted as an incident to a commercial or industrial contract.

Many other exemptions are carefully crafted to meet a specific fact situation, but it is beyond the scope of this book to enumerate all of these narrow exemptions. In many instances these sections were developed to clarify the intention of Congress after a court decision and/or an administrative determination by the Internal Revenue Service. A few examples of this type of action follow.

1. Since 1976 the income from entertainment events at fairs and expositions under the auspices of agricultural and horticultural associations is tax exempt [Section 513(d)(1), (2)].
2. Section 513(f) created a set of circumstances in which income from bingo is exempt.
3. Section 513(c) created a set of circumstances in which small hospitals could develop cooperative means to gain operating services. These rules include the requirement that each participating hospital be exempt from taxes, each hospital have 100 beds or less, and the activity be consistent with the hospital's exempt purpose.

4. There is no unrelated business income to a veterans'
    organization that collects insurance payments for the organiza-
    tion's members or their dependents if the funds are set aside for
    the payment of insurance benefits or for a charitable purpose.
    There are similar rules for this "exempt function income" for
    social clubs, voluntary employee beneficiary associations, sup-
    plemental unemployment trust benefit trusts, and group legal
    service organizations [see Section 501(c)(7)(9)(17)(20)].

Gaining this type of specificity is not always beneficial to the class
of exempt organizations. Where such rules exist, the service and the
courts tend to look at them as the exclusive means to determine tax
exemption.

   This approach was described earlier in the review of the
IRS's position on affinity cards. It has also been seen in the ap-
proach to cooperative effort between exempt hospitals [see *HCSC—
Laundry v. United States,* 473 F.Supp. 250 (E.D. Pa. 1979)].

Special Rules
for Specific Types
of Income

Chapter Four analyzes many of the special rules developed by Congress for determining the taxability of a specific income source. These rules all emanate from the underlying purpose of the unrelated business income tax. This is the desire of Congress to structure an environment of fair competition between exempt and for-profit organizations when the former generate income not associated with the principles on which the concept of tax exemption is granted.

As the type, number, complexity, and funding requirements of exempt organizations have grown, so has the need for clarity on a broad range of issues as to the tax consequences. The Internal Revenue Service is normally the first body to attempt to provide this clarity, which occurs when the IRS issues a regional ruling or a private letter ruling on a particular fact situation. When the fact situation is one of first impression (that is, the first time the issue has been addressed by the IRS), the IRS extrapolates based on the then-current Code, court decisions, and its own prior interpretations.

When an exempt group believes that the IRS's interpretation is not correct, it has the right to engage in civil litigation. Court decisions may help to clarify an issue or they may only create more confusion. The greatest clarity occurs when the United States Supreme Court rules on an issue; the greatest confusion occurs when there is a division of opinions on the various lower-level federal courts.

Congress amends the Internal Revenue Code when the IRS prevails on Congress to codify the IRS's position on a particular matter, when the division of opinions by the federal courts is such that it is compelled to provide clarity, or when public comment is such that it grabs the attention of Congress and legislators respond to constituent concerns. Irrespective of the specific motivation (particularly since World War II), Congress, the IRS, and the courts have felt the need to develop special rules for numerous income-generating activities of exempt organizations.

This chapter will review the settings that have had the most impact. As will be seen, these rules are often quite detailed and complex. Exempt organizations are urged to gain advice from attorneys and tax consultants with specific expertise in these rules before entering into an income-generating activity that may be covered by one of these rules. The information that follows is intended to provide a general overview and to give the reader knowledge sufficient to understand when these rules may come into play. Those desiring further information should either consult with appropriate legal counsel and certified public accountants or read the pertinent sections of a number of the sources listed in the references (especially Hopkins, 1987 and Treusch, 1988).

Leasing Rules

The purpose of the tax-exempt leasing rules is to restrict the federal tax benefit of leasing property to an exempt organization, as well as the federal tax benefit available to investors in partnership with taxable and tax-exempt organizations. These rules were created in response to possible abuses of "sales and leaseback" arrangements. As one reviewer noted, "The tax exempt entity leasing rules stand as a monument to the ability—if not the inclination—of Congress to react (perhaps overreact) strenuously to correct a perceived tax abuse. As these rules so starkly reflect, tax exempt organizations are not immune from this phenomenon" (Hopkins, 1987, p. 854).

These leasing rules are perhaps the most complex in the Code. Those organizations that find themselves in a situation that possibly falls within these rules should gain the assistance of an expert in this area.

These rules apply to real and personal property. The rules force investors to compute their depreciation on a straight-line basis, over a longer period of time (forty years) for tax-exempt use property than property that does not meet this definition. This has meant that investors could no longer pass along through low rental rates tax deductions not available to exempt organizations. (Note: Because exempt organizations do not pay income taxes, there is no deduction for operating expenses such as rent.) "Tax-exempt use property" is any portion of tangible property leased to an exempt organization. For nonresidential real property, tax-exempt use property is that portion of the property rented to an exempt organization through what is called a "disqualified lease." The latter is any lease of 35 percent or more of a property to an exempt organization if at least one of the following is present.

1. A tax-exempt bond or other tax-exempt vehicle financed all or part of the property and the exempt leasing organization participated either directly or indirectly through a related organization.
2. The lease gives the exempt organization, or a related entity, an option to buy. The latter must be for a set price.
3. The lease term is in excess of twenty years.
4. The lease occurs after the convenience of the property by the exempt organization, or the lease of the property from the exempt organization, and the property has been used by the exempt organization prior to the transfer or lease.

It is the last point that is intended to resolve congressional concern as to questionable sale and leaseback arrangements.

In a few instances, exempt organizations had sold property they owned to individuals and organizations with a for-profit motive and then had the property leased back to the exempt organization. The net effect of these transactions was to give the for-profit entity both a major tax deduction and an income stream, while the nonprofit organization received what amounted to a large donation based on the net return from the sale of the property and the reduced rental costs on the property. The federal government was "paying" for this type of "donation." This arrangement does not become a disqualified lease unless the exempt organization has used the property prior to the transfer and the lease. Additionally, Code Section 168(h)(1)(B)(v) requires that the exempt organization must have used the property for more than three months immediately prior to entering into the arrangement.

In 1986 Congress acted to remove a loophole in these rules. Some tax-exempt entities had created a "controlled" tax-exempt organization to act as a middleman. The Tax Reform Act of 1986 defined a controlled entity as one in which one or more tax-exempt organizations own 50 percent or more of the value of the stock. When this occurs the leasing rules apply.

Debt-Financed Property

In 1969 Congress altered the Internal Revenue Code to place a tax on the investment income of exempt organizations that can be traced to borrowed funds; prior to that time, such income was treated as passive. This is referred to as debt-financed property or acquisition indebtedness. As with the regulations on leased property, these rules are also quite complex. Here too the exempt organization is encouraged to gain professional assistance when entering into these types of arrangements. The intent of the debt-financed property regulations is to treat exempt entities like for-profits to the extent that the exempt organization purchases property with borrowed funds. The motivation for this was complaints by for-profits that when their income was treated as passive, exempt organizations had an unfair competitive advantage in the marketplace.

Property is defined quite broadly. It can be real property, stocks, or personal property—essentially anything that can be held for the production of income. Section 514 of the Internal Revenue Code states that tax liability is calculated by determining the percentage of the property financed by borrowed funds. This percentage applies to the income derived from the investment and the expenses that may be deducted. The actual tax computation is relatively complex. An equation to calculate acquisition indebtedness is:

$$\text{Unrelated business income} = \frac{\text{the average AI for the past year}}{\text{average adjusted basis of the property for the prior year}}$$

If at least 85 percent of the property's use is substantially related to the organization's exempt purpose, this rule does not apply. Also, where property is owned and used by a tax-exempt organization or a related exempt organization, or by an exempt organization related to the related exempt organization, the debt-financing rules do not apply. A related organization occurs when 50 percent of the members of one organization are members of the other.

If property is received by an exempt organization through a bequest (will) and is subject to a mortage, it is not treated as debt financed for ten years from the date of the acquisition. If similar property is received as a gift by an exempt organization, it will not be considered debt financed if the mortgage was placed on the property more than five years before the gift was made and has been held by the donor for more than five years. There is no acquisition indebtedness for taxes not yet due on property.

Since July 1984 there has been an exception to the rules on debt financing for any indebtedness incurred by a "qualified organization" in acquiring or improving real property. Section 514(c)(9) defines a qualified organization as an educational institution, any affiliated support organization or qualified trust, and a tax-exempt multipatent title-holding organization. In a number of circumstances this exception will not be applicable. The two most common settings are "income from property" financed deals or where the seller will lease back the property. The latter arrangements are covered in the prior section; the former refer to agreements where the income generated by the use of the purchased property is the means for financing the purchase of said property. Today we often see a university-affiliated organization develop a facility for the university. It is this type of relationship that the last exception addresses. The service has provided guidance on debt-financed income rules for partnerships in which one or more (but not all) of the partners are qualified exempt organizations. This can be found in Internal Revenue Service notice 90-41.

As an example, a university support organization builds a parking garage for its campus and the campus pays the support organization rent equal to the annual principal and interest payments. After the loan is retired, title to the property will transfer to the campus. A lease between two exempt organizations does not by itself create passive income (see Rev. Rul. 58-47, 1958-2 C.B. 275). In this fact situation, since the income comes from property used in furtherance of the support organization's exempt purpose, it falls within the "qualified organization" exception to debt-financed property. Thus there is no unrelated business income.

The courts are willing to define debt-financed property rather broadly. In one case a court found securities purchased on margin to fall within these rules, and another found that reinvesting the accumulated cash value of life insurance owned by a tax-exempt organization in income-paying investments is acquisition indebtedness [see *Elliot Knitwear Profit Sharing Plan v. Commissioner*, 71 T.C. 765 (1979) aff'd 614 F.2d 347 (3rd Cir. 1980) and *Mose and Garrison Siskin Memorial Foundation, Inc. v. U.S.*, 603 F.Supp. 91 (E.D. Tenn. 1985) aff'd 790 F.2d 480 (6th Cir. 1986)].

In recent years the creation of employee stock option plans (E.S.O.P.s) has become a new means for financing companies. The tax-exempt organization in these situations is the entity created by the employees to purchase shares through their company's E.S.O.P. The IRS has created an exception to the debt-financing rules to address this: "A leveraged ESOP capital growth and stock ownership objectives are part of its tax exempt function and borrowing to purchase employer securities is an integral part of accomplishing this objective" (Rev. Rul. 79-12, 1979-1 C.B. 208). The IRS warns that this is different from an employee pension or profit-sharing plan that borrows money to purchase an employer's stock.

Income from Advertising

Many exempt organizations generate income through advertising sales. This may occur in a magazine for members, the program for

GRACE COLLEGE LIBRARY
WINONA LAKE, INDIANA

a cultural or sports event, or an informational publication for the general public. It must be remembered that before examining the question of whether advertising income is passive and/or substantially related to the organization's exempt purpose, the trade or business and regularly carried on test must be passed. As was discussed in Chapter Three, if these tests are not passed, the income cannot be taxed [see *Parkland Residential School, Inc. v. Commissioner*, 45 T.C.M. 988 (1983)].

The first time the issue of advertising income from an exempt publication was presented to a federal court, it ruled that the net income from advertising was not taxable [see *American College of Physicians v. U.S.*, 530 F.2d 930 (Ct. Cl. 1967)]. This decision spurred Congress to pass Section 513(c) of the Internal Revenue Code as part of the Tax Reform Act of 1969. The Code now states that advertising income is unrelated business income unless in and of itself it is exempt.

Almost twenty years later the United States Supreme Court enunciated a standard for determining the status of particular advertising income. In its decision the Court stated that net advertising income was not automatically unrelated. The issue to the Court was whether the conduct of the organization in selling and publishing the advertising demonstrated a related function. The reviewing body examined whether the advertising presented the reader with a systematic or comprehensive presentation of a relevant good or service. It was the Court's view that an exempt organization could control the format and type of advertising in such a way as to exhibit an intention to contribute importantly to its exempt function. This could be done by coordinating the editorial and advertising content or by having the advertising restricted only to new developments. Other factors to be looked at are who solicits the advertising and whether there is an attempt to solicit only advertisements that are an extension of the editorial content [see *American College of Physicians v. United States*, 106 S.Ct. 1591 (1986)].

In practice, the standard enunciated by the Supreme Court means that almost all advertising income that meets the other tests will be taxable. In the only case to apply this standard, the Tax Court found the income to be taxable: "No systematic effort [was] made to advertise products that relate to the editorial content of the magazine, no effort . . . made . . . to limit the advertising to new products" [*Florida Trucking Association, Inc. v. Commissioner*, 87 T.C. No. 66 (1986)].

This is not to say that under no circumstances can advertising income be found to be substantially related. For instance, the IRS has stated that although ordinary commercial advertising in a bar journal is unrelated business income, the publication of legal notices is related (Rev. Rul. 82-139, 1982-29 I.R.B. 6). As a general rule, advertising is substantially related if its preparation and sale are part of an educational program; if an exempt membership organization is serving its members; or when the form, content, and manner of presentation are controlled by the editorial function.

The losses, if any, from editorial and circulation can be used to offset gains from advertising if the entire publication is found to be a trade or business. If an entire publication is not a trade or business, the costs of advertising must be separated from all other publication costs. If the right to receive a publication is associated with membership dues, special allocation rules must be followed [see I.R.C. Reg. Section 1.1512(a)—(1)(F)(4)].

Subsidiary Organizations

Tax-exempt organizations have formed both taxable and exempt subsidiaries due to legal and policy dictates. Among the law-related reasons for forming a subsidiary organization are the desire to limit potential liability and risk, to create a means to lobby, and to gain the legal status to receive tax-deductible gifts. Operational reasons for having a subsidiary are an organization's policy decision that it does not want to engage in any unrelated activity directly, as well as the belief that operating clarity and efficiencies could be derived by creating a limited-purpose organization.

There are many subgroups of exempt organizations that form subsidiaries. A trade association may create a separate organization to conduct research activities; unlike the parent, when properly structured such an organization can achieve Section 501(c)(3) status and qualify for tax-deductible gifts. Membership organizations (for example, social welfare, labor, veterans' groups, and social organizations) engage in similar behavior.

Many charitable organizations have found that they gain administrative and programmatic advantages by creating an auxiliary organization to engage in fund-raising activity. Some states have allowed their public colleges and universities to structure separate corporations to manage a broad range of support and out-of-classroom activities to limit the state's financial liability. Some charitable organizations (Methodist Hospitals and some colleges and universities) have developed operating policies that they do not want to have any unrelated activity. When these organizations engage in an unrelated activity, they form a separate legal organization. In most instances it is for one of the aforementioned policy reasons that an exempt organization chooses to create one or more subsidiaries (Small, 1984).

First the IRS and then Congress became concerned that in some instances exempt organizations may have been creating subsidiaries in order to avoid the unrelated business income tax. Like other taxpayers, exempt organizations were being advised by their tax advisers as to the legal means to minimize their tax bill. In fulfilling their fiduciary responsibility, directors of exempt organizations took appropriate steps to maximize the organization's ability to perform its exempt function. It is often difficult to draw the line between legally permissible but policy-inappropriate actions and those that are both permissible and appropriate. In any case, in the Tax Reform Act of 1969 Congress amended the Internal Revenue Code and put in place a number of special rules addressing the transfer of income from a subsidiary organization to its parent organization.

As these rules operate today, if one organization controls another, payments of interest, annuities, royalties, and rent to the parent are unrelated business income based on a ratio-of-income approach. (Note that dividends are not included in this treatment.) For an organization to be controlled by another, 80 percent of the voting stock and all classes of stock must be owned by the parent organization. If the subsidiary is also an exempt organization and the parent receives payments in the form of passive income (except dividends), the amount of taxable income is determined by "comparing the unrelated income of the subsidiary to the greater of its total taxable income (treating the subsidiary as a taxable entity) or its unrelated business income. . . . This is calculated without regard to any payments to the parent. The ratio is then applied to the noted forms of passive income to determine the parent's taxable income" (Hopkins, 1987, p. 770).

If the subsidiary is not an exempt organization and makes payments to the parent organization, a ratio approach is used to determine to what extent this income is taxable to the parent. Essentially the rules require the organization to (1) determine the taxable income of the controlled organization and (2) subtract from this the income that would be related if received directly by the controlling exempt organization. The difference of these two sums is the taxable income to the parent [I.R.C. Reg. Section 1.512(b)-(1)(3) and Hopkins, 1987, pp. 771–772].

There are exceptions to these rules when the controlled organization is also an exempt organization. If the transfer of income by the subsidiary is done as part of its tax-exempt purpose, all of the income to the parent is exempt. The most typical example is a controlled foundation making a grant to its parent organization. Also, if a separately incorporated organization is exempt on the grounds that it is an integral part of an exempt organization's function, it can generate a profit. But if this separate organization operates predominantly for sales to "outsiders," it will be viewed as a nonexempt feeder organization (see Rev. Rul. 73-164, 1973-1 C.B. 223 and Rev. Rul. 68-26, 1968-1 C.B. 272).

If the membership of the board of directors of a tax-exempt organization and its for-profit subsidiary are identical, the IRS views this as one organization. This is known as the attribution rule (see IRS Private Letter Ruling 8606056). When courts look at this, they attempt to determine whether the separate organization is a sham. The answer will be yes if the parent controls the day-to-day operation and activity of the other organization.

When capitalizing a subsidiary organization, the parent must follow the prudent investor rule to create a truly separate entity. If a contribution by the parent may not be considered prudent, the exempt parent should consider making a loan with a fair market interest rate and appropriate security. Other means to avoid these rules include a proper reimbursement of the parent for occupancy costs; shared staff and equipment; the payment of a royalty for the use of the parent's name, logo, copyrights, and patents; and a distribution of a dividend.

Exploitation Rule

As with the subject of the previous section, the exploitation rule was developed to eliminate situations in which an organization attempts to avoid taxation. The exploitation rule comes into play where an organization uses an otherwise exempt activity to generate income. In some circumstances this income may be unrelated, which occurs in the sale of advertising that exploits the goodwill and other intangibles of an exempt publication. Another example is where use of athletic facilities on a campus is given to students because of a student fee and outsiders are allowed to use the facility at no charge. If fees are charged to students, faculty, and outsiders, any unrelated business income will be determined under the "dual use facilities" rule to be discussed later in this chapter (see IRS Private Letter Ruling 7823062).

A related situation occurs with religious organizations having unrelated business income when the service of members is sold to third parties but the income goes to the religious organization due to the individual member's vow of poverty. If the individual member receives food, housing, and/or other living needs from the exempt organization for performing this service, the income to the organization is taxable.

Joint Ventures and Partnerships

Exempt organizations enter into joint ventures for a host of reasons. This vehicle is often used to acquire real estate and to purchase major pieces of equipment. In the past few years, higher education has used it as a means to take its faculty's research and turn it into marketable products. The IRS has increasingly viewed joint ventures as a means of tax avoidance. In many instances the issue for the IRS is not merely one of unrelated business income but of an organization's maintaining its exempt status.

Every partnership must have at least one general partner, and there may be one or more limited partners who assume limited risk

(risk that is confined to their capital contributions). All other liability lies with the general partner. Partnerships are not taxed directly; all profits are passed on to the individual partners, where tax liability is determined.

The position of the IRS has long been that where an exempt organization is a partner in a joint venture, it must include its share of the profits in its unrelated business income. Also, income from the sale of an exempt organization's interest in a publicly traded partnership is unrelated business income. Both the IRS and the courts have rejected the argument that as a limited partner the exempt organization lacks the ability to actively engage in the management of the partnership, thus making the income passive [see Rev. Rul. 79-22, 1979-2 C.B. 236 and *Service Bolt and Nut Company Profit-Sharing Trust,* 78 T.C. 812 (1982) aff'd 724 F.2d 519 (6th Cir. 1984)].

The Internal Revenue Service has carved out an exception to its general position when the partnership activity is substantially related to the exempt purpose of a limited partner. A private exempt university and a for-profit hospital entered into a partnership to build and operate an eighty-eight–bed hospital. The university needed the facility for its medical school program. In its analysis, the IRS noted that the exempt organization was a limited partner, the general partner bore the financial liability, and the agreement was an arms-length one. On this fact situation, the IRS concluded that the joint venture did not endanger the exempt organization's tax status and that the income to the tax-exempt organization was substantially related and not taxable (see IRS Private Letter Ruling 8432014).

Where an exempt organization is a general partner in a taxable joint venture, it is the position of the Internal Revenue Service that the organization is choosing to forfeit its exempt status. The sole limit to the IRS's position is where the principal purpose of the partnership itself is to further a charitable purpose. An organization will lose its tax-exempt status "if the charitable organization/general partner is not adequately insulated from the day-to-day management responsibilities of the partnership and/or if the limited partners are to receive undue return (private inurement) (Hopkins, 1987, p. 833). See IRS General Counsel Memorandum

39005 for this rule and General Counsel Memorandum 39444 for its application. In Private Letter Ruling 8541108, the Internal Revenue Service found that, where a partnership leases all of the space in its owned property to the tax-exempt limited partner and related charitable organizations, there is no risk to the exempt organization's tax status.

Today it is not unusual for an exempt performing arts organization to enter into a joint venture with private investors in order to fund a production. Due to the nature of the activity, the exempt organization may want to be a general partner. In this situation, where the agreement between the partners was at arms length, the cost to purchase a limited partnership was reasonable, the general partner was under no obligation to return the limited investment, the limited partner had no control over the exempt organization, none of the limited partners nor any officer or director of the joint venture was an officer or director of the tax-exempt organization, and the investors were not receiving undue compensation, a court found that the exempt group did not risk the loss of its exempt status. Nevertheless, the service fee income to the exempt organization was taxable [see *Plumstead Theater Society,* 74 T.C. 1324 (1980) aff'd per curium, 675 F.2d 244 (9th Cir. 1982)].

Dual Use Facilities

Many tax-exempt organizations own facilities that they rent part of the time to taxable activities. These are known as "dual use facilities." The determination as to whether a specific facility rental generates unrelated business income is made by the rules discussed earlier. An issue of major debate between tax-exempt organizations and the Internal Revenue Service is the appropriate means by which to determine the amount of indirect expenses that may be deducted from this active income to derive the unrelated business income. Indirect expenses include items like depreciation, utilities, cost of facility management's employee compensation, and cost of repairs and preventive maintenance. The dual use facility rule applies only to these expenses—direct expenses may be fully deducted.

It is the position of the IRS that the percentage of all indirect expenses is calculated by looking at the total time a facility could be available for use. At least one federal appellate circuit agrees with many exempt organizations that the appropriate basis of allocation is the amount of time of actual use [see *Rensselaer Polytechnic Institute v. Commissioner*, 732 F.2d 1058 (2nd Cir. 1984)].

The *Rensselaer* court endorsed the following equation to determine the percentage of indirect expenses that could be deducted:

$$\frac{\text{Deductible}}{\text{indirect expenses}} = \frac{\text{Total}}{\text{indirect expenses}} \times \frac{\text{Hours facility used for UBI activity}}{\text{Total hours of actual facility use}}$$

This formula will generate a greater percentage of indirect expenses that may be deducted. (Note: The IRS substitutes "total hours facility is available for use" for "total hours of actual facility use" in its approach.) The IRS continues to use its approach in jurisdictions that have not endorsed the position enunciated by the second circuit.

Fund-Raising Activities and Solicitations

Pure fund-raising activities of charitable organizations may give rise to unrelated business income. As with any other income-generating activity by an exempt organization, it must first be determined if the activity is a trade or business, is regularly carried on, or is substantially related to the organization's exempt purpose. The answer to these questions, as well as the exemptions for donated labor and goods and the other exemptions that have previously been reviewed, may make this a nontaxable activity.

One area of particular concern to the IRS during the 1980s was solicitations associated with a gift. In the typical fact situation, a charitable organization sent out a fund-raising letter requesting a donation and included with the letter some type of gift. It was the inclusion of this "gift," which the IRS refers to as a premium, that caused the IRS to challenge the activity and conclude that the income so generated was taxable. The issue for the courts has been whether the activity has amounted to a competitive trade or business. The rule developed by one circuit states: "When premiums are advertised and offered in exchange for contributions in stated amounts," the activity becomes a commercial one; but if the organization "had mailed the premiums with its solicitation and informed the recipients that the premiums could be retained without any obligation arising to make a contribution," the activity is not a trade or business and is not subject to the unrelated business income tax [see *Disabled American Veterans v. United States,* 650 F.2d 1179 (Ct. Cl. 1981)].

In a subsequent case, the organization "suggested" an amount to be donated in return for receiving the "free" gift. Here the court found that if a gift is included as part of the solicitation and the amount of the requested donation is close to the actual value of the gift, the so-called donation is unrelated business income [see *Veterans of Foreign Wars,* 89 T.C. 7 (1987)].

Mailing Lists

Until the past few years, taxability of income derived by an exempt organization from allowing another party to use its mailing list was determined by the rules for passive income. The issue was whether the exempt organization, in addition to allowing the use of its mailing list, had agreed to perform administrative services or some other form of active participation in order to receive the income. Where the exempt organization performed no services, the income was found to be passive [see *Oklahoma Cattleman's Association v. United States,* 310 F.Supp. 320 (W.D. Okla. 1969)], but where services were performed, the income was unrelated business income [see *National Wells Association, Inc.,* 92 T.C. 7 (1989); *American Bar Endowment v. United States,* 761 F.2d 1573 (Fed. Cir. 1985) rev'd 477 U.S. 105, 106 S.Ct. 2426 (1986); and Rev. Rul. 81-178, 1981-2 C.B. 1985].

In a series of administrative determinations on income from the use of mailing lists to sell affinity cards, the IRS initially stated that the income was a nontaxable royalty. The IRS then reversed itself and determined that since Congress had passed I.R.C. Section 513(h), this Code section now created the sole means to exempt mailing list income from the unrelated business income tax (see IRS

Private Letters Ruling 8823109). I.R.C. Section 513(h)(1)(B) states that any income derived from the exchange or rental of mailing lists between tax-exempt organizations is not taxable. This amendment became effective on October 22, 1986. Thus, income derived from the sale of a mailing list to any for-profit is unrelated business income in the view of the Internal Revenue Service.

The response of the IRS to this Code section has prompted some practitioners to recommend that exempt organizations be certain that all agreements clearly separate mailing list income from income derived for allowing the use of the group's name, logo, and the like (Kirschten and Brown, 1989). The latter is still clearly tax exempt, while uncertainty surrounds the former.

A 1990 Tax Court ruling has rejected much of the position of the IRS (*Disabled American Veterans v. Commissioner*). This Court determined that mailing list rental income is a royalty, irrespective of to whom the list is rented, as long as the tax-exempt organization is involved only with the maintenance of the list and not the providing of services to those renting the list.

Research

The desire to make scientific advances and to improve our nation's economy has been the motivation to exempt much of the research activity in our country from the federal income tax. In a number of determinations, the IRS has developed a comprehensive position on research. It has stated that research activity, whether applied or basic, is exempt if done in the United States for any federal agency or state, or subdivision thereof. Furthermore, any other research is exempt unless it is product or material testing for a commercial entity and the end use of the testing is the marketability of the product, even when the immediate testing deals with product safety standards (see Rev. Rul. 54-73, 1954-1 C.B. 160, Rev. Rul 68-373, 1968-2 C.B. 260, and Rev. Rul. 78-246, 1978-2 C.B. 175).

As a matter of public policy, the IRS and the courts find that research is often tax exempt. The criteria most often used to support this position is that the information is made available to the public, the research aids in the education of students or the treatment of disease, and there is no private inurement.

Where an organization's primary purpose is commercial, the fact that it engages in research will not enable it to gain tax-exempt status [see *American Institute for Economic Research v. United States*, 302 F.2d 934 (Ct. Cl. 1981)]. When an exempt organization does research, the courts attempt to determine whether the purpose is to promote private commercial interests. Where this is found, the income gained from this research is taxable.

The courts have attempted to define what constitutes exempt scientific research and testing. One court found that scientific research "involves experimentation to validate a scientific hypothesis" while routine testing "has measurements of specifications as its purpose" [*Midwest Research Institute v. United States*, 554 F.Supp. 1379, 1386 (W.D. Mo. 1983) aff'd 744 F.2d 638 (7th Cir. 1984)]. Another court "focused on the problem-solving nature of scientific research . . ." [*ITT Research Institute v. United States*, 85-2 U.S.T.C. par. 9734 (Ct. Cl. 1985)]. In both of these cases, the court examined the tax-exempt organizations' motivation for research. If it was scientific the income was exempt from taxation, but where the interest was on the potential economic return the income was taxed.

Chapter 5

How the Internal Revenue Code Treats Different Types of Organizations

As the previous chapters have shown, multiple issues must be resolved in determining whether specific income to an exempt organization is taxable. This chapter will focus on major categories of exempt organizations and look at how the courts and the service have applied the sections of the Internal Revenue Code applicable to exempt organizations. The analysis provided in this chapter assumes the use of the information from the previous chapters of Part Two. We will review those issues that most often cause conflict between exempt organizations and the Internal Revenue Service. It is important that each segment of the exempt community understands the precedents that have been established in rulings reviewing actions of other exempt organization segments, for it is a typical pattern for precedents established in one part of the exempt community to eventually be applied to the other segments.

In the subsection on hospitals there is extensive discussion of the current debate as to whether voluntary hospitals should be allowed to maintain their tax-exempt status, and if so, under what circumstances. It is this sector of the nonprofit community that as a whole is under the greatest attack as to its exempt status. Thus an

understanding of the issues under debate here will help other segments of the nonprofit sector to avoid similar attacks.

To assist the reader, Resource D has an extensive listing of
applicable IRS advisory opinions. Those who want to pursue a
specific issue further may do so by going to the source material and
reading the actual advisory opinion(s).

Educational Organizations

Any organization that provides instruction can qualify as exempt
under the education category in Section 501(c)(3). "Instruction" can
occur solely through study and research. It is clear that instruction
to individuals does not equate to private gain. In addition to the
traditional structure of colleges, universities, and private and public
primary schools, museums, zoological associations, symphony or-
chestras, and other similar organizations are often found to be "educational." Similarly, drug counseling, marriage counseling, birth-
ing centers, and other counseling organizations are regularly found
to be educational.

In determining whether an organization is educational, the
service will look at the method used to develop and present its ideas.
At a minimum an organization must provide a factual basis for its
views and "relevant facts" that assist a student in the learning process [see Rev. Rul. 86-53, 1986-1 C.B. 326 and *National Alliance v.
U.S.*, 81-1 U.S.T.C. 9464 (D.C. Cir. 1983)]. A key factor used to deny
exempt status is that the function of the organization is primarily
social, as is often found with Greek letter organizations. A second
major reason for denying exempt status is that the organization has
a commercial purpose.

We find that this theme of commerciality was used repeatedly
by a variety of courts in the 1980s. Where an institute was self-
supporting, a court found that its primary motivation was the
generation of income and thus it had a commercial purpose; where
an organization operated through classes that may well be educational, exempt status was denied because the organization "is a part
of a franchise system which is operated for private benefit and . . .
its affiliation with this sytem taints it with a commercial purpose"
[see *American Institute for Economic Research v. United States*, 302

F.2d 934 (Ct. Cl. 1981) and *est of Hawaii v. Commissioner,* 71 T.C.
1067 (1979) aff'd 302 F.2d 934 (9th Cir. 1981)].

The IRS has shown particular interest in organizations
whose supposed educational function is carried out via a publishing function. Where a court observes that although the published
materials may in fact be educational, the behavior of the organization mirrors a commercial firm, exempt status will be denied. Behaviors that indicate an essentially commercial purpose are
publishing and sales practices similar to commercial publishers, a
trend of increased profits, growth in accumulated surplus, and substantial increases in compensation for management staff [see *The
Incorporated Trustees of the Gospel Workers Society, Inc. v. United
States,* 510 F.Supp. 374 (D.D.C. 1981) aff'd 672 F.2d 894 (D.C. Cir.
1981) cert. den. 456 U.S. 944 (1982)]. A number of observers believe
that the growth of the "commerciality" theory could have a more
far-reaching effect than any of the statutory changes that may come
out of the current review by Congress of these Code sections.

As discussed in Chapter Three, those public higher education institutions that have the powers of eminent domain or taxation, or have police powers, are recognized as subdivisions of state
or local government. It is the position of the IRS that most public
colleges and universities are not political subdivisions of a state.
This position is most important when determining if interest payments from these institutions are tax exempt. In most instances they
are, because the institution borrows funds through or by the authority of a clearly recognized state entity. The more difficult issue is
whether related exempt organizations of these public institutions
have the same status. Historically, the IRS has treated these organizations much like their parent institution (see Rev. Rul. 63-20,
1963-1 C.B. 24, Rev. Rul. 60-248, 1960-2 C.B. 35, Rev. Rul. 57-187,
1957-1 C.B. 65, and Rev. Rul. 54-106, 1965-1 C.B. 28). Recently the
IRS has shown an interest in tightening its position; in proposed
Reg. Section 1.103-1 the organization must be a "duly" constituted
authority of a state or local government. Thus the IRS would like
to require a much more immediate relationship between the organization borrowing the funds and the sponsoring government
organization.

Many see this as simply part of the attempt during the past

decade to restrict the amount of tax-free bonds. Private-sector schools have felt this restriction very directly. Where at one point it was quite easy to generate as much tax-free financing as an organization desired, Congress has now restricted this to $150 million per institution. With the large amount of deferred maintenance that colleges and universities have accrued, this restriction has become a major factor in planning renovation programs.

Sallie Mae has recently become a source of tax-exempt financing for related exempt organizations of public colleges and universities. As of the beginning of the 1991 calendar year, exempt organizations related to the California State University system had loan agreements in excess of $11 million with Sallie Mae.

The IRS has issued literally scores of advisory rulings to assist educational organizations in determining which activities will generate nontaxable income. In some instances the IRS can clearly find a position in the legislative history of the Revenue Act of 1950. Thus items such as tuition, service fees, and residence hall fees for a school's students are clearly not taxed. But past this type of income the IRS must look at the substantially related test and convenience exception to determine the tax treatment for a given activity. The scope and diversity of the activities found in educational organizations have made this a complex task.

In reviewing income generated through the rental of a campus's residential facilities, the service may use the determining factor of who is leasing the space, what purpose the space will be used for, or what scope of service is included. If the space is leased to an institution's own students, the income is exempt. If the space is leased to an organization for instructional or other educational purposes, the income is exempt (see Tech. Adv. Mem. 7840072, Tech. Adv. Mem. 8024001, and Private Letter Ruling 8121004). The sole exception to this educational purposes test is if the facilities are leased to commercial business entities (Tech. Adv. Mem. 8246014). If the space is not leased for educationally related purposes and the services provided by the exempt organization move beyond those associated with passive income, all or part of the income will be unrelated and taxed.

In looking at alumni association and university travel programs, the Internal Revenue Service must engage in a similar depth of revue. Where the income-generating activity is substantially an educational program it is exempt, but where the activity is essentially exploiting the value of the exempt organization's name and reputation it is taxed.

When examining the modern campus bookstore, the IRS makes good use of the fragmentation rule. Materials required for coursework and other directly related educational materials are substantially related and not taxable. Novelty items, sundries, convenience goods, and an array of other items whose useful life is under one year are exempt under the convenience exemption (see Rev. Rul. 81-62, 1981-8 I.R.B. 45, Private Letter Ruling 8004010, Private Letter Ruling 8605022, and Private Letter Ruling 8025222).

The Internal Revenue Service has given many advisory rulings on a broad range of activities conducted by educational organizations. A cursory review of these rulings shows that most financial aid programs are exempt, as are international student centers; training tables for coaches and athletes; law reviews and professional journals; intercollegiate, intramural, and interscholastic athletics; national honor societies; and a broad range of out-of-classroom (but related to the classroom) student activities. Yet when the convenience exception is the basis of the exemption from taxes, to the extent that the income source is not students, faculty, or staff of the institution, the income is taxable.

As one looks at some of the proposed changes to the unrelated business income tax code sections, much of the concern is whether an activity will be considered substantially related by the IRS and the courts. In the past, the combination of the substantially related and convenience exemptions has allowed everyone concerned with these issues to be somewhat vague. If, as is the current belief of those closest to the activity of the Subcommittee on Oversight, the convenience exception is eliminated, the need for greater clarity will be upon us.

Religious Organizations

One of the founding tenets of our nation is the freedom of religion. In reviewing issues involving organizations claiming the status of religious organizations under Section 501(c)(3), the separation of church and state has made the role of the IRS particularly difficult [see I.R.C. Section 7611 and *U.S. v. Church of Scientology of Boston, Inc.*, Fed. D. Mass (1990)]. It is an area in which the IRS has shown commendable restraint, yet this posture has become increasingly difficult with the pluralization of religious entities. The second major issue of importance to religious organizations is the extent to which possibly taxable activities of affiliated groups can be attributed to the parent organization.

Today the range of religious sects in our nation is broader than at any other time. In addition to those groups whose foundations are in the Judeo-Christian tradition, we have the full range of Eastern religions, transcendental and metaphysical groups, as well as an enormous number of groups claiming a different basis of religiosity. Additionally, the past two decades have seen religious organizations expanding the scope of income-producing activities in which they engage. Compounding the difficulty of the role of the IRS is that the alternatives available to it are often very limited. In many instances the only issue is whether the organization does or does not qualify as an exempt religious organization. This difficulty is brought home with episodes like the Bakkers and the extensive commercial activity in which they engaged. Their religious organization claimed that every facet of their operation was substantially related to their exempt purpose. Certain of their activities had become so large that to rule otherwise would have endangered the exempt status of the entire organization.

As one looks at one of the proposed changes in the Code sections directly applicable to religious groups, one finds an attempt to address this difficulty. The proposed new aggregation rules would combine a church's income with its tax-paying subsidiaries'. Some feel that this will threaten the exempt status of some legitimate religious organizations. Traditional religious organizations argue that the proposed rule would (1) create dangerous government entanglement in the Internal Revenue Service reviewing these organizations, (2) reduce the current protection granted to religious organizations in the filing of information returns, and (3) reverse the current situation and impose too severe a penalty. In terms of the latter, religious organizations may either have to divest or risk the loss of their exempt status.

As one scholar notes: "One of the principal reasons for the effectiveness of churches and other charities in contributing to the overall public good has been their freedom to be unique, independent in defining and pursuing their charitable purpose" (Treusch, 1988, p. 2). In reviewing religious organizations, the historical hesitancy of Congress and the IRS has created a separate set of rules for these groups. As we approach the year 2000, the issue becomes: How does the federal government continue the protections given to religious organizations, even as we see potential abuses both in terms of the nature of organizations claiming this status and the scope of activity of these groups?

Hospitals

Today the definition of an exempt hospital is one that promotes health care. Section 501(c)(3) does not list health care as a category; the exempt status comes because it is a "charitable organization." In 1969 the IRS substituted a "community benefit test" for the "financial ability test." Under the latter, an exempt hospital had to provide care to anyone, irrespective of the individual's ability to pay. The IRS determined that the advent of third-party insurance, Medicare, and the modern economics of health care necessitated this change. It now requires evidence of the benefit to the community— a qualitative not quantitative determination.

Commentators have described this community mission as (1) improving a community's health standards, (2) providing high-quality care, (3) supporting public and ongoing professional health education, and (4) conducting research. Other attributes of a community service orientation are (1) values tailored to the service community, (2) a governance and accountability structure based on community representatives "unfettered" with financial gain, (3) a long-term service commitment to their community, (4) a physician-hospital relationship with no financial inducement to the physician, which allows the physician to concentrate on quality service, and (5) institutional volunteerism in terms of providing opportunities for individual volunteers and leadership in the community as to health care needs.

This change in policy has been supported by the federal judiciary. The courts have found that the promotion of health care per se is a charitable purpose. The key factor is whether the hospital serves a class of persons broad enough to benefit the community and to operate for the public good [see *Eastern Kentucky Welfare Rights Organization v. Simon*, 506 F.2d 1278 (D.C. Cir. 1974)]. It should be noted that, although this is the standard for federal tax-exempt status, it may not be a particular state's standard for exemption from property taxes. As will be discussed in Chapter Eight, in many local jurisdictions federally exempt organizations are seeing their local property-tax-exempt status challenged.

The underlying thrust of much of the discussion on the health service industry is whether nonprofit hospitals should be able to continue to enjoy a tax exemption. In the view of some, the difference between for-profit and nonprofit care providers has become so blurred that there may no longer be any real distinction in many instances. Those advocating this claim that voluntary hospitals are unwilling to serve the increasing number of underinsured Americans. Some even contend that proprietary hospitals provide as much indigent care as most voluntary hospitals. Added to this is the fact that the language used by voluntary hospitals increasingly sounds like market approaches commonly found in any for-profit industry. In many settings the rise of the professional staff has been paralleled with a diminution in influence for volunteers and religious groups. In some settings the voluntary hospital is no longer as closely identified with its originating community. The ability of fees for services to cover almost all costs in the 1970s has often diminished the hospital's organizational capacity to pursue donations. Finally, there is the reality of a visible and currently successful for-profit sector. When one recognizes the ascendancy of free-market theories in the body politic and the expansion of income-producing activities by voluntary hospitals, the ability to structure an argument that these organizations no longer earn their privileged position is clear.

Supporters of continued exempt status argue that although there may in fact be abuses, to alter the exempt status of these health care providers will only exacerbate the problems surrounding medical care today. The root of their position begins with an understanding of the demographics of hospitals. Hospital care is provided through voluntary hospitals (private and nonprofit), government facilities, and proprietary hospitals (for-profit). In spite of the growth of proprietary hospitals during the past decade, they still constitute a small segment of total care capacity, which only has an impact in a few regions. A study by the American Hospital Association shows that in 1964, out of a total of 781,000 available hospital beds, only 6.5 percent or 46,000 beds were provided by for-profit hospitals. Some twenty years later, in 1984, for-profits provided only 99,980 beds (10 percent) as compared to 917,077 provided by voluntary and government hospitals (Seay and others, 1986, p. 253). Thus, although in gross number of beds proprietary hospitals doubled their capacity, they continue to represent a small total percentage of all available beds.

Perhaps more important is the concentration of ownership of the proprietary hospital capacity by a relatively few organizations. The American Hospital Association data also inform us that twenty-seven chains owned some 807 proprietary hospitals in 1984. Also of note is the spread of these hospitals across the country. For study purposes the United States was divided into nine regions. In four regions proprietary hospitals represent 16 to 20 percent of total beds, in one region 9 percent, and in the remaining four regions .5 to 4 percent. This indicates that in at least half of the nation the proprietary hospitals do not affect the provision of medical care. This regionalization of proprietary hospitals leads those supporting the continued preferential treatment of the voluntary hospital to comment: "The ability or propensity of proprietary hospital investors to be market selective, to fashion opportunistic responses to market changes, and to move capital about without regard to territorial boundaries is probably related to regional market share" (Seay and others, 1986, p. 254). This concept is buttressed by the motivation of managers and investors in the for-profit sector; as the name of this sector states, the underlying goal is to maximize profit.

Advocates for voluntary hospitals would concur with the views presented in "The Non-Profit Difference" (Mathis, n.d.). This publication reviews essential differences between the nonprofit and for-profit hospital care sectors. The major difference is found in the organization's goals and the services that actualize these goals. The voluntary hospital has as its foundation the goals of community benefit, the relief of government burden, a long-term commitment to their "community," a fundamental mission of health care, and no private inurement. These goals become the behaviors of providing unprofitable services (burn units, emergency room services, and other specialty care units), in "bad" locations, to all strata of society. These hospitals are at the forefront of medical and clinical training and research. Finally, whatever profits may accrue are returned to the community through continued improved and expanded services. It is also the volunteer hospital that will assume the responsibility of responding to the "new diseases" that humans seem to spawn (for example, AIDS).

Commentators discuss the importance of the "corporate culture" in providing health care services. They believe that in a voluntary hospital the influences of physicians and other staff are much different than those in a for-profit setting. This concept is also found in the thinking one theoretician describes as the "nondistribution constraint" on the basic structure of the voluntary hospital. Hansmann argues that the fact that nonprofit hospitals are precluded from distributing profits to an "owner" means that they are less inclined to take advantage of the consumer in the ever more complex world of medical care (Hansmann, 1980). This does not mean that the supporters of the voluntary hospital do not recognize that there are abuses within this industry. These persons note that the directors of voluntary hospitals need to reexamine their mission and reaffirm their charitable function. Issues of cost and profitability must be addressed in order to assure financial survival, and there is a need to alter focus, language, and behavior in formulating policy decisions. There is a recognition that some efforts to develop new income sources to subsidize patient care cost, research, and medical training either may be inappropriate or need to be clearly handled through a for-profit entity.

The Catholic Health Association is spearheading work that calls for what amounts to a public benefits approach to budgeting and program efforts. This organization wants "official hospital plans and budgets [to] include objectives for care of the poor and that explicit mechanisms be established for processing free or reduced care" (Seay and Vladeck, 1988, p. 132). Similarly, the organization would engage in a "charitable" audit of its activities. Here the voluntary hospital would enumerate those components of its program that merit exempt status (Catholic Health Association of the United States, 1989).

The success of the voluntary hospital sector in doing a better job of self-policing and engaging in policy and expenditure reviews like those required to implement the concepts being developed by organizations like the Catholic Hospitals may well determine the outcome of its tax treatment. Otherwise more and more policy setters will concur with the view of Congressman Stark (D., California): "If they do not provide charity care equal to the total tax benefit they receive" exempt status should be denied (U.S. Congress, 1987, p. 766).

This posture has been endorsed by the chair of the House Select Committee on Aging, Congressman Roybal. In 1990 this committee held a hearing entitled "Restoring Commitment and Fairness," much of which focused on Congressman Roybal's draft bill, the Charity Care Act. If enacted, this bill will tie tax exemption for hospitals to (1) servicing a reasonable number of Medicaid patients and (2) providing charity health care of a value at least equal to the organization's tax exemption. The congressman based much of this draft bill on the General Accounting Office report "Nonprofit Hospitals: Better Standards Needed for Tax Exemption" (General Accounting Office, 1990).

Moving away from the question of whether voluntary hospitals should be tax exempt, we look at a number of other major issues. These hospitals are engaging in an ever broader array of income activities and are increasingly using sophisticated tax advice to develop new organizations that in some instances avoid unrelated business income tax. Thus we find hospitals building condominiums to be used as short-term residences by families of patients. The service has ruled that this can be a related activity (see IRS Private Letter Ruling 8427105). Although one can endorse this position in some settings, many members of the public have difficulty when these facilities are used essentially to persuade the wealthy to use a particular hospital for care because the family can stay in upscale facilities right next door. The public has similar concerns with hospital-physician joint ventures that encourage self-dealing or benefit the physician's private practice.

The National Association of Retail Druggists (NARD) has compiled information that tends to support its allegation that some voluntary hospitals purchase more pharmaceutical products than needed for their own use with the intent to resell these at a profit. Because tax-exempt organizations are excluded from the Robinson-Patman Act, it is permissible for wholesalers to sell products at a discount to them, with the underlying theory that this will assist in reducing the price to the consumer. NARD's studies show that the discount to voluntary hospitals is approximately $130 million annually. If voluntary hospitals do in fact overpurchase and sell the excess at a profit, they are at a minimum violating the spirit of the law. Of perhaps greater concern is the claim that these drugs are not properly handled by the middlemen who purchase them—it is alleged that at times these tainted medications are sold by these middlemen to retailers. To diminish this activity, NARD is pursuing stricter enforcement of existing drug enforcement laws and the passage of a new statute that would require voluntary hospitals that dispense prescription drugs to register with the Federal Drug Administration.

A phrase used in a number of publications to describe the new structure of many voluntary hospitals is "polycorp." In this structure the parent organization is a tax-exempt corporation that controls various subsidiary corporations. These subsidiaries typically include an exempt foundation for receipt of nonpatient income (such as donations, passive income, and endowment income), a corporation for ancillary services (parking garage, gift shop) that is also normally an exempt organization, a separate corporation for inpatient hospital care, perhaps one or more for-profit joint ventures, perhaps a for-profit corporation for clearly unrelated enterprises, and perhaps an exempt corporation for substantially related health care services (hospice, nursing home).

The IRS has advised that in its view the establishment of a for-profit subsidiary does not jeopardize the parent's tax status as long as the charitable entity is the ultimate beneficiary (see IRS Private Letter Ruling 8308019). The IRS has also stated that these multicorporation structures are permissible as long as the provision of inpatient care remains the central purpose. The service has cautioned voluntary hospitals that they must maintain tight control over all subsidiaries. This is due to a concern about the potential for private inurement if someone with different motives controls a subsidiary (see IRS General Counsel Memorandum 39326).

Health care in the United States has historically not been controlled by market forces. Today many people feel that health care is a right; with the advances of modern medicine, it is clear that those with access to the best care have a probability of a longer and healthier life. Thus the allocation of health care resources becomes a critical issue, as does the most efficient use of those resources. There have been various studies contending that either voluntary hospitals or proprietary hospitals tend to give the highest quality of care, serve the poor more frequently, and be more efficient. To clarify this debate, the Institute of Medicine appointed a group to conduct a comprehensive study. In a supplement to the main report, it stated: "The report shows that on average for-profit hospitals have been slightly less efficient, have charged payers more, and rendered less uncompensated care to uninsured patients than not-for-profit hospitals" (Gray, 1986, p. 205). The report concluded that proprietary hospitals had exhibited an ability to quickly attract capital. Although this allowed for quick expansion of facilities and services, it may have only encouraged the overexpansion of hospital capacity.

In an American Medical Association survey of physicians in 1984, the responses revealed that doctors themselves believe that voluntary hospitals provide superior care. In a question presented to all surveyed physicians, 32 percent felt that voluntary hospitals provided better quality service as compared to 5 percent for proprietary hospitals. In a question addressed only to physicians who had privileges at proprietary hospitals, the results showed that 24 percent believed that the care at a voluntary hospital is superior and 8 percent believed it is better at a proprietary hospital.

The past decade has seen an abandonment of the federal government's attempts to control medical costs through regulation. In its place we find in fact deregulation and efforts by large purchasers of medical care to control their costs through the establishment of maximum fee schedules and the direct purchasing of services. Although this behavior by the federal government and businesses may reduce their immediate costs, it is making the ability of the

underinsured and uninsured to gain medical care even more difficult. Our elected officials need to quickly determine how they
intend to fund this care if they reduce the historical pattern of sub-
sidization by those with the means to pay for those without this
means. Similarly, they need to determine how to support services
such as medical education, research, community health programs,
and the like, which were also partially supported through this sub-
sidization approach.

Those who advocate the federal government's continued support of the voluntary hospitals recognize that there is a need for
internal reform. These individuals see the professionalism and business mission of the voluntary hospital as a positive factor as long
as the charitable mission remains paramount in policy formulation.
As one commentator notes, there has always been a dynamic tension
between the community service and business mission. The critical
issue is how the volunteer board of directors views its responsibility
in balancing these missions (Seay and Vladeck, 1988).

Seay and Vladeck (1988) suggest that taxing authorities
should base a decision on the following criteria:

1.   There should be no private inurement (a nonprofit organization).
2.   The governing board must consist of community representa-
      tives with personal or pecuniary motives. The board members
      should have a fiduciary relationship to the service community.
3.   Admission policies should be open and assure accessibility.
      This must be viewed in light of the voluntary hospital's re-
      sources and role in the community. Admission policies should
      not be based on the ability to pay or restricted to certain phy-
      sicians' patients.
4.   The range of acute care services should be broad but not duplica-
      tive. They should be based on the needs of the service community.

The rise of the for-profit hospital is a relatively new phenomenon. Studies indicate that it is very regionally based. In much of
the country, the competition is solely between voluntary hospitals.
Before those who determine our policies alter a long history of
support for voluntary hospitals, they should be certain that proprietary hospitals can succeed in the long term and for the bulk of

society. If this does not occur, and, in frustration with medical costs and the abuses of a few, public policy is radically changed, we may find a rapid diminution in the availability of health care to less profitable sectors of society and the need for government to assume this burden.

Other Major Categories of Organizations

The growth of retail-type activities by museums has brought increased scrutiny to the income-generating activities of this type of exempt organization. Where once one had small gift shops carrying goods related to the purpose of the museum and some gift items, one now finds some museums involved in extensive catalogue sales, the operation of large specialty shops in suburban malls, the endorsement of a wide range of goods sold by for-profit companies, and other income-generating activities. This has called upon the IRS to develop an expanded position as to which activities it considers taxable. It has also developed a situation where competitors and elected officials are increasingly questioning the scope of activities in which these exempt organizations are engaged.

The IRS has made extensive use of the fragmentation rule in developing its advisory positions vis-à-vis the income-generating activities of museums. In a set of Private Letter Rulings released during the last decade, the IRS developed a relatively broad set of guidelines for museum retail activity (see *Museums* in Resource D).

1. To the extent that an item is expensive, lavish, or a luxury item, the probability increases that the unrelated business income tax will apply.
2. Items that improve the public's awareness of the museum's activity are probably not taxable.
3. Low-cost logo items are probably not taxable.
4. If the item has a utilitarian purpose, it will probably be taxable.
5. If an item "encourages personal learning experiences about the museum's collection, even though not an accurate depiction of an item in the collection, the article should be considered related" (see IRS General Counsel Memorandum 389491).

6. Sales of original arts and crafts, not specifically related to the
   museum's exempt purpose, are taxable.

An example of how the IRS will apply these guidelines occurred with a museum whose purpose is the cultural and historical
heritage unique to a particular city in the seventeenth to nineteenth
centuries. The IRS determined that the sale of furniture was substantially related because of its educational value. Although utilitarian, the furniture was an accurate depiction of that used in the
period and city of the museum presentation. The china sold was
also found to be substantially related. The IRS concluded that,
based on these particular facts and circumstances, items with a utilitarian function that had been modernized were still not taxable.
This determination was based on the design of the china and the
accompanying literature, which explained its historical signifi-
cance. Finally, catalogue sales were also found to be exempt. The
items being sold illustrated the exempt purpose of the museum (see
IRS Tech. Adv. Mem. 8605002).

In a review of the activities of trade associations and business
leagues, the controlling issue is most often whether the activity is
of benefit to the members individually or as a group. (Does it promote the common business interest?) Where the benefit essentially
accrues to the individual, the activity is not substantially related to
the exempt purpose.

This issue often arises in terms of insurance programs offered
to the members of an association. The association attempts to have
this income declared exempt as passive if it cannot be shown to be
substantially related. The position of the IRS is that the initiation,
negotiation with a broker, and other actions required to start an
insurance program in and of themselves make the association's participation active. Thus one has a trade or business and the unrelated
business income tax applies. This position has been upheld by a
number of courts in recent decisions [see *Illinois Association of
Professional Insurance Agents, Inc. v. Commissioner*, 86-2 U.S.T.C.
9702 (7th Cir. 1986) and *Professional Insurance Agents of Washington v. Commissioner*, T.C.M. 1987-68 (Feb. 3, 1987)].

One area of particular attention at the hearings of the Subcommittee on Oversight was the exemption for product safety test-

ing that the Underwriters Laboratory, Inc. enjoys. To some extent, this testimony was also addressing similar activities by colleges and universities, as well as exempt laboratories that are essentially the captive of a federal agency. This exemption was put in the Internal Revenue Code in 1954. The argument of for-profit companies is that they often engage in the same testing as exempt organizations, but they are at a pricing disadvantage because they must pay taxes on their net income while the exempt organization does not.

The Underwriters' Laboratories, Inc. has issued a number of statements noting substantial differences between its total activities and those of for-profit laboratories. In one statement it argues: "We have pointed out in Congressional testimony that several non-income generating activities, such as the preparation of product safety standards, contribution of staff expertise and expenses to organizations that develop fire and life safety installation codes and standards, Underwriters Laboratory's contribution of staff expertise to international safety standards developing organizations, would need to be eliminated or greatly curtailed if Underwriters Laboratory's tax exemption was withdrawn" (G. T. Castino, letter to author, October, 1989).

In some ways the arguments for this exemption parallel the community service mission argument of voluntary hospitals. Underwriters Laboratory also states that if its exempt status is withdrawn it "will cause increased costs to be incurred by both the government and the general public, result in an overall reduction in the safety levels enjoyed in the United States today, and further minimize consideration of American interests in international trade and development activity." Finally, this organization notes that, as with proprietary hospitals, the involvement of for-profit laboratories in safety testing is either "of recent vintage or is highly specialized and is influenced by profit potential" (Underwriters' Laboratories, Inc., 1988, p. 258).

Potential Changes
to the Internal Revenue Code

The previous chapters show the ability of Congress to alter the unrelated business income tax code sections. This chapter will look at major areas of potential legislative changes, as well as changes in how the executive branch may choose to interpret and implement these code sections in the coming decade. Chapter Six discusses the efforts of one department of the executive branch, the Small Business Administration, to lobby for major changes in the unrelated business income tax. This chapter will also review the efforts of the Subcommittee on Oversight of the House Ways and Means Committee, where any changes in these code sections must be initiated. Specific attention will be given to the hearings held by the subcommittee on the unrelated business income tax in the late 1980s, as well as a few bills that were designed to tax specific activities of some exempt organizations.

In the early 1980s the Small Business Administration began a campaign to gain the attention of Congress about alleged unfair competition practices engaged in by some tax-exempt organizations. At the Small Business National Issues Conference held in Washington, D.C., in 1984, the attending delegates voted the issue of unfair competition as the second most serious important issue, second only to the federal deficit. With this direction, the Office of Advocacy of the Small Business Administration began a public campaign to alter public policy toward tax-exempt organizations.

This campaign became visible with the dispersal of the publication *Unfair Competition by Nonprofit Organizations with Small Business: An Issue for the 1980s* (United States Small Business Administration, 1984). This pamphlet articulately presented the case of the small business, along with a broad set of proposed changes in federal laws and regulations. This publication essentially established the base from which the debate on the unrelated business income tax has proceeded.

In response to the concerns of small businesses, the House Ways and Means Committee directed the Subcommittee on Oversight to look into the alleged unfair activities. Following normal procedures, public hearings were held in 1987 and 1988. The testimony at both hearings was essentially point-counterpoint. The majority of the presentations by small business representatives utilized anecdotal testimony as to possible abuses by tax-exempt organizations. As the representative for the Business Coalition for Fair Competition stated, "At the outset, let me affirm that the manifold abuses resulting from unfair competition activities by tax-exempt organizations . . . still continue" (U.S. Congress, 1988, p. 258).

The discussion options released by the subcommittee for the second hearing spoke to most of the concerns of the for-profit sector. The tax-exempt community was clearly placed on the defensive, forced to be more self-analyzing and to recognize areas where abuses may be occurring, but the essence of its testimony did not change. The representatives of these organizations spoke of the great uncertainty that would be created by altering the substantially related test, by eliminating the convenience exception, and by implementing other suggested options. They noted the three-plus decades of administrative rulings and court decisions that provided all parties with a good base for planning. Changes of the magnitude suggested by the subcommittee, they said, could create relative havoc. Because of the speed with which the administrative and judicial processes would proceed, it would clearly be a decade or more before financial

planners and policy setters for exempt organizations would have a
clear understanding of the new rules.

There was one area on which all parties agreed: the clear
need for the collection of much more data on the activities of the
exempt community. For-profits believe these data will support their
contentions as to the growth of competition and the need for restrictive legislation. The exempt community believes these data will
show that where competition does exist, for the most part there is
no unfair competition. Although it was never clearly stated, it is
reasonable to assume that the exempt community also anticipates
that the collection and analysis of these data will take at least three
to five years. This sector continues to make ground with arguments
that Congress should not proceed with major code changes until
there is a body of fact supporting any change. If successful, this will
forestall any major changes for a considerable period of time.

Posthearing Activity:
Proposals Currently Under Consideration

In the years since the last subcommittee hearing, there have been
numerous rumors, trial balloons, and draft proposals. After a
number of days of intensive meetings and negotiations, the Subcommittee on Oversight produced a set of proposed changes in mid
1989. Although not as far reaching as the "discussion options," they
would produce many changes in the existing federal tax treatment
of exempt organizations. These proposals would leave the basic
rules about tax exemption in place: There would be no change in
the substantially related test and the regularly carried on requirement would remain in place.

Uncertainty would be created by the deletion of the convenience exception. To minimize this confusion, and to address some
concerns of the small business advocates, a set of special rules would
be established for specified income-producing activities, creating
what is referred to as "safe harbors." Some of these new rules would
simply codify positions currently held by the Internal Revenue Service, including the taxation of income from adjunct food sales,
affinity cards, and catalogue endorsements.

Retail sales operations by museums (gift shops and bookstores) would generate unrelated business income except for the sale of low-cost mementos (less than $15) and sales of items that are of an educational nature and relate to an organization's exempt purpose. Items primarily of a decorative or functional nature would be taxed. Hospital gift shop sales of items used primarily by patients would not be taxed. All other sales would now be unrelated. Universities would see rules similar to museums. Bookstore and convenience store sales of items that are not common consumer items to students and employees in furtherance of educational programs, items of low cost ($15 or less), and items with a university's logo, name, or marks would not be taxed. All other sales would generate unrelated business income.

Computer sales by colleges would also see new rules; only those sales to a student for a required course would be considered related. Furthermore, the course requirement must be certified by a faculty member and total exempt sales in any year could not exceed 50 percent of the student body.

As requested by the small business community, income from the sale or rental of medical equipment and devices (for example, hearing aids or oxygen tents), laboratory testing, and pharmaceuticals would be unrelated business income except for sales to patients. Also, income from fitness and exercise facilities would be taxable unless the facility itself serves a primarily charitable purpose and, based upon community standards, the program is available to a reasonable cross-section of the public either due to the availability of scholarships or the nature of the fee schedule. (The latter addresses concerns of the for-profit community toward YMCA-type organizations.)

The small business community also would receive most of what it wants in terms of campus travel programs. The income from these programs would be taxed unless it is part of a "degree program curriculum" and less than 5 percent of the sales is to nonstudents or faculty.

With the exception of student yearbooks and newspapers, all advertising income would be taxed. The exempt organization would be able to deduct only the direct expense of selling the advertising—there would be no deduction for production or distribution expenses.

The royalty exemption would also be narrowed. The unrelated business tax would apply to royalties measured by net income from property and royalties from property created by an organization, or where the organization performed substantial service or incurred substantial cost, except for property created in furtherance of the organization's exempt purpose.

A new cost allocation method would apply to dual use facilities. For all indirect costs, an exempt organization could deduct the "marginal cost of the activity, an allocable share of straight-line depreciation and administrative expenses to the extent that a direct nexus can be shown." In looking at idle time, the proposal states that if 75 percent or more of the facility usage is unrelated, all idle time is unrelated; if the reverse is true, all idle time is related; a sliding scale would be implemented for all other situations.

Special attention is also given to subsidiary organizations. The underlying goal of the proposal is to create more situations in which a subsidiary will be considered "controlled" by the parent organization. Furthermore, a taxable subsidiary's taxable income can be no less than its unrelated business income would be if the activity had been carried on directly by the exempt organization.

Recognizing inflation, this draft proposal also suggested increasing the standard deduction for exempt organizations to $10,000, with a phaseout at income levels above $50,000. This rule was intended to lessen the burden on the many smaller exempt organizations.

This set of draft recommendations also called upon the Internal Revenue Service to engage in a number of studies. One area of study would be hospital reorganization; a second would be possible clarification of the definition of "research for federal tax purposes." As with the discussion options, these recommendations also called for studies as to the feasibility of land-grant colleges filing information returns and studies as to the use, purpose, and effect of joint ventures and taxable subsidiaries.

If all of these draft recommendations were enacted, they would have a far-reaching effect. Although at one point it seemed that Congress might act fairly quickly on all, or part, of these recommendations, it is now apparent that quick action will not occur. The response to these recommendations came reasonably quickly and should surprise no one. Although they did not give the small business community everything they requested, these recommendations certainly responded to the majority of their concerns. Yet there are items that the for-profit community believes would not be fairly resolved even if all of these recommendations were to be adopted. Because of the direction of these recommendations, the burden of response was on the tax-exempt community. It must be recognized that even as various organizations started to formulate responses, the draft recommendations began to be modified by the subcommittee, which has made the target of responses somewhat difficult to determine.

A comprehensive review of responses to these draft recommendations is beyond the scope of this book, but a look at the response of INDEPENDENT SECTOR is instructive. This group represents a wide range of private, nonprofit organizations. In its position paper, INDEPENDENT SECTOR underscores the complexity of exempt organizations (INDEPENDENT SECTOR UBIT Working Group, 1989b), to show that in resolving one perceived problem, the subcommittee's recommendations may create a number of new issues. As examples, this group states that although it can agree to the taxation of adjunct food sales, such a rule is inappropriate for such sales at athletic and cultural events sponsored by an exempt organization. The taxation of the sale of condominiums is reasonable, but such a rule should not apply to low- or moderate-income housing programs. Similarly, taxing theme parks is not opposed as long as one differentiates historical, nature, and other facilities aimed at children from those that also have some amusement elements. In each instance INDEPENDENT SECTOR notes that the diversity of exempt organizations defies simple solutions to perceived problems of unfair competition.

The INDEPENDENT SECTOR also found many of the recommendations totally unacceptable. In this group of proposals is any taxation of royalty income, the proposed allocation rules for dual use facilities, the aggregation of subsidiaries income, and many of the facets of the special rules for the sale of goods. This organization also believes that editorial and circulation expenses should be allowed to be deducted from advertising income. It is the view of INDEPENDENT SECTOR that the dual use facility allocation rules are counterproductive: "Not allowing deductions for these costs would have the perverse effect of making it advantageous for charities to *increase* the degree to which they use facilities for non-exempt activities to qualify for deductions" (INDEPENDENT SECTOR UBIT Working Group, 1989b, p. 5).

This group cites many potential problems with the special sale of goods rules. They wonder if these rules would tax the sale of uniforms and equipment by youth organizations to their members, art goods sold by museums, devotional items sold by religious organizations, and books sold by environmental groups. Besides the uncertainty that the proposed rules may create as to what is taxable, these rules could also be harmful to small businesses from which the exempt organization acquires the goods for resale. In regard to the proposed rules on the aggregation of income of subsidiaries, INDEPENDENT SECTOR notes that this is unnecessary to assure fair competition, for these for-profit subsidiaries are already being taxed. In looking at a proposal like that for travel income, INDEPENDENT SECTOR questioned whether the subcommittee was serving public policy by taxing the day-trips of senior citizens to museums and the like, as well as taxing research trips by staff of exempt organizations.

Advocates for higher education have argued for the need to maintain the convenience exception. On one level they continue to be concerned about the uncertainty the proposed rules would create as to which sales are taxable. On a more pragmatic basis, they question what would be accomplished by taxing a range of self-generated income: "It is the net income in their Bookstores that provides a substantial component of discretionary funds to enhance the life of the institution. Elimination of the convenience exception would dramatically reduce such net profits while not enhancing the capacity of off-campus businesses to compete with them" (Francis, 1988). Continuing this line of reasoning, others argue that (1) taxing these sales would only increase the cost of a college education, (2) these sales present no real threat to the private sector, (3) where applicable these stores now pay unrelated business income taxes, and (4) there would be harm to the campus community without any corresponding societal gain (Arent, 1987). In place of "bookstore" one could substitute other activities now exempt under the convenience exception.

As groups were developing responses to these draft recommendations, members of the Subcommittee on Oversight continued informational communication on this matter. A major set of modifications came in a letter from Congressman Dick Schulze (Rep., Penn.), ranking minority member, to Chairman Pickle. In this letter Congressman Schulze suggested dropping all proposed changes on royalty income and grandfathering all existing arrangements. The IRS would then conduct a study over the next two years; based on this study, the rules for royalty income would be reviewed and amended as needed (Schulze, 1989).

In terms of advertising income, the full cost could be deducted if ads were substantially related to the organization's exempt purpose, but only 20 percent of the editorial costs could be deducted if a substantial number of ads were not substantially related. The third compromise proposal was to allow each tax-exempt organization to have one controlled subsidiary to which the aggregation rules would not apply. The response of the exempt community to these proposals does not suggest that this group sees them as workable modifications. There is grave concern as to what will occur a few years down the line after the proposed studies are completed. Exempt organizations point out that developing programs take a multiyear commitment, so that the uncertainty inherent in this approach may well stall many important projects. Although the modification on the aggregation rules is somewhat helpful, it still does not address the major issue. If the subsidiary is a for-profit, it is already being taxed. Why should there be special rules that could apply unfairly to exempt organizations?

Concerns of a different nature come from religious organizations. First, they are concerned that these proposals will effectively remove their exemption from information-reporting requirements, which in turn raises the entire discussion of government entanglement in the freedom of religion. Second, some of these organizations have large for-profit subsidiaries. Under the proposed aggregation rules, they may be compelled to either disassociate themselves from these or lose their exempt status.

The members of the House Ways and Means Committee are

uncertain as to exactly what legislation should be pursued to amend the unrelated business income tax, but there is clear agreement about the need to collect better data. In October 1988 Congressman Rostenkowski, chair of the House Ways and Means Committee, sent a letter to the commissioner of the Internal Revenue Service. The purpose of this letter was to "advise the IRS that it need not wait committee action to proceed with improved reporting and data collection." To show bipartisan support for this approach, the letter was cosigned by the ranking minority member of the Ways and Means Committee and the Subcommittee on Oversight, as well as the chair of the Subcommittee on Oversight (Rostenkowski, 1988).

The subcommittee has also "asked the Joint Committee on Taxation to develop an estimate of how much revenue would be governed by the UBIT package as it stands now" (INDEPENDENT SECTOR, 1989a). This foreshadowed the potential motivation for future subcommittee proposals. Many observers believe that the discussion on the unrelated business income tax, while couched in terms of unfair competition, is now driven by the federal government's need for additional revenue. These same observers note "corrections" to existing tax loopholes would not violate President Bush's commitment not to raise taxes. Many members of Congress have found themselves speaking at national conferences on the issue of the unrelated business income tax. Their comments at these meetings indicate support for the theory that revenue needs may be taking control of this policy review. As one congressman stated: "If the Treasury Department were interested merely in regulating business competition between for-profit and non-profit organizations, only minor changes in UBIT would be necessary. But the scope of the [Treasury's recommendations] is very much revenue driven" (Klinger, 1989).

In the review of the unrelated business income tax, one cannot ignore the context in which it is occurring. Both major political parties are committed to taking steps to reduce the federal deficit. Without a strong deficit-reduction outcome, many believe this issue is not substantial enough to have members of Congress risk suffering the wrath of the supporters of the exempt community in future elections. This factor, in combination with the general hesitancy to open the door to any major changes to the Internal Revenue Code, plays in favor of the exempt community for at least the short run.

Under this scenario no substantive action would occur until after the Internal Revenue Service had completed its compliance review and had gathered multiple years of data. With this information in hand, more carefully crafted amendments could be developed to address substantive problems and real abuses. Discussions with staff of the House Ways and Means Committee indicate that this is a possible course of behavior. Some of these staff persons also note that, as with efforts to restrict tax-exempt bonds in the past decade, "correcting" the federal tax treatment of exempt organizations could take many years.

Actions of the Internal Revenue Service

The Internal Revenue Service showed its commitment to markedly increase the information-reporting requirements for all exempt organizations in its revisions to Form 990 and Form 990T. These revised forms were released in 1990. Many who understand the complexity of meeting these proposed requirements believe that "the cost of compliance and reporting could be worse than the tax itself" ("Egregious Cost of Compliance," 1988).

The IRS is also involved in a comprehensive compliance review of exempt organizations, in which a large number of them are audited to determine whether they are acting in full compliance with the Internal Revenue Code. Audits will be conducted of organizations that have filed appropriate annual reports as well as those that have not filed. Some observers believe that nonfilers may be given special attention to determine whether allegations of widespread violations of reporting requirements are accurate. More than one source has been cited as stating that higher education will be given extra attention—some sources believe that most colleges and universities can expect to be audited in the 1990s. Lest anyone believe this is not a wise use of time, it should be noted that an audit of a large, comprehensive public university by the IRS in the mid 1980s culminated in an agreement in which the university paid in excess of an additional $250,000 in income tax. This amount is in addition to the nearly $100,000 the university had already paid for the two years the audit covered. This campus was not assessed any penalties or fines because it had filed all appropriate reports and had made a reasonable effort to comply with the law (University of Michigan, 1986).

An audit of the University of Texas at Austin is being watched with great interest. Some believe this is significant because it falls within Congressman Pickle's district, and added to this is the IRS's hard-line position on a number of issues. This audit took the IRS two years to complete, and it has demanded a tax payment of $164,000. The university is in the process of exercising the administrative appeals process. The campus has aggressively pursued this appeal and is intent on altering the position of the IRS on some, or all, of the issues in question.

This audit focused on activities and practices that occur in almost every college and university. The Internal Revenue Service determined ("University of Texas UBIT Audit," 1989):

1. Some forty-five events at the campus's Special Events Center are unrelated activities and all income therefrom (ticket sales, facility fee, concessions, advertising) is taxable. These events include concerts, ice shows, a circus, and other similar performances. The university has responded that these events are "promotion of the arts," which is part of its exempt purpose.

2. All advertising revenue from the school newspaper is taxable. The IRS based its determination on the fact that participation on the newspaper is not "required coursework" and does not contribute importantly to the organization's exempt purpose. The IRS sees advertising sales as simply a means for students to earn income. The campus responded that being a course requirement is not needed for the activity to be either educational or substantially related.

3. The advertising income for women's athletic programs is taxable because it is sold by a university employee. This makes the organization's involvement active. The university has responded that this activity does not meet the "regularly carried on" test.

4. Drug studies for commercial firms, intended to assist the firms

in gaining Food and Drug Administration certification, are taxable. The university argues that since these studies were performed by students they are substantially related and therefore exempt.

5. The cost allocation system used by the university was rejected by the IRS. The IRS wants an overhead rate for auxiliary services that does not include the cost of depreciation of academic facilities and equipment or other educational operations. The university believes its cost allocation system follows the principles of Office of Management and Budget (OMB) Circular A-21 and the process proposed by the IRS is overly burdensome.

6. The cost allocation approach for dual use facilities was also questioned. The IRS rejected the university's use of the Rensselaer Polytechnic Institute holding and insists that costs be allocated on the basis of available time for nonexempt activities.

These positions by the IRS tend to indicate a new, more aggressive attitude on its part and suggest the posture that will be taken as it conducts its compliance review.

If the determination on events in the Special Events Center is enforced, a wide range of performance activities are called into question. Will the IRS alter its position on bowl games or performances in community centers and social centers owned by religious organizations? What nature of performance activity will be considered substantially related to education and other exempt organizations that have traditionally promoted such events?

The ruling on the school newspaper creates a new criterion for a collegiate activity to be substantially related. It must now be part of the required coursework. If the convenience exception is eliminated, what effect will this have on a wide range of collegiate activities? What effect will the extension of this rationale have on the activities of other types of exempt organizations? It is interesting to note that advertising in college media is the one form of advertising that seems to have the support of the Subcommittee on Oversight to be exempt from taxation.

The IRS's position on drug testing also shows a potential change. Normally, if an activity is conducted by students as part of their educational program, it is exempt. Here the IRS seems to be saying that if the source of the income is a taxable activity, irrespective of its relationship to an exempt function, it is taxable. Please note that because this case is still under administrative review neither party is willing to share information; thus there are gaps in information on all of the facts and the IRS's rationale. This may lead to some inaccurate conclusions by those evaluating this situation.

The cost allocation issues are of particular importance. The IRS continues to take the position that it has historically held on dual use facilities. This assures all exempt organizations of uncertainty as to the proper tax treatment of these facilities until such time as there is a declarative decision by the United States Supreme Court or amending legislation. The outcome on this issue will have a major dollar impact.

The general cost allocation system the IRS wants the university to implement underlines the lack of clarity between federal agencies on this issue and the potential cost to exempt organizations to simply gather the data required to implement this approach. It underscores the concerns of many observers that at least at the federal level the real cost to exempt organizations is going to be the implementation of management information systems that will facilitate compliance with reporting requirements.

At a seminar sponsored by the American Bar Association in Houston, Texas, in early 1990, a representative of the Internal Revenue Service stated that now the position of the IRS is that income produced by an exempt organization is presumed to be taxable. The organization will need to justify its claim for every dollar of tax exemption. Although this is essentially how the current law is written, in practice many activities conducted by exempt organizations have historically not been questioned. Statements like these, and actions like the audit of the University of Texas at Austin, indicate a baseline change in the posture of the IRS.

Other Tax Legislation

In its major review of the Internal Revenue Code in 1986, Congress altered the law toward the sale of insurance by exempt organizations. In passing Section 501(m), Congress took the position that commercial-type insurance is taxable, which removed the exemption for such programs as Blue Cross and Blue Shield. The essential element is that if the sale of the insurance generates income beyond its operating expenses, the activity is not exempt, even where there is no private inurement.

The 1989–1990 congressional session saw a number of bills that would remove exempt status from particular activities. Two examples are H.R. 2275 to tax affinity card income and H.R. 3739 to tax income from the sale, lease, or exchange of membership lists. Also, the 1990 Budget Reconciliation Act passed by the House (H.R. 3299) would have limited deductions a taxable subsidiary can take for interest paid to its exempt parent, had it become law. Functionally, this bill would mean "the more interest paid the exempt parent, the less that is deductible" ("Reconciliation Provisions," 1989). Currently, Section 512(b)(3) already states that, if a tax-exempt organization owns 80 percent or more of a subsidiary, the interest paid to the exempt parent is unrelated business income. There has also been serious consideration to declaring all income derived from foreign investments by exempt organizations taxable. During this same time period, Richard Darman of the Office of Management and Budget said an excise tax on the revenue of nonprofit organizations does not violate President Bush's tax policy.

This section is not intended to be all-inclusive as to the behaviors of the legislative and administrative branches that indicate a new attitude toward exempt organizations. The examples that have been presented show a diverse set of behaviors which tend to exhibit a much greater willingness to question the activities of exempt groups. When this questioning can also assist in reducing the federal deficit, the interest level seems to increase.

Part Three

State and
Local Issues

Chapter 7

Nonprofit Tax Law
at the State Level

The Unfair Competition Debate

For most of the past decade, the focus of the debate about what government policy should be toward exempt organizations has been at the federal level. Yet it is at the state and local levels of government that the most dramatic changes with the most financial impact on government policy may occur. At the state level, the key issue is the concept of unfair competition. Chapter Seven examines this concept and the major initiatives that have been started by some parts of the small business community to dramatically limit the scope of activities that nonprofit organizations may perform. This chapter then proceeds with a discussion of legislative and judicial activity at this level of government on the issue of unfair competition and a few related issues. Chapter Seven concludes with an examination of the impact of political pressure on nonprofits to alter legally permissible behavior, responses by some segments of the nonprofit sector to the various initiatives to reduce their permissible scope of activity, and the future implications of the current debate.

There was little excitement, government interest, or advocacy about the issue of unfair competition between nonprofits and for-profits prior to the 1980s, in spite of long-term competition between these sectors. Many of the activities questioned today (such as exemption for voluntary hospitals, sales by college bookstores and museum gift shops, and recreational programs and facilities run by nonprofit organizations) have been in existence for decades. This is not to say that there has been no debate on this subject. Certainly the travel industry has been questioning components of travel programs sponsored by colleges and universities since at least the 1970s. This can be seen through a series of unsuccessful suits filed in federal and state courts. At the federal level the plaintiffs attempted to allege that travel service activities by specified exempt organizations were not substantially related. In *American Society of Travel Agents v. Blumenthall*, 46 U.S.L.W. 2195 (U.S. Court of Appeals for the District of Columbia, 1977) and *American Society of Travel Agents v. Simon*, 36 A.F.T.R.2d 75-5142 (D.D.C., May 23, 1975) aff'd 566 F.2d 145 (D.C. Cir. 1977), the federal courts easily dismissed actions filed under federal law.

This did not deter our nation's travel agents. After exhausting federal judicial remedies, they next attempted an action in a state court based on the theory of unfair competition [see *Travel Companies of Minnesota v. International Student Travel Association*, File #448502 (Dist. Ct. 2nd Dist. Minn. Aug. 4, 1983)]. This action was also not successful.

The Business Coalition for Fair Competition

In a series of White House–sponsored Small Business Administration conferences in the 1980s, the issue of unfair competition by nonprofit organizations rose from virtual obscurity at the first conference in 1980 to be ranked as the third most important issue in 1987. During this time period, the Small Business Administration increased its emphasis on the importance of this issue. In 1983 the nation also saw the creation of the Business Coalition for Fair Competition. This organization was formed as a nongovernment vehicle to address the needs of those elements of the small business community that found themselves competing with nonprofit organizations.

Although there was some activity in a few states (most notably Arizona) on the issue of unfair competition prior to the establishment of the Business Coalition for Fair Competition, it has been through the activities of this organization that the issue of unfair competition as an item of concern for state government has been articulated. This organization has been active in developing a number of publications, producing a strategy and philosophy statement, and encouraging the development of similar advocacy groups in every state. The Business Coalition for Fair Competition assisted these groups in developing their state organization, with the research and information collated since 1983, and in networking with other state organizations. For the past few years the coalition has also sponsored an annual conference in Washington, D.C.

From its inception, the coalition has stressed the importance of those actions initially proposed by the Small Business Administration to remedy existing federal tax law as the cornerstone of correcting problems of unfair competition. This has been their position because of the potential advantage of exemption from federal taxes enjoyed by many nonprofit organizations and because many states base their state corporate income tax on the Internal Revenue Code. Thus a change at the federal level would have the immediate effect of altering the laws of approximately eighteen states.

Yet this organization quickly realized that gaining changes in the Internal Revenue Code was a slow and complex matter. As a point of strategy, the organization recognized that it may be far quicker to gain incremental changes through sympathetic state legislatures than through a comprehensive change in federal tax policy. In 1985 the Business Coalition for Fair Competition published what amounts to its "manifesto on needed state action" (Burch and Pattie, 1985), which presents everything from a "how-to" guide to a state-by-state summary of activity to a detailed set of remedies. Since 1985 the coalition and those state organizations formed to address the concepts advocated by the coalition have focused on implementing the remedies stated in this publication.

In many ways the proposals for state legislative action mirror those for federal action. All told, the Business Coalition for Fair Competition enunciated fourteen remedies in this publication:

1. Establishment of a private enterprise review board
2. Statutes prohibiting competition by state agencies
3. Spending restrictions that assure that no state funds may be used by any organization to "provide goods or services which duplicate or compete with goods or services offered by for-profit firms" (Burch and Pattie, 1985, p. 14)
4. The adoption of uniform administrative requirements for assistance to local governments to assure that no state-provided resources may be used in any way to compete with for-profit organizations
5. The adoption of policies for the use of state-supported research equipment and facilities to assure that no unfair competition occurs
6. The application of the maximum separation doctrine to nonprofit organizations
7. The review by states of their corporate income tax codes and amendment per concepts proposed for the Internal Revenue Code
8. Taxation at the highest possible tax rate of the income of those nonprofits that fail to properly report unrelated business income tax per a given state's law
9. Establishment of a commission to review the state's criteria for granting a charter to a nonprofit organization
10. Establishment of a formula that determines when the level of unrelated business activity would automatically deny an organization exemption from state taxes
11. Reflection of tax factors in the decision-making process for the awarding of state contracts
12. Establishment of a permanent, independent state commission to investigate unfair competition complaints
13. Pursuit of litigation
14. Development by each state of comprehensive data on the income of nonprofits

While most of these points are self-explanatory, a few require further discussion.

Key to the philosophy of the Business Coalition for Fair Competition is that competition per se is not at issue. What is at issue is "unfair" competition. The latter occurs when one organization is granted preferential tax treatment, tax-free loans, or other advantages through government action as compared to other organizations competing in the marketplace to sell similar goods or services. It is these types of advantages that may allow a nonprofit organization to devote more funds for marketing, service delivery, or lower prices, which a tax-paying organization may not be able to match and stay in business.

The maximum separation doctrine would call upon nonprofits to create separate for-profit organizations to engage in competing business activities. This second organization would be required to be totally separate—staff, facilities, operating systems, financial structure, and equipment. Although it is becoming more common for nonprofit organizations to establish for-profit subsidiaries to perform various business functions, these subsidiaries usually share some of the elements just enumerated with their nonprofit parent for financial and operating efficiencies. It is this sharing of resources that may become a future focal point of the unfair competition debate.

The establishment of a percentage of income at which a nonprofit organization would be presumed to be taxable will be opposed by the nonprofit sector. The percentage used as an example in the publication is 25 percent of annual operating funds. Depending on what activities are specified as "business income," many traditionally tax-exempt organizations may become taxable. In this group could be most, if not all, voluntary hospitals, privately supported institutions of education, and fees-for-services-based community service and recreational organizations.

As has been articulated by the advocates of small businesses, although unfair competition is a national issue, its clearest impact is found at the state and local level. It is for this reason that much of the legislative focus has shifted to the state level.

In addition to those concepts previously discussed, advocates for state legislation point to lost opportunity denied to for-profit organizations: "The nonprofit sector has gained market share, and it is easier to document their gain rather than the small business loss"

(U.S. Congress, 1988, p. 258). In many instances nonprofits counter this argument by noting client choice and the concept that the activity of the nonprofit sector has increased the total market and therefore the business opportunities available to small businesses.

Small business advocates also argue that the "nonprofits are professionally operated, and sophisticated management will adapt to maximize resources" (Pires, 1985, p. 9). Arguments like this are perhaps most vexing to managers and layleaders of nonprofits, because for the past two decades business leaders and government officials have decried the lack of business acumen exhibited by the nonprofit community. As managers begin to show these skills their organizations face assaults on their tax status for doing that which they have been called upon to do.

As various state-based organizations attempt to alter state law, they are targeting a broad array of activities conducted by nonprofits. As enumerated in another publication of the Business Coalition for Fair Competition, areas of concern are "food service, testing labs, sale of books and computers, travel services, recreation, nurseries, day care, hearing aid sales, medical equipment supplies, pencil makers, electrical, plumbing and heating contracting, to name a few" (Pires, 1985, p. 9).

Legislative Activity at the State Level

While the federal and local levels of government have been looking at their tax policies as a means to correct potential imbalances in competition between nonprofits and for-profits, as well as a means to develop additional revenue, the legislative focus at the state level has been to limit the scope of services and goods provided by the government and organizations funded by the government. Advocates for shifting service delivery to the private sector have pursued legislation that would bar government agencies and tax-funded or favored nonprofit organizations from providing goods or services where a for-profit entity stood ready to perform. These advocates have also pursued legislation that at a minimum would allow, and if possible require, certain government services to be provided by for-profits (for example, in road construction). This concept is generally referred to as privatization.

To date, legislation to implement one or both of these goals has been introduced in most states. Many states have passed some form of unfair competition legislation, which may be as limited as a general endorsement of fair competition concepts, may create a state commission to investigate whether there is unfair competition, or may actually limit activities in which the state and its funded agencies may engage. One association that has closely monitored this issue tracked twenty-three bills in eighteen states and forty-three bills in twenty-four states during 1990 and the first six months of 1991 respectively (National Association of College Stores, 1991, p. 1).

In 1981, prior to the establishment of the Business Coalition for Fair Competition, Arizona passed House Bill 2148, currently the most comprehensive piece of state legislation implementing the goals espoused by the coalition. This act placed specific limits on competition between state agencies and the for-profit sector. It covers all state agencies, including publicly supported higher education, but it does not cover privately supported higher education or nonprofit organizations. The act also removed certain restrictions that previously required that specified health service contracts be with nonprofit organizations.

Perhaps the component of this legislation with the most impact was the creation of a Private Enterprise Review Commission. This commission was authorized to review any activity provided by a state agency covered by the act to determine if the activity was allowed by state law; for those agencies authorized by the act to compete with for-profit entities, "to determine if it would be in the public interest to contract the program" (Burch and Pattie, 1985, pp. 38–50); to review determinations by the board of regents and state board of directors as to the propriety of those goods and services authorized by them; and, by an amendment to the act, to hear complaints from individuals that covered agencies engaged in unfair competition. All members of this board are appointed. The largest single block of members must come from private enterprise and represent the small business community. The appointment process does provide a single representative for state agencies in the aggregate, one representative selected by the board of regents, and one representative of the board of directors of the state's community colleges. The mandated composition and appointment process has assured the for-profit sector of control of this board since its inception.

As with most legislation of this nature, various exceptions to the general dictates of the law were enacted. These exceptions recognize both the political realities to getting a law like this enacted and the difficulty of totally altering long-term practices. Section 11 of this act provides eight exceptions for state agencies, including the operation and development of state parks and historical monuments programs, industries established by the state's correctional institutions, and the Arizona office of tourism. This section also provides a general exemption for state community colleges and state universities. These organizations are covered in Section 12 of the act, which develops a second tier of administrative procedures for higher education. The governing boards are required to review all services and goods available for sale to the public and determine if they fall within the activities permitted by the act. These boards must also establish a first tier of review to hear complaints of unfair competition. Decisions of the governing boards may be appealed to the Private Enterprise Review Commission.

Section 12 essentially creates a "convenience exception" similar to that found in the Internal Revenue Code for goods and services provided to students, faculty, and staff. There is also a specific exemption for sponsoring recreational, cultural, and athletic events. For all other activities, higher education may not compete with for-profits unless there is a "clear educational or research advantage."

Although it does not grant advocates for the for-profit sector all that they wanted, this legislation does provide the framework of the type of comprehensive statute that with amendments could meet all of their goals. The key action element in this bill is the review board. To the extent that it is an "activist" body, small business owners can use it to eliminate competing government activity. Rulings by this board in the past decade indicate it has been such a body.

Arizona is not alone in enacting legislation of this type. In the past few years a number of other states have enacted bills mirroring many of the sections found in the Arizona legislation. The major difference in these bills from the Arizona legislation has been the enforcement process. Either to gain the votes necessary to pass the legislation, or due to an unwillingness to expend state funds to create another state agency, none of the subsequent state unfair competition statutes have created a review board with the scope of authority found in Arizona.

A number of states have specified that the governing board for state-funded higher education must develop fair competition policies and must create a review mechanism. States like Colorado, Washington, Illinois, Iowa, and Indiana have passed bills with some or all of these provisions. Since these boards were already in place, there was no cost to the state to add this requirement to their assigned duties. States enacting bills of this type have provided exceptions to areas of potential unfair competition similar to those found in the Arizona legislation.

A few states have also responded to very specific complaints from segments of the business community. Idaho has passed legislation that limits the sale of hearing aids by state-funded entities. Illinois legislation limits the extension of credit by a state-funded institution to its students. Credit may now only be extended for the purchase of school supplies, meals, and items not sold in the surrounding community. (Merchants had complained that credit sales on campus provided campuses with an unfair advantage.) A 1990 Michigan bill (H.B. 4546) would bar state universities and colleges from selling goods "at a substantially lower price than the general market." The sale of computers is the main target of this bill.

Private nonprofit organizations have not seen any restrictive legislation similar to that discussed for state agencies. Preliminary versions of the act passed by Colorado did encompass "a nonprofit religious, charitable, or educational organization which is entitled to tax exemption under Section 501(c)(3) of the federal 'Internal Revenue Code of 1986,' and any amendment thereto" (Francis, 1988). The final form of the bill omitted this wording. Many who are familiar with the process of enacting this statute in Colorado believe all nonprofits will be covered by this legislation before the end of this century.

Colorado is not the only state in which legislation has been introduced that if enacted would affect private nonprofit organizations. House Bill 1266 ("An Act Relating to Prohibiting Certain

Government Entities and Nonprofit Corporations from Competing with Private Enterprise") introduced in the Texas legislature in 1987, stated that "a government entity or nonprofit corporation subsidized by state funds may not manufacture, process, sell, lease, distribute, provide, or advertise goods or services for use by the general public if those goods or services are also available through private enterprise." Although this bill was not acted upon, the Texas House of Representatives has established a subcommittee to investigate this topic.

Review Commissions

Most states have not felt they had adequate information with which to develop appropriate statutes, and thus the more typical response to allegations of unfair competition has been to create some type of review commission. In some states this commission has either been chaired by an elected legislator or has been a committee of the legislature (Texas and Pennsylvania). Still other states have assigned this responsibility to a state agency and a specially created review body (California). It is too soon to see if these review commissions will spawn a new flurry of legislation or if they will be a politically convenient vehicle for elected officials to avoid the issue.

If one looks at California's AB 944 Task Force Report, one will see a relatively typical set of findings. This special review commission engaged in the collection of testimony, review of existing data, and a review of the literature. Its members found that while they had heard sufficient anecdotal testimony about alleged abuses to conclude that there may be issues that require legislative action, there was insufficient information from which one could draw conclusions and develop appropriate correcting legislation. This body recommended to the California legislature:

1. Appropriate state agencies (for example, the Franchise Tax Board, the State Board of Equalization, and the Attorney General's Office) should file annual reports on the status of nonprofits, with specific attention to "the nature and magnitude of competition between exempt organizations and small, for-profit businesses" (Hamm, 1989, p. 86).

2. California should act "to improve tax compliance and enforce-
    ment efforts directed toward the exempt community" (Hamm,
    1989, p. 88). These efforts would include increased sharing of
    information between state agencies, and between the state's
    Franchise Tax Board and the Internal Revenue Service, more
    systematic data collection, and an educational campaign di-
    rected toward exempt organizations about their current tax ob-
    ligations and issues involved in implementing new commercial
    ventures.
3. Further review should determine the desirability, need, and af-
    fordability of creating a review board similar in scope of au-
    thority to Arizona's.
4. Due to the lack of available data and the activity on this topic
    at the federal level, as well as to see that Recommendations 1–
    3 are properly implemented, the task should be continued.

The scope of the findings and recommendations in the California report is similar to the activity of other state review bodies.
Where the majority of those appointed to the body are predisposed
to the view of the for-profit sector, one will find proposals to enact
legislation encompassing some, or all, of the concepts espoused by
the Business Coalition for Fair Competition (as in Indiana and
Pennsylvania). States whose review bodies are more similar in sentiment to California's either conclude there is insufficient information on which to construct fair legislation and recommend
continued study or conclude there is insufficient advantage to the
state to change current law.

Proposed Model State Unfair Competition Bill

Recognizing that significant federal legislation on unfair competition–related issues would not occur soon, in August 1990 the Business Coalition for Fair Competition released "The Model State
Unfair Competition Bill Annotated." In an accompanying press
release, the coalition stated that the purpose of the bill is to promote
the growth of private enterprise and to provide "guidelines" for
government and nonprofit activities. The press release also noted
the three-part process included in the bill: "prevention of compe-

tition, accountability and strong remedies" (Business Coalition for
Fair Competition, 1990a, p. 2).

The bill itself is quite comprehensive, covering all facets of
government and nonprofit activities, including the contracting of
services to for-profit organizations. Irrespective of the form of the
organization, the clear intent is to regulate "all the commercial
activities of government and other service sector organizations"
(The Model State Unfair Competition Bill Annotated, 1990, p. 7).

If enacted in the suggested form, it would require review of
all current and future activities by any government agency or nonprofit organization. This bill encompasses what the Business Coalition for Fair Competition considers the best elements of statutes
like the Arizona law, in addition to the other concepts this organization has advocated in its previous publications. For instance, institutions of higher education would be barred from selling
computer hardware and software; a Private Enterprise Review Commission would be created with full powers to hold hearings and
adjudicate complaints; and privatized services performed by for-
profit contractors would be placed under the same restrictions as if
the nonprofit performed the service itself.

The wisdom of the coalition's strategy will be tested very
quickly. By early June of 1991 a number of states (Arizona, Hawaii,
North Dakota, Oregon, and Wyoming) had introduced clones of
this model bill, while other state legislatures had introduced bills
that addressed specific parts of it. There are indicators that legislators in other states are prepared to also introduce bills based on the
coalition's proposal. The enacting details in the proposed model
bill eliminate the loopholes typically found in legislation of this
nature. To date none of these bills have been approved.

Judicial Activity and Other State Legislation

In some instances, the business community has attempted to use
theories of unfair competition based upon either specific state statutes or common law theories to limit the activity of state agencies.
Institutions of higher education have most often been the defendants in such litigation.

Perhaps the most fully litigated case has been *Jansen v.*

Atiyeh, 749 P.2d 1230 (1988). This action was brought by small businesses in the town of Ashland, Oregon, against Southern Oregon State University. It was the view of the plaintiffs that university housing, transportation, and other related services to non-regularly admitted students was unfair competition. Ashland is a college town. Its two largest activity centers are the university and the Ashland Shakespeare Festival. The size of the hotel, motel, transportation, and restaurant business in the Ashland area is dependent on the amount of business generated from these two centers. The university has a summer residence and conference program that allows nonstudents to stay in campus residential facilities in order to attend the plays performed at the Shakespeare Festival. Along with this, the campus offers transportation and food services, as well as related programs through their extended education program.

The university responded to the suit by stating that the offering of these services was part of its mandated mission by the state and was permitted by state law. The arguments and activities presented in this litigation are mirrored in collegiate settings throughout the nation. At various stages in the litigation process, both parties were successful with their arguments. In reviewing the court record, the Oregon constitution, and state statutes, the Oregon Supreme Court determined that it was within the purview of the board of higher education to determine the permissible scope of activity for the university. This essentially concluded the litigation in favor of the university, since the board of higher education had determined that most of the activities of concern to the plaintiffs were educational in nature and thus within the mission of Southern Oregon State University.

The state of California has also seen hotly contested litigation on the issue of unfair competition by an institution of higher education and small businesses. In *First Street Books v. Marin Community College District,* 256 Cal.Rppt. 833, review granted and superseded by 260 Cal.Rppt. 182 (1989), two local trade-book stores alleged that the leasing of two community college bookstores to a for-profit vendor allowed the sale of goods in violation of the California Education Code.

California had enacted very specific legislation as to the op-

eration of "auxiliary services" at its community colleges and the
California State University system. There are different rules for each
system. The California court of appeals found that under then-
existing laws the sale of printed material was limited to required
and supplemental textbooks. The sale of all other books, magazines,
and similar printed material was not permitted. The ruling did not
affect the sale of any other goods.

While the case was on appeal to the California Supreme
Court, the community college system successfully pursued amending legislation. As signed into law on October 2, 1989, Senate Bill
1590 allows any community college district to establish one or more
full-service bookstores on its property. The statute does not differentiate as to the scope of permissible service based upon how the
bookstore is operated. It does specify that if the bookstore is to be
privatized, an open and competitive bid process must occur. The
enactment of this statute made the civil case legally moot; that is,
there was no longer an issue to be litigated.

It should be noted that the fact that the community college
district had leased its bookstores to a for-profit company had no
legal bearing on this case. That is, the law applied equally to an
institutionally operated store and to a privatized store, yet the local
competitors did not become concerned about the sale of these items
until the district had privatized the stores. As will be reviewed in
more detail later in Part Three, local for-profit competitors of exempt organizations often do not become concerned about the activities of the latter until they choose to privatize a service.

As noted in a previous discussion of travel service litigation,
in the case of *Travel Companies of Minnesota v. International Student Travel Association,* File #448502 (Dist. Ct. 2nd Dist. Minn.
Aug. 4, 1983), an unfair competition suit based on state law proved
unsuccessful. Here the plaintiff was found not to have standing to
challenge the defendant's exempt status. This means the case was
dismissed at the pleading stage and the court did not rule on the
substance of the allegations.

There has also been an attempt to use state law to limit the
research activity of a nonprofit organization. In *Structure Probe,
Inc. v. Franklin Institute,* 450 F.Supp. 1272 (E.D. Pa. 1978), the
plaintiff contended it was unfair competition for a nonprofit orga-

nization to engage in research activities in competition with a for-profit organization. The court found no violation of state law.

This set of litigation shows the typical deference courts will give to administrative bodies charged with interpreting and implementing state laws. It also demonstrates that without a clear pronouncement in state law to the contrary, courts will not normally attempt to apply common law equity theories to this area. The very sparsity of litigation indicates that these factors are recognized by the small business community.

In addition to litigation and the types of legislation discussed in the prior section, state legislatures have engaged in a number of other activities in response to complaints from small businesses. In many states, nonprofits enjoyed certain exemptions for sales taxes, but in the past decade a few states have recently seen fit to eliminate some or all of these exemptions. For instance, in 1988, Utah applied the state sales tax to all cash food sales on college and university campuses. The unfair competition argument to eliminate these types of exemptions is that those entities that are not required to pay sales-type taxes are able to charge lower prices.

Some states are holding very focused legislative hearings and/or auditing activities of state agencies to review allegations of unfair competition. Once again one finds higher education gaining center stage, with the sale of personal computers and accessories the focal point.

During the past decade computer manufacturers chose to offer higher education major discounts on the sale of personal computers and accessories to students, faculty, and staff. For-profit businesses engaged in selling this equipment often feel that these large discounts create a setting of unfair competition. It is their belief that this educational discount program is costing them income. Those companies offering these discounts and the higher education community responded with a two-fold argument: (1) The societal benefit of putting technologically advanced equipment less expensively in the hands of students far outweighs current economic losses to a relatively small segment of the business community, and (2) these programs will over time actually expand the total sales of these goods by the for-profit sector.

Both the Kansas and Michigan legislatures have investigated

these collegiate computer sales programs. The Kansas review took the form of a Performance Audit Report, while the activity in Michigan was a legislative hearing. The Kansas audit found that state funds were not subsidizing these sales and that the campuses reviewed acted in reasonable compliance with the contract terms. (Note: The typical educational discount program requires that sales be limited to a specified class of students, faculty, and staff. Furthermore, only one personal computer may be sold to an individual and the equipment is to be used essentially for higher-education-related purposes.)

The Michigan hearing consisted of the typical point-counterpoint, anecdotal-type testimony. Both the Kansas audit and the Michigan hearing brought forth evidence that there were some sales under the educational discount program that violated the terms of the agreements. That is, equipment was sold to persons who were not in the permitted class or the equipment was to be used for non–higher-education–related purposes. Because the magnitude of these sales is large ($3.5 million over a two-year period at the University of Kansas and Kansas State University and $13 million worth of goods in a single special two-day sale at the University of Michigan), groups like the Business Coalition for Fair Competition believe this is prima facie proof of unfair competition. State higher education officials note the small percentage of documented improprieties and again argue the overall benefit to society.

The Use of Political Pressure

Many of the businesses affected by the competition between non-profit organizations and for-profits are truly in the small business category, often in the "mom and pop" class. That is, they are owned and operated by a single family who typically have all of their financial resources tied up in their business. Persons in this situation often have great difficulty in looking at the overall picture as to what is best for the country in terms of service delivery and the economy. What they perceive is a nonprofit organization engaged in a competing endeavor that they believe is costing them business. These persons are often unaware of the financial and legal constraints faced by nonprofit organizations, do not understand under what circumstances nonprofits do pay taxes, and are not knowledgeable about the pressures on the nonprofit sector to become more self-supporting.

It is not surprising that in this highly personal and emotional setting the term "unfair competition" is used without any precise definition. To the layperson fighting for financial survival, unfair competition is the perception that a competitor has been allowed some type of advantage by the government. Many small business owners automatically assume this is true for all nonprofits.

Particularly in locally based elections, small business owners can have an impact far greater than their numbers. This makes an area's state legislators, as well as local government officials, highly responsive to concerns of the small business community. Recognizing their capacity to exercise some political muscle, some small business owners who believe they are in competition with nonprofits have chosen to approach these officials to pressure the policy setters for the offending nonprofit to alter its scope of services.

Institutions of higher education provide a number of publicly documented examples of this activity. These incidents involve efforts both by the academic sector of the institution and the auxiliary service sector. The University of Pittsburgh, for example, had faculty engaged in research on radon. From this research a radon-testing program was developed. For-profit businesses engaged in similar testing felt that it was unfair for the university to offer this service, and they complained to university officials, elected officials, and the local media. Although it did not concede any wrongdoing on its part, the university chose to discontinue the testing program. It was its belief that the potential negative consequences of continuing this program outweighed the program's positive attributes. Based on the available information, it seems the university's radon-testing program was fully within all applicable state and federal laws. The university simply made a political decision affected by external pressure.

The student union building at the University of West Virginia underwent a major renovation in the late 1980s. As part of this renovation, the campus developed space for a bank and a number of other small commercial ventures. The campus went through a public bidding process to have for-profit entities come onto the campus to operate these ventures. The planning and execution of this process was done in full public view, with the knowledge of the local business community. As the construction of the project was nearing completion, the campus prepared to conclude the bid process and to award contracts, but at this point local business leaders pressured local government officials to approach the campus to discontinue the awarding of contracts. The term "unfair competition" was loosely bantered about as the legal justification for this request.

Here too there was clearly no legally supported unfair competition activity. The real concern of the business community surrounding the campus was that the addition of services within the campus proper might alter the banking and buying patterns of students. That is, students would go through the downtown area less often and would engage in fewer discretionary purchases. Even if these fears had actually been borne out as correct, this is not unfair competition from a legal sense. This fact situation is particularly interesting because the actual proposed providers of the service were for-profit entities and would operate under the same laws as the complaining businesses. Although there might be some advantages due to the nonapplicability of property taxes and proximity to the student body, the disadvantages as to mandated service hours, permissible advertising vehicles, and other campus-mandated contract constraints would have offset these advantages.

To many of the persons involved in the multiyear effort to develop this renovation and facility expansion project, the campus's decision to place this process on hold was quite frustrating. Campus officials felt compelled to respond to the potential negative effect of completing the project on campus-community relations and on fund-raising efforts. They were also keenly aware of inferences that if the business community and their political allies failed to persuade the campus to voluntarily alter their course of action, the potential of facing a fight in the state legislature was very real.

It should be noted that the initial decision to use for-profit organizations to operate the bank and other commercial services was made partially to avoid unfair competition complaints. A second reason for this approach was found in the financial plan to support the construction and ongoing operation of this space.

Through the use of multiyear leases, the campus would be guaranteed a minimum level of income. This allowed the planners of the project to calculate the income-producing capacity of the building and thereby know the financial obligations that could be incurred. This focus on the self-supporting capacity of the project was in direct response to external desires that nonacademic campus functions be totally self-supporting.

Even where there is an applicable state law, political pressure can be applied to those local officials charged with interpreting the statutes. A North Carolina statute (the Ulmstead Act) bars public institutions from selling goods or services in competition with the private sector unless the activity is substantially related to the organization's mission. It is the responsibility of the local district attorney to enforce this act.

A coalition of small businesses challenged certain sales activities occurring at the University of North Carolina, Chapel Hill. Most of the challenged activity centered on sales through the campus bookstore to students, faculty, and staff. The Orange-Chatham County district attorney was confronted with the task of responding to the complaints of these businesses. After review by his office, and lobbying by all parties, this official concluded: The sale of greeting cards; candy and nuts sold by the pound; gifts, posters, and novelties without the campus logo; stuffed animals, and photo processing must be discontinued. All other sales activity, including challenged sales of personal computers, was permissible.

The campus argued that the challenged items were either substantially related to servicing the campus population or were the type of convenience item permitted under federal law and expected to be found on a campus of its nature. Students had also submitted a petition to the district attorney about the importance of the sale of personal computers. They strongly argued the importance of being able to acquire these goods at the pricing the campus store could offer, as an important tool for their academic success.

Computer sales also led to political pressuring and litigation in the state of Illinois. Here the target of off-campus retail computer stores was the University of Illinois. After much acrimony and debate, the campus agreed to close its store and to contract with three off-campus stores to sell computers to its students. This action ended litigation against the university as well as the need for elected officials to respond to requests for legislation.

Although publicly supported higher education has been a very visible target for allegations of unfair competition and the resulting political pressures, litigation and debate surrounding voluntary hospitals, centers for social and recreational activity, and long-term publicly supported charitable organizations such as the Salvation Army have also not been immune from this activity. Since most of these efforts have been played out in the arena of local property taxes, specific incidents will be discussed in the next chapter.

Responses in the Nonprofit Community: Policy Formulation

Because higher education has been the focus for many of the unfair competition complaints by the for-profit sector, it is not surprising that many of these institutions have developed policies to respond to public concerns. These efforts have occurred through national associations and individual campus action.

The National Association of College and University Business Officers (NACUBO) had a task force address this issue in 1986. After gaining the approval of its executive committee, NACUBO released a combined "Policy Statement and Guidelines on Educational Business Activities of Colleges and Universities." NACUBO's membership consists of most of the colleges and universities in the United States. Due to the diversity of its member institutions as to size, funding sources, governance structures, mission, and scope of services, the document speaks in broad concepts. It has been the expectation of its writers that individual campuses would use it as a roadmap from which to develop campus-specific policies. As William Erickson, chair of the NACUBO Task Force on Fair Competition, stated in an article in the *Chronicle for Higher Education:* "If we had gotten much more detailed, it wouldn't have been useful to our members. The intent of this whole thing was for use as a guide" ("Colleges Are Reviewing . . . ," 1988, p. 25). Part of the intent of NACUBO in developing this statement was to show elected officials and the business community that the educational community had heard their concerns as to potential unfair competition and was endeavoring to respond. In the same article, Joseph O'Neil, chair of the Business Coalition for Fair Competition, welcomed the efforts of NACUBO: "It is healthy for an industry or profession to police itself. If they can control abuses, it will make the problem less serious" ("Colleges Are Reviewing . . . ," 1988, p. 25).

A number of individual campuses and state higher education systems have used the NACUBO statement as its authors intended. Among those who have articulated fair competition policies are the University of Minnesota, the Utah State Board of Regents, the California State University system, the University of Washington, the University of California system, and Texas Tech University. Each of these statements is crafted to the nature of the individual campus and the setting in which it is located.

These policy statements encompass an array of issues. The University of Minnesota statement requires that a service be economically feasible and/or necessary for the conduct of the mission of the university. Specific attention is given to sales to noncampus community members and to contracting for services. It also has a review and approval process for all existing and proposed business services.

Due to the nature of its institutions, the Utah statement discusses items like its medical school program and the sale of by-products from research and instruction. This policy statement also bars all advertising to the general public.

Many campus statements provide some type of complaint vehicle for local businesses. The Texas Tech statement charges its vice president for finance and administration to: "Address questions from the external community about specific sales programs" (Bookman, 1990, p. 40).

A number of institutions of higher education had developed initial policy statements on this issue before it became a topic of national debate. The board of regents for the University of California system approved such a policy statement in 1977, which covered the nine campuses in the system. It enunciated a three-part test to determine the permissibility of an activity: (1) importance to the university mission, (2) reasonable price or convenience, and (3) determination that no unfair competition is present. The regents charged the chancellor on each campus with implementation responsibility. (Note: This policy was revised in May 1981. Although the new policy is more detailed, it continues the basic premise of the original one.)

Higher education is not the only component of the nonprofit sector to develop policy responses to concerns of unfair competition. The responses by other types of nonprofit organizations are as diverse as the nature of these groups and those charged with policy development for them.

In the area of voluntary hospitals, one finds a number of actions and recommendations. For instance, the Methodist Hospitals have taken the position that they will not engage in any unrelated business activity. A number of academicians and supporters of voluntary hospitals advocate the development of community benefit standards and self-policing by hospital accrediting bodies as to the scope of activities engaged in by voluntary hospitals (Mathis, n.d.; Seay and others, 1986; Seay and Vladeck, 1988). Underlying these concepts is the self-policing endorsed by the leadership of the Business Coalition for Fair Competition. The Catholic Health Association has taken a different tangent, focusing on the basic mission of charitable and service nonprofit organizations. To assure an organization's compliance with its exempt purpose, this association has developed a "Social Accountability Budget" (Catholic Health Association of the United States, 1989b). Through the use of this concept, an organization assures itself that in developing its annual operating priorities the organization's service responsibility to its community will be preeminent in importance. This in turn allows a proper balancing of the organization's service mission with its business mission. The former is the organization's reason for existence; the latter is a means to ensure financial integrity.

Somewhat akin to this approach is the action of the governing body for the YMCA of the United States, which in 1987 adopted a document entitled "The Reaffirming of the YMCA Mission." This document restates the historical purpose of the YMCA and calls upon the individual community YMCAs to reevaluate their programs to ensure compliance with these historical purposes.

The Future

At the state level competition between nonprofits and for-profits generates highly personalized responses. Although government and business in general want nonprofit organizations to become better managed and more financially self-reliant, the competing small business person is most concerned with a loss in income. This dichotomy has been recognized by many involved in this process. The chairman of the Pennsylvania Task Force to Study Ways to Reduce Competition Between PA and Private Enterprises and the Select Committee to Study Nonprofits, Representative Italo S. Cappabianca, stated in a 1986 report:

> Nonprofit firms argue that in many cases, they are responding to mandates from government when moving into areas which have until recently been the exclusive province of for-profit firms. For example, many of the current initiatives Pennsylvania universities are involved in regard new products or processes stemming from state or local government programs which specifically request universities to take on a new role. Mentioned in this category were the Ben Franklin Partnership and the Software Engineering Institute at Carnegie-Melon University. . . . Representatives of nonprofit firms feel that, in responding to charges of unfair competition in these areas, they are being forced to meet two conflicting standards of behavior mandated by government [Meyer, 1987].

These conflicting mandates, with the concurrent risk to a nonprofit in terms of negative consequences, often compel politically based decisions to be made. As one author states, "In all this, an institution must weigh whether the benefits justify the financial and political cost" (Small, 1984, p. 26). The potential consequences are negative public relations with a reduction in donations, the cost of defending litigation and political lobbying efforts, the cost of complying with new reporting and audit requirements, and the potential loss of tax exemptions or the opportunity to engage in specified activities.

It is not terribly surprising that in light of this many nonprofit organizations are having greater difficulty gaining volunteer board members. Those serving in these capacities are, on an increasing basis, having to decide whether to discontinue program offerings or actively engage in efforts to offset the efforts of small business advocates. Whichever course they choose will displease a part of the public and will conflict with the desires of some elected officials.

It must be remembered that the types of services where organizations like the Business Coalition for Fair Competition see potential unfair competition are in a broad category. Among the areas for concern are "food service, testing laboratories, the sale of books and computers, travel services, recreation, nurseries, day care, hearing aid sales, medical equipment supplies, pencil making, specialty advertising, janitorial services, waste hauling, electrical, plumbing and heating contracting, to name just a few" (Stanion, 1989b, p. 9). Thus the potential effects of the full compliance with the wishes of this organization would be far reaching.

Chapter 8

Local Government
and Property Tax Exemptions

For many nonprofit organizations, exemption from property taxes is a critical financial matter. Chapter Eight examines the history and rationale for this exemption, and Chapter Nine gives detailed analysis of a number of specific settings. As will be seen, for both philosophical and financial reasons, since the first property tax exemption statutes were put in place, individual local governments have been challenging in state courts property tax exemptions to specific activities of nonprofit organizations. The past few decades have seen increasing discussions between nonprofit organizations that own large land masses and local government officials as to how local government can recover some of the funds lost through the taking of land off the property tax roles. This chapter takes a close look at these activities. Chapter Eight concludes with a review of efforts by state courts to develop workable judicial tests to determine under what circumstances a property tax exemption should be denied.

As in the federal arena, the growing sophistication of the activities of nonprofit organizations has made this an ever more complex issue to determine. Since many of the state laws that govern property tax exemptions have not been updated to stay abreast of these changes, on an increasing basis state courts are feeling compelled to interpret these statutes to cover behaviors that are not specifically addressed.

Every state provides property tax exemption for a specified set of nonprofit organizations. The greatest effect of this exemption is felt at the local government level, since property tax income has historically been a significant funding source for cities, counties, school districts, and other special assessment districts. The role of property taxes in funding local government has been reduced in some states due to both the implementation of new tax vehicles and court orders for the equalization of funding in areas like K-12 public education. Nevertheless, property taxes still play a major role in the funding of local government in all states.

In 1988 approximately 50 percent of the cities in the United States had deficit budgets. In the same year close to two-thirds of the cities increased fees, while some 40 percent raised property taxes. The reasons for these funding difficulties are multiple and often affected by local economic conditions. Clearly, efforts to lower the federal deficit, which has eliminated revenue sharing and other state and local government funding from the federal government, has been a major contributor to this problem. Also, the practice of one level of government mandating new programs that a lower level of government must provide and fund has been a second major contributor to the funding dilemma for local government. These factors, combined with the long-recognized fact that the voting public can most easily vent its frustration with taxation and service levels at locally elected officials, have created near-crisis situations for local governments in many states.

Of the advantages a state can grant to nonprofit organizations, a study in New England found that exemptions from property, sales, property transfer, capital gains, and corporate income taxes are the most important (Moody, 1982, p. 125). The relative importance of a specific tax source in a given state is dependent on the tax structure in the state. Of these taxes, property tax exemptions generally have the greatest impact on local government. The impact increases if a significant percentage of a local government's total land mass is owned by nonprofit organizations and government entities exempt from taxation under state law. The most aggravating fact about these exemptions to local government officials is that they have no direct say in who has them. The decisions as to which organizations are granted these exemptions are decided at the state level of government.

It should be noted that the various levels of government own far more exempt land than nonprofit organizations. Yet the capacity for local government to in any way affect the taxation of these land masses is essentially nonexistent; thus, the general focus of local government officials when attempting to alter the effect of property tax exemptions is nonprofit organizations.

Property Tax Exemption Litigation

Based on the same theories that compelled the federal government to exempt nonprofit organizations from income taxes, from the very founding of our nation states have granted property tax exemptions to specified nonprofit organizations. The scope of organizations exempt in each state is based upon local custom. Some states' courts have given a broad definition of these exemptions. These states tend to look at who actually receives the benefit from the land [see *Worthington Dormitory, Inc. v. Commissioner of Revenue*, 292 N.W.2d 276 (Minn. 1980), *Southern Illinois University Foundation v. Booker*, 425 N.E.2d 465 (Ct. App. Ill. 1981), *State ex. rel. Wisconsin Building Corporation v. Baries*, 257 Wis. 497, 44 N.W.2d 259 (1950), *District of Columbia v. Catholic Education Press*, 199 F.2d 176 (1952) cert. den. 344 U.S. 986 (1952), *Cleveland State University v. Perk*, 26 Ohio St.2d 1, 268 N.E.2d 577 (1971)]. This is often referred to as the "equitable interest or beneficial ownership theory."

Juxtaposed to this, many states use a "strict construction" approach: "These exemptions (property tax) are usually 'strictly construed' to the end that such concessions will be neither enlarged nor extended beyond the plain meaning of the language employed" [Kaplan, 1985, p. 398, and also see *Cedars of Lebanon Hospital v. Los Angeles County*, 35 Cal.2d 729, 221 P.2d 31, 34 (1950), *Commonwealth v. Progressive Community Club of Washington County*, 215 Va. 732 (1975), *Cook County Collector v. National College of Education*, 41 Ill. App. 633, 345 N.E.2d 507 (1976), *City of Ann Arbor v. University Cellar,* 401 Mich. 270, 258 N.W.2d 1 (1977), *Princeton University Press v. Borough of Princeton,* 35 N.J. 209, 172 A.2d 420 (1961)]. Resource C provides over fifty cases in which state courts have interpreted local property tax exemption laws.

Since the inception of exemptions from property taxes, local officials have challenged what they perceived as abuses, which has resulted in extensive litigation in many states. Those nonprofits with large land holdings and budgets, and therefore exemptions with a very real impact on the income of local government, have historically been of the greatest interest to local officials. As local government has faced increasing financial pressure, and as society in general has become enamored with free-market theories during the past decade, it is not terribly surprising that entities like colleges and universities, voluntary hospitals, and fee-supported social and recreational facilities have increasingly been of interest to local tax assessors. As one author notes, "Tax assessors with an eye out for the public dollar look yearningly at multi-million dollar university complexes" (Alexander and Solomon, 1972, p. 211).

Higher education has long found itself involved in litigation interpreting property tax laws. Some of this litigation has addressed the practice of creating foundations, technically separate from the campus, to provide certain services. In this situation, whether a state's courts use the equitable interest theory or a strict construction approach will often determine the outcome.

In *City of Ann Arbor v. University Cellar,* a property tax exemption was denied to the defendant, even though it provided traditional college bookstore services to a state university. The court determined that since the land itself was not legally owned by the state, the use to which the land was put was irrelevant. In Michigan the property tax exemption statute specified that it applied to "property belonging to the state." In another state, where land was used by an entity covered by the property tax exemption but this entity leased the land to a for-profit company, a property tax exemption was also denied [see *Follet's Illinois Book and Supply Store, Inc. v. Issaacs,* 27 Ill. 600, 190 N.E.2d 324 (1963)].

On similar facts, state courts have come to opposite conclusions. In *University Auxiliary Services at Albany v. Smith* (N.Y.

App. Div. 1980) 433 N.Y.S.2d 270, an organization similar to the defendant in the *City of Ann Arbor* case was granted an exemption. A similar ruling, upholding an exemption, resulted where property was used to house community college students [*Worthington Dormintory Inc. v. Commissioner of Revenue*, 292 N.W.2d 276 (Minn. 1980)]. In both of these cases the "equitable interest theory" was the basis of the decision.

This dichotomy of legal theory has also affected nonprofit organizations other than higher education. Strict interpretation theories have resulted in the denial of property tax exemptions in Washington, where the law provides an exemption for "schools," not student and faculty housing [see *Adult Student Housing v. State Department of Revenue*, 705 P.2d 793 (Wash. Ct. App. 1985)]; to a head-start school in Virginia, where the law grants exemptions to colleges and other similar institutions [*Commonwealth v. Progressive Community Club of Washington County*, 215 Va. 732 (1975)]; and in a state whose law required the property to be owned by the exempt group, a college that leased land for student housing [see *Wheaton College v. Department of Revenue*, 508 N.E.2d 1136 (Ill. App. Ct. 1987)].

In some situations the use of a strict interpretation approach has been of assistance to a nonprofit organization. A prime example occurred in North Carolina where the State constitution says all property owned by the state and its subdivisions is exempt from taxation irrespective of the use of the property [see *Matter of the University of North Carolina* (N.C. 1980) 260 S.E.2d 472]. Some nonprofit organizations have state charters that grant them their exemption and preclude any further review by the courts [*Butler University v. State Board of Tax Commissioners*, 408 N.E.2d 1286 (Ind. App. 1980)].

Where possible, most jurists prefer to analyze the actual fact situation and the intent of the state's property tax exemption statute in rendering a decision. Thus in *Blair Academy v. Blairsstone*, 95 N.J. Sup.Ct. 583, 232 A.2d 178 (1967), the court found that even though the food service was contracted, its primary purpose was to service the school. In a similar fact situation, but with different determining factors, some courts have found land taxable when leased to a for-profit company. This has occurred with a college bookstore (see *Follet's Illinois Book and Supply Company, Inc. v. Issaacs*) and another college's food service [see *Stevens v. Rosewell* (Ill. App.) May 2, 1988].

In other fact situations the court has not been as concerned with who the actual owner or user of the land was as with how the land would be used. Thus when Rutgers University built a 20,000-seat stadium while having a student body of 1,700, the court had little difficulty in denying an exemption. Yet in Ohio the courts found the fact that the income to be generated by property owned by a state university, but leased to an entity not related to the university, would be used to support the university's general operating budget to be controlling. Here the granting of the exemption essentially lessened the amount of funds the state would need to directly contribute to the support of the campus.

Illinois showed its more conservative approach to granting property tax exemptions in a case with a somewhat similar fact situation. Where a private university leased its tennis courts to a church, an exemption was denied. Similarly, a press associated with a private university was denied a property tax exemption where its printed works were used by others for a profit [see *Princeton University v. Borough of Princeton*, 35 N.J. 209, 172 A.2d 420 (1961)].

The homes of campus presidents have received much attention from local tax assessors. As a general rule, courts tend to grant an exemption based upon the actual use of the home, not its locale or other factors [see *Appeal of the University of Pittsburgh*, 407 Pa. 516, 180 A.2d 760 (1962), *Cook County Collector v. National College of Education*, 41 Ill. App. 633, 345 N.E.2d 507 (1976), and *Trustees of Boston University v. Board of Assessors of Brookline* (Mass. App. 1981) 416 N.E.2d 510].

Housing for fraternities and sororities has also attracted the attention of tax assessors. The court's determination is often based on the involvement of the group's college or university in the housing. Where the campus owns the land, the campus specifies housing rules, and the primary basis of the program is education, not social and recreational activities, there is a better chance an exemption will be granted. It should be noted that the Internal Revenue Code classifies fraternal organizations separate from educational organizations. Thus this general approach is consistent with the underlying thinking in the federal government's approach to income tax exemption. [See *Alford v. Emory University*, 216 Ga. 391, 116 S.E.2d 596 (1966), and *Alpha Rho Zeta of Lambda Chi Alpha v. Inhabitants of the City of Waterville* (Me. 1984) 477 A.2d 1131.] An interesting twist to this area of litigation occurred where a fraternity successfully gained a property tax exemption on the basis of its relationship to its campus, but the court awarded the refund to the college [see *City of Waterville v. Colby College* (Me. 1986) 512 A.2d 1039].

Courts also like to examine who the actual users of property are in relationship to the property owner. Thus Stanford University was able to retain a property tax exemption for its golf course, which was used 49 percent by its students, 46 percent by alumni, and 5 percent by the general public [see *Board of Trustees of the Leland Stanford Junior University v. County of Santa Clara*, No. 337067 (Sup. Ct. Santa Clara Cty.) 1978]. Amherst College was granted an exemption for property used as short-term housing for persons visiting the library, but it was denied an exemption for a vacant lot, which was not currently used for an educational purpose [see *District of Columbia v. Trustees of Amherst College* (D.C. App. 1986) 515 A.2d 1115]. Still another campus gained an exemption for an apartment complex used to house students, faculty, and staff, but only in proportion to its ownership of the property [see *Indiana University Foundation v. Tax Commissioners*, 527 N.E.2d 1166 (Ill. Tax 1988)]. Colleges have been denied exemptions for recreational facilities where the primary users were the general public and students from other campuses, or the land was not used for an exempt purpose [see *In re Middlebury College Sales and Use Tax*, 137 Vt. 28 (1979) and *President and Fellows of Middlebury College v. Town of Hancock* (Vt. 1986) 514 A.2d 1061].

In other situations, courts have based their decisions on either the need for the service or the fee level charged. Thus where a campus provided housing for its staff but in a setting where ample rental property was available, an exemption was denied [see *Tusculum College v. State Board of Equalization* (Tenn. App. 1980) 600 S.W.2d 739]. A similar denial occurred where the nonprofit organization charged more than a nominal rent and the space was put to a commercial use (*In re Board of County Commissioners*, 225 Kans. 517, 592 P.2d 875 (1979)].

In the past few years an increasing number of nonprofit organizations have been having their property tax exemptions challenged on the basis that they are not providing sufficient "charitable" service. This has been the underlying theory to challenges affecting voluntary hospitals and specific YMCAs [see *City of Pittsburgh v. Board of Property Tax Assessment*, Court of Appeals No. 3067 C.D. (Pa. 1989) and *Utah County v. Intermountain Health Care, Inc.*, 13 Utah Adv. Rept. 14 (Sup. Ct. Utah) 709 P.2d 265 (Utah 1985)]. Due to the importance of this rapidly expanding theory, various cases in which it has been utilized will be examined later in this chapter and in the last two subsections in Chapter Nine.

Litigation: Exemption from Other Local Government Taxes

In frustration with what some cities perceive to be disproportionate benefits accruing to nonprofit organizations located within their borders, local officials have attempted to apply other taxes to them. For the most part these efforts have not been successful. When the city of Morgantown attempted to charge a state university a 2 percent entertainment tax, state courts ruled against this [see *City of Morgantown v. West Virginia Board of Regents*, 359 S.E.2d 616 (W.Va. 1987)]. Similarly, Boston was stopped in its attempt to charge a user fee for fire services to exempt organizations [see *Emerson College v. City of Boston* (Mass. 1984) 462 N.E.2d 1089)]. Where a state's laws exempted collecting sales tax from nonprofit organizations, the nature of the income-producing activity was not relevant [see *Regents of the University of New Mexico v. Bureau of Revenue*, 62 N.M. 76 (1957)]. Yet Seattle was allowed to charge a state university a street user fee and require the campus to remove a sky bridge [see *Washington University Board of Regents v. Seattle*, 741 P.2d 11 (Wash. 1987)].

Property Tax Exemption Statutes

In some thirty-six states, constitutional provisions either specifically provide a grant of property tax exemption to specified nonprofit organizations or allow the state legislature to do so. In other states either the constitution expressly gives the legislature the authority to develop policy in this area or has been interpreted to provide this authority.

Periodically, a local government considers implementing some type of tax on college students, which generally takes the form of a head tax, or a tax on tuition and fees. The Illinois General Assembly has considered a bill that would ban such taxes because "it's horrible public policy to allow municipalities to tax students or tuition" (Blumenstyk, 1990, p. 21).

As with the Internal Revenue Code and the exemption from the federal income tax provided to many nonprofit groups, through legislative or judicial action states have developed a variety of tests to determine whether an organization qualifies for a property tax exemption. As one would anticipate, the variances in these tests and their specific applications are as diverse as our fifty states, the District of Columbia, and other segments of our nation (for example, Puerto Rico).

Analysts looking at these tests have identified what amounts to organizational and operational tests. There are two major organizational tests: (1) The entity must be organized in a nonprofit form and there must be no private inurement and (2) all assets must be irrevocably granted to further the organization's exempt purpose. In many states the last test requires a section in the organization's articles of incorporation specifying who will receive its assets if the group disbands. This clause must demonstrate that the assets will be given to another nonprofit organization dedicated to accomplishing similar purposes.

Because property is the focal point of this exemption, it is not surprising that the use of property is the first test to be reviewed in an application for exemption. The majority of states require the property in question to be used exclusively for exempt purposes. In practice, when administrative bodies and courts interpret this requirement, in almost all cases they take a practical approach and allow incidental use of the property for nonexempt purposes.

Some states have eased the burden for the interpreting government agency by passing a "primary use" test. In these states the law requires that the primary use of the property in question be for exempt purposes. Still other states take a dual use approach; they allow substantial nonexempt use of the property but grant a tax exemption only to the extent that the property is used for an exempt purpose. This dual use approach is beginning to be described as the "modern approach" to this operational test.

In some states, both the courts and the legislature are indicating a preference for this modern approach. As early as 1950, California courts began to utilize this theory. In looking at a YMCA that had a dormitory, as well as a set of commercial services (restaurant, tailor, and barber shop, with the latter open to the general public), the court allowed a partial tax exemption. That percentage of the property used for the dormitory was found to be in an exempt use and no tax was levied. The remainder of the property was taxable [*Y.M.C.A. v. L.A. County,* 35 Cal.2d 760 (1950)].

In 1989 the California legislature showed its support of this approach when passing a bill specifically addressing campus bookstores. This statute states that to the extent that a college or university bookstore generates unrelated business income as defined in federal legislation, local property tax districts may assess a property tax. This particular statute again underlines the effect actions of the federal government have on state and local government in regard to tax policies toward nonprofit organizations.

A second test applied in most jurisdictions addresses who is intended to be served. Here the issue is whether an "indefinite class" will be or is being served, a class that may not be limited to a specific voluntary or self-selected subgroup. It is for this reason that most states deny property tax exemptions to fraternal organizations. But where membership in a class is limited to an involuntarily created subgroup, there is no legal problem; in the latter group are organizations dedicated to serving the young, the elderly (in most settings), the poor, and the infirm.

Either in their constitution and/or legislation, all states have enumerated the type of organizations to which an exemption may be granted. Typically, states use a definition similar to that found in Section 501(c)(3) of the Internal Revenue Code. Thus educational, religious, and charitable organizations generally may be granted an exemption.

Some states specifically enumerate certain of such organiza-

tions. This often occurs when the courts have denied an exemption
to a particular organization and the legislature feels compelled to
clarify its intent. Perhaps the most visible example of such action
has occurred in regard to YMCAs and similar service organizations.
Some fourteen states have specific exemptions for these types of
organizations, with state statutes that either specifically name the
covered groups or create a descriptive definition of them.

Texas took such action in response to a 1926 court ruling
denying a property tax exemption to a YMCA [see *City of San
Antonio v. YMCA*, 285 S.W. 844 (Tex. Civ. App. 1926)]. Through
an amendment to its constitution, Texas provides an exemption to
organizations "engaged in promoting the religious, educational,
and physical development of boys, girls, young men or young
women operating under a state or national organization of like
character" (Tex. Const. Art. 8, Sec. 2).

No jurisdiction bars a property tax exemption simply because a group collects fees for its services. Some states do have legislation that requires a portion of an organization's income to be
from charitable contributions. Where such a provision is present, an
increasing number of states recognize government subsidies as a
form of charitable contribution. Still other states focus on the availability of charitable services. In some jurisdictions, "charitable" is
defined as free, while in other states a sliding fee scale based on the
ability to pay or fees are no greater than costs is sufficient. There
is also a set of states that will only grant a property tax exemption
if services are provided irrespective of the ability to pay.

In many settings courts have found it necessary to develop
tests to apply legislation to actual fact situations—particularly
when looking at the nature of a group's activities. Here we see a set
of tests that also seem to rely heavily on theories involved in the
exemption from the federal income tax. Among the tests developed
by courts are

1. A community benefit test: Does the community as a whole re-
    ceive some form of underlying benefit from the group's
    activities?
2. Who is being served: This is essentially a test based on the class
    of persons served. Some states require that service may only be

rendered to a permissible class (Iowa), while other states permit incidental use by others. As noted previously, classes of persons such as the young, poor, sick, and infirm are generally recognized as charitable. Some courts will look past the age factor and also look at the financial and physical health of the elderly set of persons being served. For this reason we find some courts granting a property tax exemption to residential retirement communities constructed by nonprofit organizations for the elderly, while other courts deny exemptions. Grounds for the latter rulings most often are that the persons served are in relatively good shape financially and are in good health.

3. Relief or reduction of a government burden: Most courts look at this on a theoretical basis. This may be in the form of assuming all or part of an existing government function or a function often performed by government. A minority of jurisdictions require an actual reduction in government expenditures (Iowa and South Dakota).

4. Financial support tests: Most states that consider the issue of fees look to see if the organization's primary purpose in charging a fee is to make a profit and whether fees are reduced for some clients, or at a rate at or below costs. Some states require some free services, while others require that services be provided regardless of ability to pay. A few states require public support through actual donations (Minnesota, Nevada, and Utah).

5. Commerciality test: A minority of courts look at the actual operating behavior of the nonprofit organization. Where the group's actions seem to be based on the same motivations as a for-profit organization, a property tax exemption is denied. Thus we find a split in jurisdictions for exemptions for YMCA residential facilities and federally subsidized housing owned and operated by nonprofit organizations. Using a community benefit test, some courts grant an exemption; other courts want to look at the class of persons using the facility and how residents are selected. Where there are income limitations, restrictions giving priority to the ill or handicapped, services in addition to simply housing, and measurable public support either through donations or government subsidies, courts tend to grant a property tax exemption. In looking at these multiple

factors, courts usually take a holistic approach and do not focus on any single item.

In more recent litigation we are beginning to see courts develop multipart tests. This has occurred in at least six states (Idaho, Illinois, Minnesota, Oregon, Pennsylvania, and Utah). The litigation is typically based on the denial of a property tax exemption to a self-supporting voluntary hospital or a self-supporting retirement home. A number of the hospital cases will be discussed later in this chapter, as well as in Chapter Nine. The Idaho court's test exhibits the type of factors courts are tending to want to consider:

1. A charitable purpose test: Is the group organized for a recognized charitable purpose?
2. Does the activity amount to a "gift" available for general public use?
3. Is the activity supported by donations?
4. A test based on the ability to pay: Must those desiring to use the service pay for assistance?
5. A public benefit test: Is an indefinite class benefited? Is there relief of a public burden?
6. A commerciality test: Do the activities generate a profit?
7. Another version of a commerciality test: Is financial need taken into consideration?
8. An organization test: What is the group's stated purpose?

[See *Canyon County Assessor v. Sunny Ridge Manor,* 106 Idaho 98, 675 P.2d 813 (1984)].

As with other courts creating these types of tests, the jurists clearly state that there is no precise formula in applying the multiple parts of these tests. Like the substantially related test under the Internal Revenue Code, the court must look at all of the factors at play in a given circumstance and then render a decision. In developing and applying these tests, courts have been aided by specificity in state law. Thus if state law requires a specific test and defines it in whole or in part, the task for the court is clarified.

What we find courts most typically struggling with is the application of constitutional provisions and state laws developed

decades ago for a different societal setting. The nation's economy
and system for delivering social services are far different today than
at the turn of the century. Similarly, the scope of services government has attempted to provide has altered the expectations of the
citizenry. Where the legislature has not updated its state's policies
on property tax exemption to address these changes, courts find
themselves attempting to develop some type of balancing test that
is often responsive to the mores in a particular state. Thus, although
the issues analyzed by these multipart tests may be quite similar, the
determinations may be far different.

Community and Nonprofit Organization Relationships: Political Alternatives

In spite of our nation's historical support of voluntary nonprofit
associations, there has often been a tension between these organizations and their host community. This tension may arise due to
differences in philosophy (pro- and antiabortion rights groups), the
large influence the organization may have on the total community
(colleges and universities), the perceived financial drain created by
nonprofits that consume large land masses (hospitals), and a host
of other variables. In the past few decades tension between for-
profits and nonprofits competing for the same market has added a
new factor to this equation.

As a review of the cases in Resource C will show, tax districts
have been challenging property tax exemptions since the inception
of these exemptions. The difference today is that we are seeing these
challenges occur with a greater urgency on the part of local governments. Added to this is the position in some areas of the country that
certain types of nonprofits may no longer justify tax exemptions.
The latter is particularly true for voluntary hospitals and fee-
supported organizations providing recreational and social services
(for example, YMCAs). This questioning and urgency seem to be
spurred by the dire financial straits confronting many local governments. On the last rung of the taxing ladder, they are unable to pass
either the cost or responsibility to provide services on to other
agencies.

The debate and litigation as to the property tax status of

nonprofit organizations are centered in a few generic settings. Much of the struggle is occurring in cities where large land masses are being consumed by a relatively few nonprofit organizations. In this type of setting, the real debate is how local government can generate needed funding without increasing taxes on those who already believe they are taxed to the limit. A second type of setting is where a cadre of for-profit businesses strongly believe their livelihood is being threatened by "favored, tax-exempt organizations." The latter, at least in the minds of the owners of the small businesses, are functionally no different from the taxed, for-profit operations.

Another significant setting essentially merges the first two factors. Added to this in some settings is the perception that some nonprofits have altered their mission to such an extent that they no longer earn this favored status. In other settings, the strength of support for free-market approaches, combined with the belief that there are for-profit organizations prepared to provide those services now being provided by nonprofits, produces the catalyst to challenge historical practices.

In 1981 many of the fiscal legislative proposals for the city of Boston addressed nonprofit colleges and universities. This particular city perhaps has the largest concentration of these institutions of any other large city in the United States. The proposals recommended that the state (1) repeal the tax-exempt status of college-owned housing, (2) make in-lieu payments for colleges and universities to make up for the lost tax revenue, and (3) provide local government the option to impose an excise tax on students.

Oregon has been the initial locus of challenges to tax exemptions for some YMCAs. The thrust of these challenges came from business owners of competing gyms who saw the local YMCA organization open new, state-of-the-art facilities, which seemed to differ from their own operation only to the extent that the YMCAs operated in a nonprofit form (for example, no private inurement) and did not pay "their fair share" to support local government. These local businesspersons, soon to be joined by some local government officials, felt that specific YMCAs had divorced themselves from the traditional role they played in the community and had forfeited their privileged tax status.

The states of Utah and Pennsylvania have seen significant

activity as to the tax status of voluntary hospitals. Although the challenge typically begins with a single local taxing entity, in both states there has been statewide interest. The perception of some government officials in these settings has been that these hospitals require significant government services, are being given a large government "grant" through a property tax waiver, and no longer provide sufficient charitable services to earn this grant. Where taxing authorities are successful in charging these types of organizations property taxes, the income generated to local government is often quite large. Typically the property owned by these hospitals generates a tax well in excess of $100,000 annually, with some exceeding $1 million annually.

Nonprofits are not without their advocates for retaining their tax-exempt status, nor do they lack strong arguments for the continuation of their historical treatment. Many of these arguments rest on the theories that motivated the original granting of tax-exempt status to nonprofit organizations. A second tier of argument is built on the economic value to a community of having these organizations. Studies by numerous colleges and universities have shown that the total economic return to the host community far exceeds the cost of hosting them. Unfortunately, there are relatively few data as to what would occur if higher education, voluntary hospitals, and other nonprofit organizations were compelled to pay property taxes. One source states that "if private colleges were forced to pay property taxes, the operating budget of some would rise 40%" (Moody, 1982, p. 129). This in turn would require schools to increase tuition and/or shrink in size; the net result would be greater demands on public institutions and a reduction in income to the local community.

Options Other Than Property Tax Exemptions: State Subsidies

Recognizing that property tax exemption statutes are approved at the state level, some states have developed formulas by which they compensate local government for lost property tax revenue, tending to provide compensation only for those entities that have a statewide value. In Connecticut, therefore, the state gives local government 40 percent of the lost property tax revenue from private colleges and universities, Maine provides a similar reimbursement at the rate of 50 percent, and Massachusetts reimburses local government for foregone taxes on the land (but not the buildings) of public higher education institutions, except community colleges.

Here too there are no systematic studies as to state subventions to local government for lost property tax income. One pilot study by Cornell researchers of fifteen institutions of higher education found that in 1982

- California provided reimbursements totaling $820 million.
- Connecticut provided $67 million, with a reimbursement rate of 40 percent for private colleges and universities.
- Massachusetts provided reimbursements totaling $36 million.
- Michigan provided reimbursements totaling $14.3 million.
- New York provided reimbursements totaling $38.4 million [Kay, Brown, and Allee, 1989].

This same study found that on a per-student basis the total cash transfers from the university or college to local government were a low of $22 to a high of $314 per student. Total payments varied between $155,000 and $4.1 million annually. These payments came from a combination of fees for specific services (such as sewer and water), state subsidies either for specific services or as a percentage of foregone tax revenue, and fees in lieu of taxes.

Options Other Than Property Tax Exemptions: Fees in Lieu of Taxes

Local governments have been entering into agreements with nonprofit organizations for the latter to pay a fee in return for a commitment that the taxing authority will not attempt to collect property taxes. This concept is referred to as "fees in lieu of taxes." The conceptual framework for these agreements is that the presence of certain nonprofit organizations makes heavy demands on a city's police, fire, road maintenance, and an array of other services. This is particularly true of institutions of higher education and, to a lesser extent, medical facilities. Some nonprofits have entered into these agreements as a policy matter in order to be "good citizens" and as a pragmatic strategy; that is, the institution avoids a messy public, political battle and all of the attendant costs.

The pressure to pursue these types of agreements tends to occur in states where local government relies heavily on property tax income and/or where much of the total land mass is consumed by tax-exempt organizations. Thus it is not surprising that Ann Arbor, Michigan, where 50 percent of the land mass is tax exempt, has vigorously pursued funding from the University of Michigan and the state. One sees a similar pattern in Chapel Hill, North Carolina. Much of the unfair competition and property tax exemption litigation is occurring in Illinois, where cities receive approximately 85 percent of their funding from property taxes.

Both Yale University and Dartmouth University have agreed to fees-in-lieu-of-taxes agreements that generate in excess of $1 million annually to local tax authorities. In their host states, local government receives approximately 85 and 75 percent of their funding, respectively, from property taxes. Other institutions of higher education make similar payments to their local governments (for example, Princeton University pays $35,000, University of Scranton $50,000). Recently three campuses of the University of California system have entered into agreements with their local governments. In the case of Santa Cruz and Davis, these agreements concentrate on issues of city planning and growth. The agreement between the University of California, Berkeley, and its host city guarantees a payment in excess of $200,000 annually.

Local taxing authorities have also pursued fees-in-lieu-of-taxes agreements with voluntary hospitals. A few years ago the city of Pittsburgh and Presbyterian University Hospital entered into this type of agreement. It was quite clear that a major motivation for the hospital was the avoidance of litigation: The hospital recognized that at a minimum litigation would force it to incur the cost of defending and the negative public relations; additionally, there would be no guarantee as to the outcome of the case. Sources estimate the total payments to the city to exceed $10 million annually.

In Lehigh County, Pennsylvania, government officials have also seen hospitals as an income source. In the late 1980s the county was receiving approximately $600,000 per year from two voluntary hospitals. In 1988 this county attempted to reach agreements with a total of four voluntary hospitals, but these efforts failed and litigation resulted.

Judicially Created Multipart Tests
and Other Court Actions

As the issues involved in challenges to property tax exemption have become more complex, and as large amounts of dollars hang on the determinations reached by the courts, a number of state judiciaries have developed multipart tests to determine whether an organization complies with a state's exemption requirements, in addition to the Idaho standard reviewed previously.

In enumerating the standard for review, the courts rely on pertinent sections of their state constitution, state codes, and prior judicial decisions. Generally, these tests rephrase the basic tenets of what constitutes an exempt nonprofit organization, as previously discussed in this chapter. It is in the application of these tests that the courts endeavor to apply local beliefs and recognize the evolution that has occurred in some segments of the nonprofit community. As the Utah court's action shows (please see Chapter Nine for a detailed review), this combination of local beliefs and attitudes toward this evolution can work against some nonprofit organizations.

The multipart tests enunciated by the state courts have been quite similar. Recognizing the lead role Pennsylvania has played in litigating property tax issues, a short review of its test seems in order. In *Hospital Utilization Project v. Commonwealth*, 507 Pa. 1 (1985), the Pennsylvania Supreme Court stated a five-part test. To be considered a "purely public charity" under that state's constitution, an organization must (1) advance a charitable purpose; (2) donate or render at no charge a substantial portion of its services; (3) benefit a substantial and indefinite class of persons, who have an appropriate charitable need; (4) relieve the government of some burden; and (5) operate absolutely free of any private profit motive. For the vast majority of organizations that have traditionally been granted a property tax exemption, these standards present no difficulty. But for those that rely significantly on fees for services to support their programs, the third standard can present a major difficulty. Looking at the cases discussed previously on voluntary hospitals and YMCAs, it is a matter of definition as to whether these organizations provide what amounts to sufficient gratuitous services. Organizations such as the YMCA argue that the combination of scholarships for low-income persons, providing volunteer experiences, working to develop moral ethics, providing significant volunteer leadership to their community, and the like meets this test. Voluntary hospitals believe that their policies to admit all persons irrespective of ability to pay, to provide medical training and research centers, to provide a variety of high-cost special services (burn wards and emergency care units), and to engage in public education efforts provide abundant gratuitous service to meet any reasonable standard.

The tests developed by other states are very similar to those described for Pennsylvania and Idaho. In the application phase of this process, what seems to differentiate the states is whether they place a value on the items such as those just discussed for YMCAs and voluntary hospitals, whether they view government subsidies as gifts, and the extent of actual unpaid service that is required. Some states merely require that the ability to pay not be a criterion for service (Oklahoma), and others seem to want to see a significant amount of donated services. Clearly the court's position in Utah is that donated services should at least be equal to the value of the property tax exemption. Unfortunately, in putting forth this standard, the Utah court did not state how one places a dollar value on the many services provided by a voluntary hospital at less than full compensation.

Local governments are not challenging only YMCAs and voluntary hospitals on exemption issues; these disputes have an impact on every sector of the nonprofit community. Higher education comes in for special attention in many areas of the country. In some settings the dispute is a straightforward property tax issue. Thus in March 1990, local governments in Pennsylvania challenged the tax-exempt status for dual use facilities at six institutions of higher education. In each instance the challenge was for specific buildings, not the entire campus. Each of these facilities is used for clearly educational and therefore exempt purposes, but each is also used for potentially nonexempt purposes. As with the Carrier Dome dispute in Syracuse, New York, these facilities are also used for cultural, sports, and entertainment events. (For a complete discussion of the Carrier Dome case, see Chapter Nine.)

A dispute in Madison, Wisconsin, shows how a local government can use its authority to grant building permits to compel an action by a nonprofit organization. The University of Wisconsin needed a zoning variance to build a parking garage as part of a housing and shopping center complex. Local restaurant owners were concerned that the university might place a pizza parlor in the student housing facility; therefore, to get the variance, the university had to agree not to locate such a restaurant there.

This fact situation graphically demonstrates the extralegal effect a small component of the for-profit sector can have on local government actions. Because the small business community tends to be very active at the local government level, at times this group can gain its end goals for a perceived competitor in the nonprofit sector through local government action on a seemingly unrelated issue.

When renting their facilities, organizations exempt from property taxes must also be very alert that they do not violate requirements as to exclusive charitable use. A Kansas chapter of the Salvation Army lost its exempt status when it leased space to a branch of Weight Watchers, Inc. The Salvation Army believed that this use of space furthered their exempt purpose of improving people's health and self-esteem. The trial court in this case only wanted to know whether the party leasing the property was a for-profit organization and whether the latter charged a fee for their service. Once this was answered in the affirmative, there was no need to go any further—the court ruled against this nonprofit organization.

Overview of Property Tax Exemption

The application of local property tax exemption statutes is unique to each state. The sole common factors are that all states grant property tax exemptions to "charitable" organizations and no state automatically deny an exemption because an organization charges a fee for its services. Although there is great symmetry as to what each state sees as the key requirements to determine which organizations qualify for a tax exemption, there is equally great individuality as to how these standards are applied in a given jurisdiction. At times this individuality is not only seen between jurisdictions but also in how a jurisdiction applies its standards to particular segments of the nonprofit community.

Factors that seem to influence the degree of litigation in each state include the condition of the economy, the financial viability of local government, the degree to which local government relies on property tax income, and the aggressiveness of the small business community in raising its concerns. It is also clear that some segments of the nonprofit community are more likely targets for challenges to their tax exemption than others. Organizations primarily supported by fees for services fall into this group, as do those organizations that simply have very large budgets. Perhaps the thinking of many locally elected officials is expressed in this quotation from Mr. Donald E. Lifton, member of the county board of representatives and a graduate of Cornell University: "there's only one billionaire in Tompkins County and that's Cornell University. It doesn't make sense to go after smaller potatoes" (Stanion, 1989a, p. 154).

Chapter 9

Community Disputes
Over Property Tax Exemptions:
Lessons from Specific Cases

The previous chapter analyzed property tax exemptions for non-profit organizations. In this chapter we will focus on a few specific settings to examine how local governments and nonprofit organizations interact and how both parties have attempted to resolve specific disputes. The settings that will be reviewed involve those segments of the nonprofit sector that are garnering the greatest level of attention from local government as to continuation of their property tax exemption. As has been noted previously, the actions a particular level of government takes toward one segment of the nonprofit sector have over time been applied to other segments of this sector. The settings examined in this chapter are those involving higher education, YMCAs, and nonprofit hospitals, but the concepts discussed have an impact on all nonprofit organizations.

There is little substantive research on how segments of the nonprofit community affect their host cities. The first subsection looks at one area where some research has occurred—the relationships between institutions of higher education and their host cities—reviewing studies done by the League of Cities and Cornell University. To the extent that nonprofits can show local officials that their total effect on the community is quite positive, they are able to strengthen the argument for continued property tax exemptions. This information is followed by a concise review of a particular dispute between an institution of higher education and its host city. In this situation, an initial inability to reach an agreement on a project that was of benefit to all entailed significant costs to both parties. This case study shows how politics as usual can often be of disservice to both nonprofit organizations and local government.

The remainder of this chapter focuses on YMCAs and nonprofit hospitals; much of the current property tax debate and litigation are being played out around these two segments. By examining key judicial decisions, the reader will be able to gain a better understanding of the pivotal legal issues and how different jurisdictions are resolving these issues. These subsections also contain information on actions being undertaken by these segments of the nonprofit community to maximize the probability of continued property tax exemption.

Higher Education

Recognizing the importance of higher education to their host cities, the National League of Cities' University Caucus commissioned a study that was released in 1989 (Kane and Rosen, 1989), which garnered responses from eighty-two cities, ranging in size from 5,350 to 785,000. For the vast majority of the respondent cities, less than 10 percent of the city's land was held by institutions of higher education. The focus of this study was not solely on income transfers but also on relationships, mutual perceptions, and areas of cooperation and support.

Some 42 percent of the cities had a formal joint relationship committee with campuses in their area. On the whole the respondent cities viewed their relationship with their college and/or university favorably. Eighty-six percent gave a rating of "good" or "very good" and only 1 percent as "poor." (Note: The latter city has over 50 percent of its land mass owned by one campus, with which it has a history of political battles.) The major positive attributes of a campus's presence in the community were stated as the effect on economic development, education, libraries, transit, parks and recreation services, and education. Those areas where a negative effect was most often found were police and fire services, as well as streets and roads. Most cities and their institutions of higher education cooperated on matters of police and security, economic development, city planning, environmental issues, mass transit, technology use, and vocational education.

Not terribly surprising to anyone involved in city-campus relationships, the most common university presence problems mentioned by the respondents centered on parking and traffic problems. Others mentioned by a minority of the respondents were housing, provision of services to the tax-exempt campus, and student behavior. These latter responses could often be traced to either specific community events (student behavior) or state tax structure (provision of services to exempt schools).

Even for those factors most often mentioned as a negative, the responses are very divided. Thus, although 42 percent of the respondents were concerned as to the effect on police, 20 percent gave this a positive rating. Similarly, the effect on fire protection was given a 33 percent negative rating and a 19 percent positive rating. On the other hand, those factors noted above as being rated positively tended to have an overwhelming positive response: The effect on economic development was 90 percent positive and 3 percent negative, and the effect on education was 81 percent positive and 4 percent negative.

All of the respondent cities received some payments from their colleges and universities; most common were payments for sewer (91 percent) and water (97 percent) services. At the other end of the spectrum, only 22 percent were compensated for police services and 36 percent for fire services. Cities mentioned arrangements for payments in lieu of taxes in 11 percent of the settings, while 15 percent noted university-related state payments. In no case did the subvention from a campus yield 10 percent or more of any reporting city's revenue.

Institutions of higher education consistently point to economic returns to their host city other than direct payments in the form of cooperative efforts, programs run by the campus that are utilized by the host city and its residents, and the income flow created by the presence of these large monetary centers. The responses of the cities tend to support these claims. Of those cities that responded to the individual question, positive cooperation was mentioned by 96 percent for police and security issues, 96 percent for student internships, 77 percent for small business assistance, 86 percent for economic development initiatives, 75 percent for city planning, 68 percent for environmental issues, 60 percent for transit issues, 60 percent for adult education, 53 percent for technology use, 51 percent for vocational education, and 48 percent for energy initiatives. Although this survey did not attempt to gather any information quantifying the economic value of having a college campus located in a city, these responses indicate the very real value received by a city and its residents from these types of tax-exempt organizations.

It is interesting to examine the data broken down by city size. In cities where the total population is either less than 25,000 or greater than 100,000, the responses tend to be most favorable. Cities whose populations fall in between these two ranges show the greatest dissidence, but even in these cities, there is only a majority negative rating for the effect on police services.

The responses as to positive and negative effect follow a pattern somewhat similar to the flow of payments between a city and its institution(s) of higher education. Cities believe that they receive from all sources (campus and state) less than full reimbursement for police, fire, and transit 86 percent of the time, and hazardous waste disposal 50 percent of the time. For all other services, a range of 59 to 87 percent stated they were in a "pay-as-you-go" mode of operation. The survey also found that not all cities provided police, fire, and other services to their campuses.

The growth in the positive responses on economic issues from two previous surveys conducted by the League of Cities is quite significant. In its initial survey in 1979, only one respondent noted positive cooperation on economic issues. As the statistics above show, essentially 100 percent of the campuses and their host cities are engaged in multiple cooperative economic development areas. Most often mentioned as areas of economic cooperation were (1) management and technical assistance to local small businesses; (2) promotion of new small business "incubators"; (3) provision of research parks; (4) data analysis by universities and projections on key economic indicators; and (5) joint community development efforts.

A smaller survey conducted by Cornell University researchers yielded very similar results. In their preliminary comments to their data, these researchers stated, "Defining the concept of 'fair share' is as much a political as a research task" (Kay, Brown, and Allee, 1989, p. 2). They commented that in addition to the historical societal concepts for tax exemptions, in developing the decision-making equation one also needed to consider the cost to local government to provide services, the value of the property tax exemption, business brought to the community due to the presence of a campus, and the community and social enrichment that occurs due to the presence of a campus. This type of equation thus consists of some objective factors and an equally important set of subjective factors. To these researchers the underlying issue is whether there is a disproportionate burden on local payers of property taxes due to benefits conferred by the state that assist all of the state.

This survey showed that neither cities nor campuses had any systematic approach to totaling payments. Of the campuses surveyed, state law always provided an exemption for teaching-related property, but there is no consistent pattern for other property owned by institutions of higher education. In their review of the data, the researchers found that the extent to which local government depended on property taxes as a revenue source was directly related to the level of concern about the exemption. They also found that it was in these settings that campuses had agreed to pay the largest dollar value of fees in lieu of taxes.

This survey generated information on an array of programs, unique to a given setting, which show noncash contributions from a campus to its community. Among those enumerated were joint operation of an ice rink, a police and fire mutual aid pact, child care programs, joint studies, assistance to local public schools, and economic development programs.

Case Study: The Syracuse University Carrier Dome

The multiyear dispute between Syracuse University and the city of Syracuse provides an excellent example of how a major nonprofit corporation and its host city should *not* go about problem resolution. It graphically shows how both parties can expend a significant amount of economic resources and goodwill in the political and judicial arenas and finally recognize that only through mutual cooperation can a fair resolve be achieved.

After the heady days of rapid enrollment growth and growth in the local economy in the 1960s, Syracuse University and its host city found themselves in at best a steady state pattern in the following decade. On the advice of a consultant, the university decided to develop a domed football facility, because market studies indicated that by upgrading its football facility, the university would improve its ability to recruit quality players. Better teams would in turn attract a broader range of students, which would in turn offset expected enrollment decrease. It was the view of the leaders of the university that "the increase in student numbers and spin-off income from the dome would allow the university to improve its educational program. The dome 'was seen as an answer to the University's problems for the next twenty years'" (Kirby, 1988, p. 44).

The university had developed a diverse funding package for this project. Of the $27.5 million needed, the campus persuaded the state of New York to contribute $15 million. The remaining funds came from gifts, the largest of which gained the name for the stadium, and internal funds that the campus could generate.

In the time period preceding construction of the stadium, there were attempts to develop a positive campus, city, and surrounding community approach. But when agreement was not reached on a timely basis from the university's perspective as to where to locate the new stadium, the campus proceeded to build it in the middle of an already overcrowded campus. This decision strained relationships between the university and its immediate neighbors.

The campus thought it had a financial and service agreement with the city, but once the stadium went into operation, it quickly developed that there was disagreement on many key terms. Part of what complicated this issue was the financial condition of the city. Between 1965 and 1980, the city had a rapidly shrinking property tax base, a result of a major downturn in the local economy, which in turn reduced the value of assessed property. At the same time, the value of the land owned by Syracuse University (were it taxable) had nearly doubled in this period and now equaled approximately 50 percent of the city's tax base.

In the first eight months of operation, many of the events in the Carrier Dome clearly were not educationally based. In this period programs such as a major boxing match, a political benefit fund-raiser, major rock concerts, and the like grossed over $8 million. These events were quite costly to the city, since it had to provide extra police officers to control traffic and crowds. The heavy usage in the area also created additional city costs and further alienated the university's neighbors.

Recognizing that an agreement would not be reached, and in very real need of funds to cover both direct expenses related to the stadium and new revenue, the city filed suit. The city's basic claim was that this dual use facility no longer merited a property tax exemption. Although the action was based on state law, much of the legal theory underlies the current debate at the federal level as to the taxation of dual use facilities.

After an initial trial and one level of appeal, both parties had partial victories. The city succeeded in its main legal argument: To the extent that the Carrier Dome was used for activities unrelated to the university's exempt purpose, it was subject to taxation. At the same time the court also lowered the assessed value of the property, which reduced the potential tax to the campus.

In the process of this litigation, both parties suffered income losses. After the city filed suit, the university decided to use the Dome only for athletic events and other clearly campus-related programs. This cost the campus significant rental income and the city in toto lost the income from funds that would have otherwise been spent there. Although they could not be measured in dollars, "town/gown" relations suffered terribly from this dispute.

Instead of continuing the debilitating process of litigation, the parties recognized the need to reach a compromise. The agreement that was finally negotiated has the university paying a surcharge on all nonacademic events with ticket prices over $2 and 5,000 or more in attendance. The minimum annual payment will be $100,000. At the rate of the minimum payment, it would take the city four years to simply cover litigation costs.

After the entire episode was completed, campus leaders discussed the difference between brinkmanship and an approach based upon dialogue and cooperation. The process initially engaged in by both parties was that of brinkmanship: Each party, with some reasonable justification, felt it was in the legal and moral right and saw the issue from its own perspective and not the perspective of the greater community or the other party. This generated personal and institutional acrimony; as previously noted, it also proved to be very expensive to all involved. The final resolve compelled the campus to yield on the position it had taken on not paying fees in lieu of taxes. With these philosophical issues resolved, the parties were then able to address the functional problems associated with the use of the Carrier Dome.

Recognizing the critical place this university has in the local economy and the financial difficulties confronting the city, the entire community should have supported the development of the Carrier Dome. Clearly, the improved financial strength of the campus was of benefit to the entire city. Also, the new income that the noneducation events brought to the area was to everyone's advantage. Yet tunnel vision by all parties toward their own agendas allowed the project to proceed in a way that caused disharmony and negative financial consequences (Kirby, 1988).

Case Study: The YMCA

For more than a century, the tax status of individual YMCAs has been periodically questioned by local government officials. Until the past few years, the focus of this concern has been the residential facilities, restaurants, and other commercial-like ventures of a given YMCA. In all instances, the dispute has arisen as to the activities of a particular YMCA.

Perhaps the earliest case involving a YMCA was *YMCA v. Mayor of New York*, 113 N.Y. 187, 190 (1889). Based on then-existing New York law, the YMCA was denied a property tax exemption. Just four years later, 1893, the state amended its codes on property tax exemption to include organizations whose primary purpose was similar to that of a YMCA. This effectively overturned the court decision.

This pattern is not unique to New York. Today more than a dozen jurisdictions have either a specific constitutional clause or legislation designed to provide a property tax exemption for a YMCA (including Alabama, Delaware, South Carolina, District of Columbia, Wisconsin, Nevada, New Jersey, Indiana, Michigan, and Texas). Some acted in response to other states where advocates for YMCA-type organizations successfully garnered legislation to foreclose the issue, and other states, like Texas, acted in response to a court decision [see *City of San Antonio v. YMCA*, 285 S.W. 844 (Tex. Civ. App. 1926)].

The decisions reached by courts during the past century have been based upon a combination of their state's property tax exemption statutes, their general approach to interpreting these statutes, and the prevailing attitude among the state's citizenry. This makes it quite difficult to generalize as to how a state that has not had litigation on this issue in the past would now respond.

A review of cases during the first half of the twentieth century sees courts ruling both for and against a particular YMCA. Yet even where a property tax exemption was denied, it was only for specific elements of the total program espoused by the YMCA movement. This differentiates earlier litigation from that which has occurred in recent times. In recent disputes in Oregon, Pennsylvania, and Kansas, the challenge has been to the full range of a YMCA's possible offerings.

A Nebraska case [see *YMCA v. Lancaster County*, 106 Neb. 105 (1921)] presents a typical challenge to a YMCA for its collection of fees. This state's courts take a broad interpretation of what is charitable; thus the court determined that the collection of fees, even if they are the primary source of income for a nonprofit organization, would not act to deny a property tax exemption. California courts exhibited a similar position in ruling that an organization need not exclusively serve the poor and that it may charge reasonable rates [see *YMCA of Los Angeles v. Los Angeles County*, 35 Cal.2d 760 (1950)]. In a New Hampshire case [see *YMCA v. Portsmouth*, 89 N.H. 40 (1937)], the courts also granted a property tax exemption, but on different grounds. This court found that the operation of room rentals and a cafeteria was directly related to the YMCA's social and welfare program.

In looking at requested property tax exemptions for residential facilities operated by a YMCA, Pennsylvania courts have come to different decisions. Cases in this state find the courts looking very closely at the specific fact situation. In one case, where the rental rates were comparable to that for commercial property and the residents had to pay additional fees to use other YMCA facilities or participate in other programs, an exemption was denied. Here the court found the YMCA was not engaged in charitable activity [see *YMCA of Germantown v. City of Philadelphia*, 323 Pa. 401 (1936)]. Two decades later, a Pennsylvania court reached a different conclusion in granting a property tax exemption to a YMCA's residential facility. Once again the court looked very closely at the specific fact situation. This court found that the nonprofit organization engaged in comprehensive interviews of potential residents, it gave preference to persons of low income, it encouraged participation in other YMCA activities, and there were no other charges to participate in other programs. On this set of facts the court determined that this YMCA facility was engaged in charitable activities. [See *In re YMCA of Pittsburgh*, 383 Pa. 175 (1955).]

Most of the media attention on more recent litigation about property tax exemption affecting a YMCA has focused on those incidents in which the YMCA has lost an exemption. Before reviewing these cases and the rationales used in them, it is important to note that this has occurred in very few settings. Also, YMCAs have won more disputes than they have lost during this time span, so where the exemption has been denied, it is to a narrow spectrum of YMCA. As some of the earlier litigation addressed specific YMCA component programs that seemed to operate from a financial perspective like a for-profit organization, the more recent denials of exemption have occurred where the entire YMCA operation was found by the court to mirror that of a for-profit organization.

Perhaps the beginning of this trend was in a 1972 case in North Dakota [see *YMCA of North Dakota State University v. Board of County Comm'rs*, 198 N.W.2d 241 (1972)]. This case is somewhat unusual, since the YMCA in question served only a particular university's student body, operating an apartment complex for foreign, graduate, and married students. The court found that commercially comparable room rates were charged, the apartments were nicely appointed, the residents were encouraged but not required to participate in other YMCA activities, and income exceeded expenses. The court ruled that this facility was not being used to carry out the YMCA's exempt purpose, and the exemption was denied.

This fact situtation is far different from that found in a Rochester, New York, dispute [see *YMCA of Rochester v. Wagner*, 96 Misc.2d 361, 409 N.Y.S.2d 167 (N.Y. 1978)]. This court found the challenged residential facility to be far different from just a low-cost hotel. Here the YMCA provided counselors for the residents, efforts were made to involve the residents in other YMCA programs, and the rental rates were low. This court found this type of service, located in the area it was in, to be aimed at the YMCA's charitable purpose of promoting mental and moral improvement and on this basis the residential program was a charitable service.

YMCAs in Kansas and Oregon lost cases involving their property tax exemption in the late 1980s. These cases challenged the exemption for YMCA facilities whose major program centered on recreational service programs for a fee. These facilities are among what I refer to as the "new breed" of YMCA. Based upon market studies, a number of local YMCA organizations have chosen to develop new "upscale" units intended to appeal to a more affluent membership; they tend to be a "state-of-the-art design." To the traditionalist, these units are far different from the more typical YMCA facility. They are usually very nicely appointed, not terribly crowded, and have only the most modern equipment. Like it or not, on the other hand, most people equate the typical YMCA with a somewhat rundown facility, with a set of mixed and matched equipment, which is heavily used and always in need of additional work.

Looking at one of these newer types of YMCA programs, the Kansas tax board denied it a property tax exemption. Kansas law requires that, in order to be granted an exemption, property must be used exclusively for exempt purposes. A section of its codes, added in 1986, does allow an organization to collect "some fees" and still qualify for an exemption. The board found that the major funding source for this YMCA was fees for services to its adult users. The fees were at a rate that enabled the YMCA to use the excess to subsidize other offerings. In the initial hearing, the board determined that 23.5 percent of the users of the YMCA received full or partial scholarships.

The board ruled that the property was not being used exclusively for an exempt purpose. It stated that recreational services are not per se charitable in nature; thus an exemption must be based on service to the poor. The board found that this YMCA's primary purpose was providing recreational services to a clientele that pay full market rates. As for the 1986 amendment, the board interpreted it to permit fees for services that at most covered actual costs. [See *In re YMCA,* Dkt. No. 6285-86-Tx (Kans. Bd. Tax App., May 4, 1987) aff'd on rehearing (Kans. Bd. Tax App., Sept. 9, 1987)].

The Oregon case also involved these "new breed" YMCAs. The Oregon statute is also quite similar to that of Kansas, requiring that property be exclusively used for charitable purposes. As for the issue of fees and potential competition with for-profits offering similar services, a 1974 case involving a YMCA resolved this. The court found that fees for services and competition with for-profit organizations alone were not grounds for the denial of a property tax exemption. [See *YMCA v. Department of Revenue,* 268 Or. 633 (1974)].

Local operators of for-profit gyms became alarmed when the YMCA of Columbia-Willamette opened two new facilities. One facility was located in a business district and intended to serve that area's adult population; the second was simply a fully modern recreational center. After gaining some appreciable public attention, the operators of these competing enterprises were able to get the Oregon Department of Revenue to review the tax-exempt status of these facilities.

After this review the YMCA was given a $400,000 tax bill. The Oregon Department of Revenue determined that "[the two fitness centers] are not operated in a charitable manner because of their policies to serve a small segment of the community, their pricing structure and the minimal element of giving" ("Tax on YMCA Upheld," 1988, p. 6). The department contrasted this with other YMCAs that "by and large, advance charitable purposes." A significant factor in the board's ruling was that out of some 3,500 users only 154 received some form of financial assistance. In rendering its decision, the Department of Revenue granted the continuance of a property tax exemption to all of the Columbia-Willamette branch of the YMCA's property except the Metropolitan facility and the personal property at the Commonwealth site.

On appeal, the court essentially concurred with the department's ruling (see *The Young Men's Christian Association of Columbia-Willamette v. Department of Revenue*, Or. Tax Ct. No. 2717, 1988). Key to the court's ruling was that under Oregon law each facility "must qualify on its own merits" ("Tax on YMCA Upheld," 1988, p. 6). This was a critical determination because much of the plaintiff's case was built upon the contributions from the two disputed facilities toward the support of the YMCA program for the entire area.

In footnote 1 to its opinion, the court notes that competition with for-profits alone is not justification for the denial of property tax exemption. The court engaged in an exacting review of the data on membership demographics, the number of subsidized users (both individuals and organizations), the fee schedules, and the actual programs in place at each facility. In comparing these facilities to other YMCAs in the general area, where the focus was on youth service, the court found a far different focus. Among its findings was that unlike most YMCA facilities that encouraged full family activities, the Metropolitan facility allowed children under sixteen years of age in only at limited times. Another finding was that other YMCAs had fees that were approximately 25 percent of those charged at the questioned units. Based on this information, the court concluded: "Plaintiff has not sustained the burden of proving its right to a charitable exemption" ("Tax on YMCA Upheld," 1988, p. 6).

Pittsburgh has challenged the property tax exemption of its YMCA a number of times, but prior to its most recent challenge, it found no succor in the courts [see *In re YMCA of Pittsburgh*, supra, and *City of Pittsburgh v. Board of Property Tax Assessment*, Court of Appeals No. 3067 C.D. (Pa. 1989)]. The Pennsylvania constitution allows a property tax exemption only for that portion of a facility "actually and regularly used for the purposes of the institution" [Penn. Const. Art. VIII, Sec. 2(a)(v)]. Current state laws allow a property tax exemption for all property used by a charity as long as all revenues are used to support its programs and facilities only. To gain an exemption, based on court precedent, the nonprofit organization must be able to show that (1) it is a "purely public charity," (2) it was organized as a public or private charity, and (3) it is operated as such. The central issue in this case was the actual use of the subject property.

Unlike the Oregon court, this court clearly recognized the differences in serving our current society from the setting when most of the laws in place were developed. On this basis, the court concluded that fees for services and the upscale nature of the facilities by themselves were not grounds for denying an exemption. As with the Oregon court, this court focused very much on the specific facts. Lacking the relevant data, the court remanded the case and asked for findings as to (1) the use of each floor of the facility; (2) whether the fees charged to members are greater than actual costs, and if so, how much; (3) whether the fees charged to outside organizations meet expenses; (4) how excess fees are used; and (5) a quantification of subsidized and nonsubsidized membership. The court indicated that if the income generated is used to subsidize others, granting an exemption to the entire facility may well be appropriate. But if it is found that this is not the case, only a partial exemption will be granted.

The opinion in the Pennsylvania case is reasonably supportive of the approach espoused by the YMCA movement. To clarify the underlying purpose of the YMCA, its national board reviewed the mission statement developed initially over 130 years ago. It is the position of the national organization that "charitable organizations must be mission-driven."

Functionally the YMCA movement operates like other large, voluntary, nationwide associations. In classical terms, it is more of a confederation than a hierarchy-controlled entity. The direction for each local YMCA organization is determined through the locally elected board of directors. To assist these local organizations, the national board developed and released a document restating the YMCA mission (YMCA of the United States, 1987). In doing this the board recognized that a local YMCA may appropriately conduct programs similar in form to for-profit entities or the government, but this is appropriate only if these programs "strengthen the uniquely YMCA aspects" of the organization.

The mission statement enumerates these aspects:

1. "Instill Christian values, emphasize the development of leadership skills, self-esteem, and respect for others, strengthen family ties, and even promote international understanding."
2. There must be community control through volunteer boards and volunteers to "lead and support" programs.
3. Each YMCA should "affirm its commitment to serving the poor and disadvantaged." Local chapters should have a "proactive financial assistance policy."
4. There is a need to "preserve donated funding and volunteer support." This expresses concern that some chapters may be relying too much on earned income and paid staff.
5. Reaffirm that membership in a YMCA means a commitment to community service. A YMCA is not simply in the business of selling memberships to engage in recreational programs, but it strives to have members involved in an array of offerings: "Wide-spread use of multi-tiered memberships and program participation by non-members significantly erodes this traditional YMCA strength."
6. "Emphasis on youth and family programming" notes concern as to aspects of "adult only" programs.

In defending challenges to tax-exempt status, local YMCAs use many of the items enumerated in the mission statement of the YMCA of the United States.

YMCA-type organizations have been offering services that some consider to be in competition with the for-profit sector and government since their inception. Robert Boisture, general counsel of the YMCA of the United States, defines the real question as being not an issue of competition but whether they are "really doing the same thing" (1989, p. 47). In this article he states that "in return for tax exemption, not-for-profits accept important responsibilities that commercial businesses, by their very nature, cannot be expected to address." Among items that he believes differentiate the offerings of a YMCA and its typical commercial counterpart is the commitment to serve all people, irrespective of ability to pay. He also notes the reliance on community philanthropy, in terms of both cash contributions and volunteerism. In 1987 over 400,000 individuals volunteered their time to a YMCA program and there were contributions of approximately $180 million. Finally, the "YMCA also accepts a social responsibility to provide continuity of service in good times and bad."

Mr. Boisture is particularly concerned with attempts to define the YMCA's charitable mission as only providing direct services to the poor. The history of the YMCA's capacity to serve the poor is built upon its capacity to attract those more affluent into its program. Once brought into the scope of YMCA activities, these members are often converted into the volunteers needed to operate the many programs serving those in need. Additionally, these persons act as the role models often required to assist others to improve their social standing. It is his belief: "Narrow the YMCA's role to serving only the poor, and you risk severing the very relationship that keeps the YMCA alive and working for all" (Boisture, 1989, p. 47).

Case Study: Voluntary Hospitals

The property tax status of voluntary hospitals has been increasingly debated in recent years at the local level of government. Much of the debate somewhat echoes the discussion on the YMCA. The central concern tends to be the fact that voluntary hospitals are essentially user fee supported.

Some argue that in terms of day-to-day operations, the behavior of many voluntary hospitals is no different from for-profit hospitals. Contributing to this identity confusion in some settings is the growing practice of voluntary hospitals of forming chains, which, although it may make sense from a fiscal standpoint, has created a community identity problem for some voluntary hospitals.

Throughout most of the history of voluntary hospitals, property tax questions have focused on their ancillary operations. This includes gift shops, parking garages, office buildings, research centers, and the like. Some states have chosen to limit property tax exemption only to patient care facilities [see *In re Queen's Medical Center*, 66 Hawaii 318 (1983)]. This is one of the areas where states have tended not to follow the standard used in interpreting the Internal Revenue Code. A second area of dispute has occurred in those states that require gratuitous (free) services. The question that has required judicial review is: What constitutes sufficient gratuitous services? This is a very individual issue in terms of how states address it.

The Iowa courts have rejected a community benefit test similar to that used in Internal Revenue Code disputes. In one case a property tax exemption was denied where all patient costs were paid either privately or through various government welfare programs. The court stated that there must be some level of truly free service [see *Iowa Methodist Hospital v. Board of Review*, 252 N.W.2d 930 (1977)].

Ohio also has a gratuitous service requirement. In one case where a hospital provided charity amounting to approximately 6 percent of its expenditures, an exemption was granted [*Vick v. Cleveland Memorial Hospital Foundation*, 2 Ohio St. 30 (1965)]. A few years later the court denied an exemption to a nursing care facility that had only one charity patient [*Crestview of Ohio v. Donahue*, 14 Ohio St. 121 (1968)].

Close to fifty years ago an Oklahoma court was confronted with this question of what constitutes gratuitous services under its statutes. This court framed the question as follows: "Are the doors of the hospital open to all, poor patient and pay patient alike? If the answer is yes, it is a charitable hospital . . . if the answer is no, it is not a charitable hospital" [*In re Farmer's Union Hosp. Ass'n.*, 190 Okla. 661 (1942)].

A recent Utah case has created grave concerns within the voluntary hospital community. In a 1986 decision, the Utah courts created a standard to achieve charitable status that few voluntary hospitals could meet and included this standard within a six-part test of "charitable purpose" enunciated by the court [see *Utah County v. Intermountain Health Care, Inc.*, 709 P.2d 265 (Utah 1985)]. Before stating and applying its test, the court first went to great lengths in describing its view as to the evolution of voluntary hospitals. The court returned to the founding of the voluntary hos-

pital movement in our country and spoke in very positive terms of
these almsgiving, social welfare institutions. In contrast, this court
found that typical voluntary hospitals today had become simply
"medical treatment centers" and had great difficulty in differentiat-
ing these hospitals from the typical for-profit hospital. In light of
this analysis, the court's determination to deny tax-exempt status to
these defendants was a foregone conclusion.

It should also be noted that Utah has always placed a heavy
reliance on a quid pro quo approach to property tax exemption. In
an early case, the court stated that "the reason for (tax exemption)
is that the state . . . is presumed to receive benefits from the property
equivalent at least to the public revenue that would otherwise be
derived from it" [*Salt Lake Lodge No. 85 B.P.O.E. v. Groesbeck,* 40
Utah 1 (1911)].

The defendants in the *Intermountain Health Care* case were
two hospitals that were part of a chain of twenty-one nonprofit
hospitals. As operating policy, both hospitals accepted patients irrespective of their ability to pay. The hospital chain, also as an
operating policy, attempted to charge patients for all service whenever possible. Thus most patient bills were covered either through
private insurance, Medicare or Medicaid, or private funds.

The six factors that the court stated must be evaluated, and
the court's application of these factors to this case, were:

1. Is the stated purpose of the entity to provide a significant ser-
    vice to others without immediate expectation of material re-
    ward? The defendants passed this test.
2. Is the entity supported, and to what extent, by gifts and dona-
    tions? The defendants failed this test. The court determined
    that patient fees covered all operating costs because these fees
    were comparable to those charged by for-profit competitors and
    there was no evidence that donations lowered prices. The court
    discounted the fact that the hospital had welfare patients whose
    costs were covered by Medicare and Medicaid. It also found
    evidence that there were significant capital contributions,
    which were immaterial unless the defendants could show that
    these contributions had a material effect on current operations
    and maintenance.

3. Are the recipients of the charity required to pay for the assistance received, in whole or in part? Defendants also failed this test. Here the court stated its key holding: It ruled that there must be a "substantial imbalance between the value of the service it provides and payment it receives" (709 P.2d 274). The court discounted the hospitals' policy of admitting all patients irrespective of ability to pay. Part of its rationale was that the free-care policy was not widely advertised and the hospitals attempted to collect from patients whenever possible. As a gratuitous aside, the court also speculated that most for-profit hospitals would have similar open admission policies on their books.

4. Does the income from all sources produce a "profit" in the sense that income exceeds operating and long-term maintenance expenses? The defendants also failed this test. The court based this conclusion on the possibility that accrued income might be spent on capital construction in other states. It also put forth an unfair-competition-type argument. While the court stated it might allow an organization to use net income in other than the year earned, it would not allow this if a tax exemption gave one an advantage in the marketplace (see 709 P.2d 276).

5. Are the beneficiaries of the charity restricted or unrestricted? If restricted, does the restriction bear a reasonable relationship to the entity's charitable objective?

6. At dissolution, are the assets available to private interests? Is the entity organized and operated so that commercial interests are subordinate to charitable ones? The court concluded that the defendants passed the test imposed by the last two factors.

(See 709 P.2d 269-270 for specific wording for these factors.) The court stated that these factors were not absolute. That is, in a given fact situation, the inability to fully comply with a specific area of concern to the court might not deny a tax exemption.

The voluntary hospital community was appalled by this decision, and their concerns were echoed by other segments of the nonprofit community, civic, and political leaders. An initiative was hurriedly brought together and put before the people in the next general election to overturn the court's decision. The vote was almost evenly divided, but the negative votes did prevail. Because the voting electorate have very few opportunities to vote directly on tax issues, the pattern most typically is of a "conservative" vote. The fact that the vote was very close, and that few individuals had felt any negative consequences from the court decision when the vote occurred, suggests that public sentiment might be more supportive of tax exemptions for voluntary hospitals in Utah than was initially concluded.

In the very next term, the court applied its new factors to a housing facility for low-income elderly and handicapped persons. [See *Yorgason v. County Bd. of Equalization*, 714 P.2d 653 (Utah 1986)]. In this case, all of the residents paid fees based on their ability to pay. The capacity to discount fees was present due to government subsidies. The court determined that this organization met all of its factors, using a very minimal gift to the community standard in this case. It found the commitment to repay the construction loan, some minor miscellaneous expenses, and volunteer hours committed to planning and operating the facility sufficient.

The court also created a new standard for its "substantial imbalance" concept by enunciating a "material reciprocity" test. Because the cost to the tenant was based on ability to pay, fees were not fully covering all operating costs. It is the difference between tenant fees and total expenses that creates the requisite gift. In reaching this conclusion, the court found that the difference "paid" by a government subsidy was not important. In this instance, the government subsidy was found to be no different than private donations.

There is certainly much difficulty in reconciling these two Utah cases. Only time will show if the standard for voluntary hospitals will be more severe than the standard for other charitable entities. The fact that there has not been a rush of litigation between voluntary hospitals and local taxing districts may indicate that there is a perception that the court went a little too far in the *Intermountain Health Care* case.

A review of property tax litigation shows that the state of Pennsylvania has been more litigious than most states. This reflects a more aggressive attitude on the part of local tax authorities toward segments of the nonprofit community and also the important role property taxes play in funding segments of local government. As with areas like YMCA and higher education, taxing authorities in Pennsylvania have been very aggressive in attempting to either recover fees in lieu of taxes or litigate to deny tax exemptions with voluntary health facilities.

Blood collection centers have rarely had their tax status challenged. Yet a few years ago, in a precedent-setting action, the Revenue Appeals Board of Northampton County, Pennsylvania denied a property tax exemption to the Samuel W. Miller Memorial Blood Center. This may well be the first time in the nation a nonprofit blood collection center was so treated.

As mentioned previously, Lehigh County had successfully negotiated fees in lieu of taxes from a number of nonprofit hospitals. When the renewal for these agreements came due, the hospitals determined they had erred in agreeing to these fees. The county then proceeded to give four hospitals property tax bills for 1988 totaling in excess of $2 million. These bills are now being challenged in court by the hospitals. The parties have recognized that these cases center on the question of what the standard should be for tax exemption for voluntary hospitals. In framing this question, it is realized that the standard for the modern hospital may need to be different from the earlier standard. A key question, from the perspective of the judiciary, is whether voluntary hospitals must provide a percentage of free care in order to qualify for a tax exemption.

In the Lehigh County case, litigation of this nature creates odd antagonists at times. Among the parties wanting to deny a tax exemption to the hospitals are public school districts. For them the issue is clearly one of money. School district representatives argue that they are as important to the community as hospitals; therefore, hospitals should pay property taxes in order to support this service. As with the small business persons who see their livelihood threatened by a nonprofit organization, the argument of the school districts seems to be rather self-serving and potentially short-sighted.

The judge in this case recognized the quandary faced by voluntary hospitals today. Judge Young stated: "The thing is, you want your hospitals dealing in large sums of money and you want them to be business-like, yet you don't want them to be businesses.

The bottom line should not be money. That's the dilemma we are facing" (Gaul, G., 1989, p. 11E).

A number of parent organizations for voluntary hospitals are working to find solutions to this dilemma. Previously there was discussion of proposals for the voluntary hospital organizations in this country to develop standards. The concept is that there should be a minimum set of essentially objective standards by which a hospital can be reviewed to determine if it is "charitable" in our current world.

As mentioned earlier, the Catholic Health Association of the United States has spent considerable time and energy in developing a process it entitles the "Social Responsibility Budget." This 100-plus-page publication gives one both the philosophical rationales of why charitable organizations need to visibly reaffirm their charitable missions and a detailed process to implement these missions. Those organizations that follow the process outlined in this publication will be able to assure their community that their expenditures are synonymous with their charitable mission and will also have categorized and quantified all charitable services. In Chapter Ten, this process will be reviewed in much greater detail. Properly implemented, a social accountability budget can be a key part of a nonprofit organization's action plan to maintain quality community relations and to respond to challenges about their preferred tax status.

Perhaps comments by the president of a nonprofit hospital in Vermont best summarize the issue. Vermont has seen litigation similar to the Utah case. The city of Burlington wanted to tax the Medical Center of Vermont; the city in fact gave the hospital a property tax bill for $2.83 million, arguing that to be considered charitable, an entity must gain its income mainly from donations. The Vermont Supreme Court determined that the amount of free care or charity is not determinative under state law.

Reflecting on the entire episode, the president of the medical center, James Taylor, stated: "A hospital's charitable heritage shouldn't be put aside in the zeal to demonstrate business-like management. The image offered the community will mirror the vision the hospital has of itself. An organization that hasn't maintained the spirit of charity, the sense of service, compassion for the sick and injured, and the leadership to address community needs will not be successful in holding itself out to be charitable. If not-for-profit hospitals allow themselves to be viewed as just another commodity or just another service industry, they will have surrendered a basic and important value" (National Association of Retail Druggists, 1989d, p. 19).

Part Four

Guidelines
for Action

Chapter 10

Ensuring Compliance with the Law and Dealing with Potential Challenges

Chapters Two through Nine reviewed statutory, judicial, administrative, and political activity as to the taxation of nonprofit organizations. Chapter Ten recommends a set of behaviors in which all nonprofit organizations should engage. Emphasis is placed on how each nonprofit organization should prepare itself for a possible government audit and develop an action plan to be in a proactive posture in the current debate on what government policy should be toward the nonprofit sector. To assist organizations in implementing this proactive posture, examples are given of processes and actions of a number of nonprofit organizations. A key concept in this chapter is that irrespective of its size, every nonprofit organization should strive to adapt the recommendations that are presented.

What the Law Requires

The starting point for all tax-exempt organizations is to make every effort to comply with applicable federal, state, and local laws. At the federal level, the main legal requirements address the proper reporting of activities and income by those organizations claiming an exemption from corporate income taxes. The Internal Revenue Service is currently engaged in its first comprehensive compliance review of exempt organizations. At its completion, this review will provide the most comprehensive data to date as to the number of organizations that attempt to comply with these requirements, as well as the relative accuracy of these efforts. From the existing data, it seems that significantly less than 50 percent of all nonprofit organizations even attempt to file the required information report (Form 990).

In addition to filing Form 990, all organizations with unrelated business income must legally file Form 990T. This form has an organization enumerate its income sources, as well as grounds for exemption from taxation for portions of this income. It is also the form on which the organization states those expenses that may be legally deducted from the unrelated business income.

At the urging of the Subcommittee on Oversight, the IRS has made major revisions in the reporting requirements and the forms just mentioned. To properly complete these forms will require more detail on income and expenses, as well as more detailed information as to grounds for exemption and those expenditures that may be deducted. It must be understood that the filing of these reports is not a discretionary action: With very few exceptions, it is legally mandated. To minimize the burden for those exempt organizations with minimal unrelated business income (less than $5,000), the IRS has developed a short form. If an organization has not been fully complying with these requirements previously, it may well find that the collection of the requisite financial data, the analysis as to exemptions and expense deductibility, and the actual completion of the forms may prove to be a major task. All organizations are urged to allocate sufficient resources to do this properly. As necessary, the organization should use tax accountants, tax attorneys, and other external resources to assist in this process.

Although the major legal requirements for exempt organizations at the federal level center on the corporate income tax, nonprofit organizations need to be certain they are operating in compliance with other federal codes that give them special privileges. The area receiving the greatest attention at the present time is bulk mailing rates. Managers for nonprofit organizations are urged to determine that they are acting in full compliance with all federal statutes and administrative regulations.

As an ancillary issue to the corporate income tax, nonprofit organizations need to be aware of their mandated public disclosure responsibilities. The IRS has two major areas of concern about disclosure requirements. The first is for those organizations that solicit donations to accurately disclose the extent to which these donations are deductible to the donor. The second addresses those portions of an exempt organization's tax filings that must be available for public review. These items were covered in Chapter Two.

Each state has some form of exemption from corporate income taxes. The states most typically model their rules for nonprofit organizations on the Internal Revenue Code. Managers of nonprofit organizations must be aware of their individual state's requirements and fully comply. As a general rule, if an organization is fully complying with federal requirements as to reporting and payment of unrelated business income, it will have all of the information on hand to comply with state requirements.

As discussed in Chapter Seven, the real issue at the state level is not compliance with existing requirements. It is the creation of laws intended either to limit the scope of activity in which an exempt organization may engage or to expand the scope of activity for which an exempt organization is required to pay income taxes. A number of states have passed statutes addressing these and related issues (for example, Arizona, Colorado, Washington, and Illinois). It is incumbent upon the managers of nonprofit organizations to stay abreast of these changes in state laws and to take action to assure full compliance.

Property taxes are the focal point of concern at the local level for nonprofit organizations. The legal issue here is not that of reporting but instead the need to fully understand state law in this area. All states grant tax exemptions to some nonprofit organizations, but statutory law, and judicial interpretation of these statutes, differs in every state. All too often an organization loses all, or part, of its property tax exemption due to a lack of knowledge as to the permissible scope of utilization of property under its state law. Managers also need to be aware of the level of agitation in their area to challenge property tax exemptions and the likely behavior of the

judiciary in response to such a challenge. Additionally, managers
need to stay abreast of similar actions in other states that could affect
them.

As an example, if a state's judiciary seems to be moving in
the direction of the Utah Supreme Court, the managers of nonprofit
organizations must understand the underlying basis of the court's
decision. This will empower the manager to collect the requisite
information, and perhaps alter some of the organization's existing
behaviors, to be in the best position to defend against a similar legal
challenge.

Developing and Implementing an Action Plan

In 1980 very few nonprofit organizations had an operating plan to
address the taxation concerns discussed in this book. Similarly, national associations had not begun their efforts to develop policy
statements and educational programs on this topic for their membership. Yet today almost every national association representing
nonprofit organizations has in place some type of policy statement
on the issues of unfair competition and the taxation of their
member organizations. Similarly, regional and national conferences
now tend to allocate significant time to educational sessions on
these issues.

Yet even with these actions, too many individual nonprofit
organizations continue to debate the need for policy statements on
these topics and an organized plan to respond to them. In some
ways this is not terribly surprising, since the majority of nonprofit
organizations operate essentially with volunteer management and
leadership. These persons are struggling to simply provide the services their organization was created to perform. Yet too many large
nonprofit organizations with professional staff also continue to allocate far too little time and energy in this area.

The decision by nonprofit organizations not to develop an
action plan on the issues raised in this book, or to engage in only
a minimal effort, may well be one of the greatest gambles these
organizations will ever take. In some ways it is akin to taking an
organization's endowment income and cash on hand and risking it
on a roll of the dice. Certainly those organizations that have been

audited by the Internal Revenue Service and handed tax bills would have preferred to have avoided the tremendous cost of engaging in these audits, challenging administrative determinations through appropriate procedures and perhaps having to pay the additional taxes, interest, and penalties. Similarly, it is highly likely that those nonprofit organizations affected by unfair competition statutes passed during the previous decade would now prefer to have been far better prepared to combat these legislative initiatives. It is not difficult to surmise that the YMCAs in Oregon, hospitals in Utah, and other nonprofit organizations that have lost property tax exemptions in the past few years would have preferred to have prepared differently for the possibility of litigation.

The first action all nonprofit organizations should take is the commitment to develop a comprehensive policy statement as to their mission, the rationale for their tax exemptions, their process for determining what activities they will engage in (with a particular emphasis on those activities that may compete with for-profit organizations), and their commitment to comply with all appropriate legislation. Implicit in the latter statement is full compliance with all tax codes, which includes the payment of all taxes, all reporting requirements, and all mandated public disclosures.

Besides being the right thing for a nonprofit organization to do from a planning perspective, and as an ethical matter, it is an absolutely necessary political action. Although some involved with nonprofit organizations view political activity as anathema to their purpose, part of operating within our society is the recognition that politics is a part of an organization's life. In this sense, politics is the process that defines an organization's legal relationship with society. The latter is represented by the various tiers of government.

A policy statement can serve as a bridge between a nonprofit organization and the communities it interfaces with. In many instances it can help to eliminate the many pieces of misinformation most people have as to the financing of nonprofit organizations. Properly developed, these statements can substantively diminish opportunities to challenge an organization's scope of activity and can serve to develop allies within the community at large should challenges occur. Equally important, the process of developing this statement can show an organization areas where it appropriately needs to alter its behavior.

One of the most difficult problems confronting organizations faced with some type of unfair competition or tax challenge is the lack of historical documentation. Simply developing the policy statement and its action plan will compel an organization to collate information on its prior activities. Once in place, the process required by the policy statement should compile the information on current activities that will more fully prepare an organization to respond to any such challenge.

Fortunately for those organizations that have not as yet developed a policy statement and the plan to actualize it, many nonprofit organizations have done so in the past few years. In an organization's preparation in developing its policy statement, management should survey other nonprofit organizations to learn what they have done. In collecting this information, in addition to giving particular focus to organizations with similar missions, management should request information from other nonprofit organizations in their area, who will yield information on steps others have taken in a particular locale and the relative success of these actions. Appropriate national associations should also be contacted, many of whom have developed recommended policy statements and/or conducted other research in this area.

This information will assist a nonprofit organization to identify the full scope of items that need to be addressed and may also suggest steps that should be followed in developing and implementing the policy statement. In soliciting this information, be certain to find out who was involved in developing the policy statements, particularly those persons from outside the organization who were brought into the process. As an organization engages in this step, it should also review existing systems, policies, and activities. Only by systematically collecting this information can an organization conduct a comprehensive review.

To do these steps requires an organization to assign this responsibility to a single person. The task of collecting information, developing an initial statement, implementing the statement, and providing ongoing enforcement requires a clear line of responsibility. To assist the individual given this responsibility to gain cooperation from all areas of an organization, many nonprofits have found it useful to create a task force to develop the initial policy statement and to conduct periodic reviews. These task forces often include community representatives, who help to ensure that attention is given to the full range of external concerns. Properly selected, these community representatives can act as intermediaries between a nonprofit organization and those in the surrounding community concerned as to its scope of activity. By helping each side to understand the concerns of the other, as well as to clarify misinformation, these persons can play a key role in minimizing conflicts.

As part of its activity in developing this action plan, the organization needs to conduct a comprehensive review of existing statutes, judicial decisions, administrative opinion letters, and the like. At the federal level, the Internal Revenue Service provides a variety of advisory opinions. The three major vehicles for such opinions are private letter rulings, technical advice memorandums, and general counsel memorandums. These advisory opinions are based on specific fact situations, and as such the service is careful to point out that they have no legal value as precedent. Each general counsel memorandum includes this statement: "Caution: Each G.C.M. is directed only to the specific case that caused the request for advice from counsel. It must not be used or cited as precedent." In spite of this caution, these advisory opinions are often used to provide guidance in similar fact situations. Administrative organizations at other government levels may also provide advisory letters.

Once the policy statement is completed, the organization needs to publish it widely and to incorporate it into other official policies. The statement is meaningless unless those involved with both the organization and the greater community are aware of it. Similarly, unless the organization shows its commitment to the statement by its inclusion in all appropriate official policies, there is little use in engaging in this process.

In releasing the statement, the organization needs to make a good faith effort to solicit feedback. After gaining this feedback, the task force should review its initial effort and determine whether modifications are needed. Those who have commented on the statement should receive some type of response indicating how their concern was handled. The nonprofit organization should then make every attempt to solicit statements from civic and business leaders endorsing its action. Statements from these persons in support of the policy statement can prove very useful should a challenge occur in the future.

Key to this statement is a definition of the organization's mission. The mission statement must cover the full scope of an organization's purpose for existence, yet not be so general as to provide little clarity, an effort that can be assisted by developing subordinate mission statements for all major components of the organization. Particular attention should be given to those areas where conflict with other segments of the economy is most likely. The statement needs to have supporting rationale for everything included in it in order to give guidance for implementation and oversight.

Specific criteria should be stated for engaging in income-producing activities, with as many categories as needed and a rationale for each category. The latter may also specify on which activities an organization will pay taxes. Finally, it may discuss under what circumstances an organization will voluntarily choose to discontinue an activity.

The organization should detail the process it will use to determine whether an activity is taxable. Similarly, the statement should discuss the process used to determine whether competition exists with the for-profit community, whether the competition is "fair," and under what circumstances it would decide not to engage in a potentially competing activity. This section of the statement should identify a process by which persons outside the organization could raise concerns.

For a policy of this nature to be truly implemented requires significant effort. All organizations (for-profit, nonprofit, and government) are resistant to change, which means that responsibility for implementation and oversight must be given to a single person who is senior enough in the organization to gain the needed cooperation. Implementation of this policy must be consistent throughout the organization—there can be no "sacred cows" that are allowed to behave differently from the other components.

In developing an implementation plan, management may

need to consider a multiphase process, because some activities with long histories may require a longer time period to bring them into full compliance with the organization's policy statement. Where this occurs, a specific timeline and review process should be enumerated, which assures that these areas will be brought into compliance within a reasonable time period.

There needs to be full documentation of the entire implementation process, which should specify a periodic audit process to ensure compliance throughout the organization and should also set out a plan to review proposed new activities. Among the items management should consider developing for the implementation process are (1) a checklist of review steps, (2) a document authorizing each income-producing activity with a tie-in to the mission statement, (3) a comprehensive internal reporting system, (4) a management information system designed to facilitate compliance with all tax-reporting requirements, and (5) a review committee and other feedback mechanisms.

The Audit Process

Historically, the tax compliance arm of the Internal Revenue Service has not focused on nonprofit organizations. This is basically because nonprofits are not large income tax producers; as a resource allocation matter, few resources were therefore allocated to this audit function.

The attention focused on the nonprofit sector since the mid 1980s has altered this historical pattern, however. As already noted, the Internal Revenue Service is currently engaged in a compliance audit review of nonprofit organizations. Many states have had some type of unfair competition review committee recommend increased data collection by state government to determine if there is a need for state legislation. In parts of our country, local government interest in the income production of nonprofits as it applies to state property tax exemption has also increased. This increased interest level in all segments of government has dramatically increased the probability that a nonprofit organization will be audited.

Individuals conducting audits for the government are public servants—these persons should not be viewed as the enemy. They are charged with the responsibility to determine if potential taxpayers are acting in compliance with laws that apply to all of us. Treat them with the same dignity and courtesy you want to be treated with. Although this will not gain you a favorable review if you are not in conformance with the law, it will develop a setting for the most favorable "people" relationships.

If you are audited, immediately put one person in charge of all communications with the auditors. This person should not be the organization's chief administrative officer. You want to create some distance from top management as a tactical matter, which gives the organization time to reflect on issues raised by the auditors, as well as an opportunity to determine the depth of the auditors' concerns prior to rendering an official response. The individual should be at a level that yields full access to all needed records and knowledge of the organization's intention to act in compliance with the law. The auditors should be nicely, but firmly, told that all communications are to be initiated with your designee.

At the first contact with the auditors, the organization should immediately reach its attorney and tax adviser. These individuals need to be aware of all issues raised by the auditors and be prepared to give advice as needed.

The organization's staff should assume a passive posture. Designated staff should respond to all reasonable questions but should avoid offering information; in this type of audit, an inappropriately worded response can be very damaging. If a nonprofit organization has implemented the type of policy statement that has been recommended, and has appropriately filed all tax returns and information reports, it has taken the most important steps to minimize audit difficulties. This assumes the organization has made a good-faith effort to be certain it is acting in full compliance with the appropriate statutes, judicial decisions, and administrative rulings.

The action statement should include steps to ensure that all income has been appropriately segregated into taxable and nontaxable groupings, with full citation of Code sections, administrative regulations, and the like. It will also ensure that proper procedures have been implemented and documented for a reasonable cost allocation system. Additionally, needed research and writing can occur

before an audit to support the organization's position on those
issues in the gray areas.

An audit is a costly activity to engage in; the staff time needed
to assist the auditors alone is a drain on resources. To the extent that
an organization needs to compile additional data, engage in last-
minute technical advice on the issues raised by the auditors, pay
back taxes due to the audit findings (and potentially incur interest
expense and penalties), and respond to possible media inquiries and
litigate determinations by the auditors, the costs may become very
significant. Additionally, the political damage from a negative
audit could harm the organization in the eyes of its service community and could lead to negative legislation. Simply put, as time
consuming and costly as developing the type of action plan that has
been recommended is, it will be found to be an excellent investment
when it assists in minimizing all of the potential costs of an audit.

As part of developing the organization's action plan, the
needed consultation with legal counsel and tax counsel should occur. Those nonprofit organizations that have external auditors
should include in the auditors' scope of responsibility review for
compliance with all tax requirements. These advisers should assist
the organization in developing a training process for those responsible for information collection and compliance with all tax requirements, as well as a plan to be implemented when an audit does
occur. As with all areas of specialty, the inappropriate use of language can be very damaging; staff need to understand the buzz
words of the audit world and be certain these words are used
correctly.

The organization should also give a single individual the
responsibility to remain current with tax and unfair competition
issues—normally the same person responsible for implementing the
organization's action plan. Due recognition needs to be given to the
time needed to accomplish these tasks.

Public spokespersons, lobbyists, senior staff, and board
members should be informed that an audit is in process. On an as-
needed basis, these persons should be advised of the areas of concern
for the auditors and the areas of dispute. It is critical that these
individuals not find themselves in a setting where they are queried
about the audit but cannot respond due to a lack of information.

This can prove very damaging in the public and political arenas, even if the specific issue proves to be insignificant by the end of the audit process.

Immediately remind all staff who might be approached by the auditors as to your protocol, including which items a person should respond to, which items need to be referred to others, the need for specificity in the use of language, and which communications need to be reported to other staff. For issues of dispute with the auditors, assigned staff should forcefully present the organization's position. In doing this, appropriate legal points and authorities must be cited. If the organization determines there are issues it cannot win with the auditors, it should either concede them or agree to disagree, continuing to pursue those items that it is on solid ground with.

Remember, the site audit is the first stage of a possible multistep administrative review process. Your goal at this stage of the process is to develop as complete a record as possible, gain clarity as to the specific grounds for each area of disagreement with the auditors, and resolve favorably as many issues as possible.

Ask the auditor to provide everything in writing to the organization's lead person. This should begin with the initial purpose of the audit and continue for all items of requested information, findings, statutory, regulatory, and judicial justification for positions taken, up through the actual audit report. The auditor should also be asked to present the anticipated timeline for completing the audit, which will assist the organization to develop a complete case history and focus on the most important issues. Make it clear at the outset that you expect the auditors to review their preliminary reports with your staff. This should include an opportunity for the organization's staff to provide information and support arguments that might alter the report.

The organization should document everything that is part of the audit. This includes all meetings with the auditors, all requests for information, all responses by the organization, the time period it took the organization to respond to requests, and the staff time required to develop these responses. To accomplish the latter, the person who has been put in charge of the audit process should attend all sessions with the auditors. This person has two roles: (1)

to act as the historian for the organization and (2) to correct errors in information presented by other members of the organization's staff. Because many people are intimidated by an auditor, this person's presence may help to reduce the intimidation factor.

Many auditors are not as familiar with standard procedures for nonprofit organizations as they are with those of for-profit organizations. Similarly, their knowledge of pertinent codes may not be as detailed. The nonprofit organization should emphasize these differences to the auditors and insist that the auditors stay within the scope of their mandate. Questions about resource allocation and policy matters that are not related to the audit are not proper topics of review.

The organization must remember that these audits are not limited to the information provided by them in their tax filings. In an audit by the Internal Revenue Service, questions may appropriately be raised about items not mentioned in the organization's Form 990 or Form 990T. It is these omissions that may cause a nonprofit organization the greatest distress.

All administrative agencies have internal administrative review procedures. A nonprofit organization should make full use of these procedures, but to do so the organization must first gain competent advice on this process. Critically important is whether issues resolved favorably to the organization at one level of the process can be altered at a higher level. As a tactical decision, an organization must determine the potential to improve decisions on issues that are partially resolved in favor of the organization in the site audit. If the probability of positive gains is small in the administrative process, the organization may not wish to pursue this course of action.

From a philosophical vantage point, issues that raise important policy questions should generally be appealed, yet an organization must consider the cost to it of engaging in an appeal, as well as the possibility that it may lose. As with other adjudicated matters, the lower in the decision-making hierarchy an issue is resolved, the greater are the limits of its value as a precedent in future disputes. In addition to using administrative appeal procedures, a nonprofit organization can choose to exercise its rights to a judicial remedy. Again, the organization must consider its out-of-pocket expenses, potential negative public relations, and the possibility of losing.

The decision to engage in an extensive appeal process should include the counsel of persons skilled in the legal and accounting issues raised by the particular fact situation.

The federal government provides an extensive administrative and judicial appeals process after a tax audit, but these procedures change periodically, so the organization should gain advice as to the procedures then in place. The positives and negatives of how to proceed need to be fully weighed by the organization's leadership.

State and local audits for income tax, sales tax, property tax, and other taxes will also provide administrative and judicial remedies. Due to the diversity of approaches, there will be no effort to review them individually. As with an appeal of an Internal Revenue Service decision, the decision as to whether to appeal audit decisions at these government levels is an ethical, financial, and tactical one.

A Recommended Proactive Program: The Social Accountability Budget

Across the nation individual nonprofit organizations and their national associations are taking steps to address concerns about the continued justification for tax exemptions. For some, one key action is developing management information systems that facilitate the collection of needed data. As Bruce Hopkins, an authority on the legal issues affecting tax-exempt organizations, has stated: "The worst thing that a nonprofit organization's management can do at this time is to ignore these developments and trends. A 'head in the sands' attitude will not work." This statement was part of an article in *The Nonprofit Counsel* in which Hopkins argues for improved accounting systems to facilitate reporting, particularly in multiorganization structures ("UBIT Preview," 1989, p. 5).

As one of the tools to gain public support for funding for public higher education, campuses began estimating the total economic advantage they bring to a community. This analysis looked not only at the gross budget of a campus but how funds were expended. These expenditures in turn supported various local businesses, which enabled them to purchase goods locally and employ local residents. As a general rule, the typical college or university found that for every dollar they brought directly into their community, the total economic benefit was equal to approximately three times this amount.

Recognizing the usefulness of this argument with civic, business, and political leaders, the American Council on Education saw the need to develop a standard means for a campus to measure its total economic value. Such a tool was developed in the past decade and is now available from this association, an instrument that can be particularly useful because it was not developed for a single organization nor to "sell" a particular view. Instead it is a well-researched economic model that can withstand the rigors of challenges of bias (American Council on Education, n.d.).

The Catholic Health Association of the United States has taken a somewhat different approach in developing an instrument utilizing financial data. During the 1980s it engaged in a number of studies examining health care services to the poor, the role of the members of the Catholic Health Association in the delivery of health care to the poor and the community as a whole, and the rationale for granting tax exemptions to voluntary health care organizations. From these reviews, this organization saw the need to develop an instrument that would assist its members both to ensure that their expenditures of funds matched their service mission statements and to gather this information. The instrument that they have developed is entitled the *Social Accountability Budget: A Process for Planning and Reporting Community Service in a Time of Fiscal Constraints.*

In his foreword to this publication, Bruce C. Vladeck, president of the United Hospital Fund of New York, shares some sobering thoughts about nonprofit organizations and the value of using the Social Accountability Budget. One of the supporting doctrines of nonprofit organizations is their accountability to the community. The lack of a profit motive and volunteer governing boards of community members are thought to create greater community accountability than the profit motive and the need to meet the financial goals of business owners. Vladeck notes that while in theory this is true, "Formal mechanisms for assuring institutional compliance with these expectations are limited and incomplete" (Catholic Health Association, 1989b, p. viii).

The phrase "these expectations" refers to what the service

community believes a nonprofit organization should be doing. As this leader in the voluntary hospital movement is saying, most nonprofit organizations rely on good intentions to ensure symmetry between community expectations and the actual behavior of the organization. Today, with the many demands placed on nonprofit organizations and the questions being raised as to their privileged legal status, there is a need for more than "good intentions" to ensure community accountability.

Vladeck then proceeds to discuss the value of the Social Accountability Budget (Catholic Health Association, 1989b). In his view it is an important communication tool. In terms of the community at large, the general public, it shows a commitment to self-evaluation and its finished product allows the organization to quantify its services to the community. Yet its greatest communication value may be in regard to the internal community of an organization. Vladeck notes that the most successful organizations share the trait of a "common culture": That is, there is a "unity" of purpose as to what the organization is doing, why it exists, and how it should go about its tasks. As an organization's staff (paid and volunteer) and governing board work through the many steps required to develop its Social Accountability Budget, they will collectively define this common culture. This in turn will facilitate the commitment of the entire organization to the implementation of the plan derived from the Social Accountability Budget on a day-to-day basis.

The Social Accountability Budget also allows a nonprofit organization to "reflect and reaffirm" the tradition of volunteerism inherent in these organizations. For persons like those who develop the Social Accountability Budget, one of the key values to society of nonprofit organizations is their capacity to allow people to serve the community. It is through this type of commitment that the values of our society are molded, and it is the nature of our nation's voluntary associations that in many ways differentiates us from other countries.

"The Budget of any institution is arguably its primary religious document. It reveals the institution's de facto value commitments and practical sense of mission as they are implicitly embodied by its allocation process" (Catholic Health Association, 1989b,

p. xi). So argues James E. Hug, S.J., in the preface to this publication. If one substitutes a phrase like "purpose statement" (although this does not have the same depth of impact) for "religious document," this statement is applicable to all nonprofit associations. It brings home to all of us the importance of the budget process and its finished product.

Hug also notes that the Social Accountability Budget assists an organization in identifying and quantifying its community services, which allows one to examine the congruency between an organization's stated mission and its actual behavior. But he also presents a note of caution: "This can be a chilling exercise where our practice does not match our rhetoric" (Catholic Health Association, 1989b, p. x). In this regard, Hug argues that the pressure of those questioning exempt organizations can be turned into a positive, if those involved in these organizations use it to pursue more "honest and in-depth" evaluation. As he states, "This can be a service to an organization even when it makes the people involved quite uncomfortable" (Catholic Health Association, 1989b, p. x).

To Hug, one of the main values of the Social Accountability Budget is that it highlights the full range of community services. It enables an organization to better identify not only its charitable care for the indigent but also the many medical services and educational programs of value to the entire community. This totality of program review allows an organization to raise questions as to governments' responsibilities to "the people." The truly successful organization not only does its part in direct service delivery but must also challenge the social, political, and economic structures now in place that are not addressing so many issues for far too many people. One specific example of such a deficiency is the fact that, since 1979, there has been a 30 percent increase, approximately one million persons, in those who are without medical insurance (Catholic Health Association, 1989b, p. xiv).

The Catholic Health Association describes the Social Accountability Budget as an instrument that was "developed to help manage the tension" between service mission and fiscal constraints (Catholic Health Association, 1989b, p. xxi). In a survey, the Catholic Health Association found that while its members did a great deal of charitable service, there was no systematic way to identify these services. This meant that when queried for such information, the individual hospital was unable to fully present the value of the totality of its service to its community. The Catholic Health Association survey only mirrors what exists throughout the nonprofit community. This lack of information has made it very difficult to fully present the case for nonprofit associations to legislative bodies, in litigation and to the public. For the Catholic Health Association, the resolve has been to create a vehicle to assist its members to engage in self-evaluation and the documentation of their services.

The Social Accountability Budget is envisioned as a means to "help Catholic healthcare providers broaden the debate" (Catholic Health Association, 1989b, p. xxii) at all levels of government. While conceding the importance of addressing services to the poor, the Catholic Health Association strongly argues that its members' service to the entire community are at least equally important in terms of justification for tax exemptions.

The Catholic Health Association defines three classes of service populations: (1) the indigent—those whose income is at 150 percent of the federal poverty level ($18,000 for a family of four); (2) other population groups with special needs—the elderly, substance abusers, AIDS victims; and (3) the entire service population. It is the amalgamation of service to each of these population groups, based upon quality evaluation of the needs of an organization's service community, which should justify tax exemptions.

The body of this book is approximately 100 pages of detailed information about how an organization develops its Social Accountability Budget. It is quite process oriented, providing a step-by-step means to create the budget. Each section contains a set of proposed guidelines, self-appraisal questions, and work sheets and model formats. Each set of guidelines is discussed in sufficient detail to allow one to understand how to use them. The self-appraisal suggestions act as icebreakers for those involved in the process and facilitate a quality review. The work sheets and model formats give an organization examples of how to collate, quantify, and present data on community services.

Wherever possible, the Social Accountability Budget's authors provide definitions of all terms. As an organization develops its own Social Accountability Budget, it must decide whether to use these definitions or to present its own. In either case, there needs to be absolute clarity as to what all terms mean. As an example, the Catholic Health Association provides a definition of where non-billed service equals charity care, whereas prior to this, it gave definitions for both nonbilled services and charity care. It is this attention to detail that helps to make the Social Accountability Budget such a useful vehicle.

The Social Accountability Budget also provides explicit directions where needed. As an example, users of this document are directed: "Ensure that your charity policy includes:

- An active policy of providing care to all acutely ill persons, regardless of insurance status or other ability to pay
- Clear and uniform procedures for determining charity eligibility prospectively and for converting a bill to charity status in the event that a billed patient cannot pay
- Timely notification of potential eligibility for charity care
- Ongoing efforts to ensure that practice follows policy" [Catholic Health Association, 1989b, p. 11]

Each of these points is followed by a discussion as to its meaning and implementation.

In scope, the Social Accountability Budget is more than simply an inventory of services and a quantification of their use. It also requires an organization to engage in a complete review of its policies and procedures for delivering its program offerings. Status quo programs are not the goal of the Catholic Health Association. Thus the Social Accountability Budget next requires the organization to take a leadership role in needs assessment (see Chapter Three). Using the needs assessment information, the organization now engages in the plan and budget for services (see Chapter Four). It is in this part of the process that an organization sets its priorities and community service goals.

The Social Accountability Budget requires explicit and quantified goals, not loose general statements of intentions. Among the guidelines in Chapter Four are the requirement to "establish explicit budget amounts for each of the community benefits" and "build explicit amounts into the annual budget, including revenue and expenses" (Catholic Health Association, 1989b, p. 36). It is in this degree of detail that the Social Accountability Budget compels an organization to transform its mission statement into actual programs. It is also these types of specific commitments that allow a nonprofit organization to present its strongest case for tax exemption.

This publication includes two additional areas. Recognizing that a budget document is still only a plan, the Social Accountability Budget also has an organization measure and monitor services (see Chapter Five). This chapter gives one a set of steps that assist in tracking actual behavior and adjusting this behavior. The budget recognizes that one organization and its service community may be different from another, and groups are urged to adjust specific factors to fit their mission and their setting. As a practical matter, it presents suggestions on how to modify an organization's management information system to capture financial data for uncompensated and other community services.

From an internal standpoint, if an organization engages in each of the steps recommended in the Social Accountability Budget discussed up to now, the work would essentially be completed. But the Catholic Health Association recognizes that part of being a community service organization is reporting to the community. It is also a political realist and notes the critical need to report community benefits (see Chapter Six) in an organized way to elected officials, civic and business organizations, and the general community.

Here, too, the Catholic Health Association shows that it has learned from the negative experiences of other nonprofit organizations. It makes good use of the experience in Utah in determining the types of information an organization needs to have available and the best means to showcase this information. This publication discusses the need to be careful in simply releasing the data generated by the Social Accountability Budget. In presenting information to any individual or group, the organization must be certain not only that the information is absolutely accurate but that it also presents the case the organization is striving to build.

Two other points made in this chapter need to be mentioned. An organization should not present information only on its services to the poor: The Catholic Health Association strongly believes that it is the totality of a nonprofit organization's community services that should gain government endorsement through tax exemptions and other means. Furthermore, this set of services will include some items that do not lend themselves to quantification (for example, the effect on a community's value structure of the presence of strong volunteer associations). These items, too, need to be included in reports on community benefits.

Finally, the Social Accountability Budget itself is not the main means to communicate but is essentially a process instrument, which as one of its outcomes allows an organization to capture much of the information it will want to include in these reports. Each organization must identify the best means to communicate this information in its own setting.

At the outset, the authors of the Social Accountability Budget warn that it is not intended as simply "an academic exercise." The detailed process it calls for requires the absolute commitment of the governing board and top management. This is a commitment not only of staff time and other resources to engage in this process but also of openness about what is learned from the process and willingness to alter practices that are not consistent with the organization's mission.

Other Proactive Examples

As service organizations, nonprofits have always engaged in some level of community relations. As a policy matter, some sectors of the nonprofit community have made a concerted effort to involve themselves in their surrounding community. One particular sector, public higher education, markedly increased these efforts as an outcome of campus activities in the 1960s and early 1970s. Across the nation, campus after campus upgraded its administrative unit responsible for community and legislative relations. Those persons working in these units were expected to carry the positive service message of a college or university to its various publics.

In its policy statement on unfair competition and the unrelated business income tax, the Association of College Unions-International included as its first recommendation: "Wherever feasible, the union or other appropriate campus entity should join and become active with the Chamber of Commerce or Convention and Visitors Bureau. Rationale: This will enable the institution to establish networks with important business leaders while actively monitoring concerns and activities." Its second recommendation stated: "The union or other appropriate entity should engage the business community in a dialogue that is educational and that produces consensus on how the campus determines whether to engage in new retail-type operations or services. Rationale: Criticism is less likely when open dialogue and participation in decision making have occurred" (Gerard, 1988, p. 4). This voluntary association of administrators involved in the management of student centers throughout the United States and other nations saw the need for those in the business and service components of their campuses to involve themselves directly in the day-to-day activities of the surrounding business community.

As the author of the position paper on which this association based these recommendations, I drew from my personal experiences. It had been my experience that where those persons responsible for the operation of units that may be perceived as competing with local, for-profit businesses had developed working relationships with the latter prior to specific disputes, the probability of a mutually positive resolve was much greater. The more people get to know each other as people, and not simply as possible competitors, the greater the capacity to discuss differences of opinion.

In one setting, the organization responsible for the operation of the campus bookstore, food service, and other quasi-commercial operations had engaged in a series of discussions with local business associations about the appropriate scope of its services. From these discussions came an unwritten agreement as to how that campus would decide to add any new unit whose income was to be based on fees for services. This agreement encompassed the types of factors the campus would take into consideration and the interaction that would occur with representatives of the business community, prior to reaching a final decision. This particular organization buttressed its position by purchasing goods whenever possible from local businesses and by including a representative of the business community on its advisory committee that made recommendations on these types of services.

Institutions of higher education have recently become more aggressive in developing internal policies on potentially competing services. In some settings, they have also entered into formal agreements with the local government on a broad range of relationship issues. In Chapter Seven the efforts of campuses and higher education systems to develop policy statements on unfair competition was discussed. One of the more interesting of these statements is one approved for the University of California system in 1981 (University of California, 1981), an updating of an initial policy statement released in 1977. This is of particular interest because it was put in place a number of years before this issue had become one of national import and before any of the national education associations had addressed the issue. Also, due to the size and complexity of this nine-campus system, it needed to address any issue that might arise within the higher education sector.

In a cover letter accompanying the policy statement, Donald L. Alter, director of corporate accounting for the University of California, stated: "Under this policy, auxiliary enterprise operations are to be conducted in a manner to serve primarily students, faculty and staff, and only incidentally serve members of the general public. Before a new auxiliary enterprise can be established by a campus, the cost and benefits of providing the intended goods and services by the local community, rather than the University, must be fully assessed" (D. L. Alter, letter to the author, Nov. 1989). In this one sentence, this nonprofit organization has voluntarily placed a set of constraints on itself in terms of providing services that might be offered by the for-profit community. It has also clearly defined its primary service community in terms of these types of offerings.

The formal policy statement embodies many of the elements proposed earlier in this chapter to be part of an organization's action plan, including a section that discusses the rationale for establishing and operating auxiliary enterprises. This last term had been defined previously in the document. Included in this definition is a set of characteristics of an auxiliary enterprise. From the standpoint of the tax-paying public, perhaps the most significant characteristic is that the unit be entirely self-supporting through mandatory student fees and/or fees for services. This means that no tax dollars are used to support these programs, including the construction, maintenance, and operation of facilities required for the unit.

This policy statement required a review of all existing programs and also specified that all programs must be reviewed on a five-year basis. This review requires a written justification and sign-off by a senior administrator designated by each campus's chancellor.

Recognizing the sensitivity to the creation of new auxiliary services to the business community, yet also quite aware of pressures on campus administrators to develop new, self-supporting units, the policy statement also enumerated a special process for the establishment of any new auxiliary enterprises. New auxiliary enterprises must gain the written authorization of the chancellor. In making this decision, the chancellor must look at the need for a campus-operated unit. This means looking at the availability of the service to the surrounding community, as well as the costs and benefits of direct university management rather than by the local business community. To assist the chancellor in this review, and to assure the capacity for self-sufficiency, complete financial projections for the first three years of operations must accompany the proposal. This type of policy statement by a nonprofit organization, if properly implemented, builds part of the foundation needed to respond to critiques. Although it does not foreclose all areas of potential business community concerns, at a minimum it narrows the scope of the debate.

Although a good number of institutions of higher education have developed policy statements for potentially competing enterprises, another means of building a basis for improved campus/community relations is through formal operating agreements that in some settings are part of a package that includes a commitment for fees in lieu of taxes. In other settings they address issues of joint planning and cooperation. These latter agreements also may include specific financial commitment for future projects and/or the conditions under which a college or university will assist in paying for a project. An example is an agreement reached in 1989 between the city of Davis and the University of California, Davis. In response to my letter of inquiry on this agreement, Gerald B. Hallee, executive assistant to the executive vice chancellor, advised me that the agreement was the result of California communities' concerns with growth and "their inability to plan, finance and manage that growth." Both parties also felt that improved communications would help each of them to improve their planning efforts. The action that pushed the parties to actually sitting down together and formalizing an agreement was the California Environmental Quality Act. This state statute requires "public agencies to assist in mitigating the impacts of their projects on neighboring communities" (G. B. Hallee, letter to the author, Nov. 1989).

The formally executed "Memorandum of Understanding UCD LRD [Long Range Plan]" (University of California, Davis, 1989) has as its main focus the merger of the campus and city master plans. Among the topics addressed in this agreement are student population size, use of campus land, housing for students, faculty and staff, air quality control, parking and enforcement, and street and road improvements. The agreement also enumerates a series of financial issues. Included among this grouping is a set of street and public facility projects to which the university makes specific financial commitments and joint funding of a number of studies (one example, a multimode transportation study). There is also a section discussing commercial developments on the periphery of the campus. In one of the possible projects is the recognition that it will generate appreciable new tax revenue to the city. If this project proceeds, the city has agreed to offset this new revenue against campus financial commitments.

As one looks at it as a whole, this agreement discusses most of the potential issues for dispute that arise between a college and its host city. Because Davis presents a college town setting, however, the items discussed are to some extent different from issues for a similar agreement between an urban campus and its host city.

Perhaps the next-to-last section of the agreement is really the most important. This section addresses the need for "ongoing communications" and establishes a means to accomplish this. The latter includes commitments for "front-end dialogue" on planning issues and at a minimum an annual " 'review and prospectus' program to discuss all items of mutual impact" (University of California, Davis, 1989).

Applicability to Individual Organizations

Nonprofit organizations are extremely diverse in their size, sophistication, and purpose. The actions suggested in this part of the book need to be modified by each organization to fit its characteristics. A small organization should not feel overwhelmed by the actions of other nonprofits. Based on the organization's level of resources and setting, it needs to take those steps that are appropriate. Yet as the many for-profit, small businesses that annually go out of business have learned, an organization without a documented plan is not likely to succeed in its mission. Thus all nonprofit organizations should develop a process intended to accomplish the goals of the Social Accountability Budget.

Because all organizations must engage in some data collection for tax purposes, the need to implement appropriate accounting systems is generic to nonprofit organizations. Yet an individual nonprofit organization need not go about this task alone; a broad range of local, state, and national associations can assist it as it goes about these tasks.

The examples used in this section occurred in the health care and higher education arenas, but with the substitution of a few nouns these concepts apply equally to all nonprofit organizations. Those that choose not to engage in these types of proactive steps do so at their own risk, and at the possible expense of the entire nonprofit sector.

🙏

Chapter 11

Influencing Public Policy
Toward Nonprofits

Government policy toward nonprofit organizations is seeing its most significant review since our nation's founding. What the current discussion should be focused on is not allegations of unfair competition but the role we want nonprofit organizations to have in the future, because it is through government policy expressed in tax codes, postal rates, corporation codes, and the like that we determine this role. To move the discussion in this direction will require courage by elected officials, as well as by officials representing small businesses and nonprofit organizations. It will require a movement away from advocacy politics, to a searching for information and approaches that will allow for the best resolve for society as a whole. If such an approach is achieved, it will be in the best interest of both sectors, for as a nation we will continue to need an evolving and expanding nonprofit community as well as a prosperous small business community.

Part of the means to allow the small business community to move away from its cry for immediate and encompassing legislative action to rectify perceived unfair competitive advantages is for the nonprofit community to become far more self-critiquing. It is my

213

belief that nonprofits have used their diversity as a means to avoid the development of meaningful standards. Here I am not talking about the type of accreditation standards used in education and many service areas but instead about standards that underlie the service mission of an organization and should structure the reason for the organization's business mission.

In this book, actions taken by the Catholic Health Association, the governing board of the YMCA of the United States, higher education associations, and individual colleges and universities have been discussed as key examples of positive behaviors within the nonprofit sector to respond to valid external criticism. As positive as these actions have been, however, they are not sufficient.

The reaffirmation of its charitable mission by the YMCA of the United States is an important policy statement. In so doing the individual YMCAs across the country were advised of the importance of having members engage in volunteer activities as well as participate in YMCA-sponsored activities. They were also reminded of the particular need to provide services to persons of low income. The importance of gaining donations as a symbol of community support was underlined, as was a concern that some YMCAs might be too reliant on fees for services. These and other factors underscored in this action, if implemented by every YMCA, would negate most of the arguments presented by small business advocates. But as structured, there seem to be no negative consequences should an individual YMCA choose to ignore significant portions of this action by the parent body. The only negative consequences seem to continue to be potential legislative or judicial action. As such, the small business sector understands that if it wants to see a somewhat speedy resolution to its concerns, it will need to continue to engage in high-profile political advocacy.

The organizational structure of the YMCA movement allows each individual community organization substantial independence. For the most part this is a virtue, in that it allows for responsiveness to local needs and encourages local initiatives. Yet when it comes to the implementation of minimum standards to achieve the privilege of the name YMCA, there may be too much independence. It is my view that the YMCA movement should take its mission statement and use it to develop a set of standards that all member organizations must meet. These standards would go beyond the minimum requirements of qualifying as a tax-exempt organization and instead would speak to the factors already enumerated by the YMCA of the United States as their reason for being. In the development of these standards, due consideration should be given to those factors that have caused others to criticize particular YMCAs and some courts to rule against a number of individual YMCAs. There needs to be sufficient flexibility in these standards to take into consideration requirements presented in different states.

If the YMCA of the United States were to state its intent to do as recommended herein, it would take significant action toward self-regulation. If along with this statement came a detailed process to develop and implement a set of standards, a timeline for the process, and a means for input from affected small businesses, a very impressive proactive plan would be put in place.

Similarly, the Social Accountability Budget developed by the Catholic Health Association is an excellent vehicle for, among other things, ensuring an organization's focus on its charitable mission. It is my impression that the Catholic Health Association intends to work with its member groups to assist them in utilizing this instrument.

As with the action taken by the YMCA of the United States, the Social Accountability Budget must be placed in the context of a set of standards that include levels of negative action if an organization does not utilize the instrument and meet these standards. These negative actions could be as minimal as a set of recommended correcting steps to be reviewed in a given time period, or as severe as an organization's decertification, which would mean not being allowed to claim any affiliation with the parent organization or association. Although these actions would not in and of themselves alter an organization's tax status, they would have an impact on the "halo effect," to the extent that it exists, and would distance the national or regional association from the actions of the individual organization. The analysis developed in the Social Accountability Budget would be useful to any nonprofit organization, but it is a particularly helpful approach for voluntary hospitals.

Similar standards need to be developed for other segments of the nonprofit community. For example, in developing standards for museums, the question of whether a museum should endorse unrelated products, develop sales locations in malls and other retail settings, and engage in other questioned income-producing activities needs to be addressed. The listing of any specific issue does not presume a specific answer; it is simply intended to note the types of issues that must be responded to by segments of the nonprofit community.

Higher education has a very special place in our nation. Its associations and its leadership must take steps not only to protect this special status but also to be certain it is not used inappropriately. Actions to date to develop fair competition policies are important initial steps, but unless there is a set of minimum standards and a process of implementation, the use of these policies will be very uneven. Over time, this may well compel more state legislatures to take action and to develop standards themselves.

Nonprofit organizations need to ask themselves if they are inappropriately taking advantage of gaps in technical rules. As the review of the history of the Internal Revenue Code as it applies to tax-exempt organizations showed, this type of behavior tends to come back to haunt these organizations. Congress has repeatedly shown the capacity to develop very intricate rules to foreclose particular behaviors.

As an ethical matter, nonprofit organizations must attempt to act in full compliance with the law. This means that there should be no debate about whether all covered organizations should file appropriate tax reports and meet public disclosure requirements. To the extent that this does not occur, all nonprofit organizations suffer in the eyes of the government and the people. When nonprofit groups are found not to be acting in compliance with the law, they should not complain about the law's enforcement. The audit of alumni associations abusing their discount mail privileges, and the subsequent public statements of some alumni officials complaining about the application of the law to them, is certainly part of the justification of those calling for a change in this privilege.

The for-profit sector needs to broaden its role and perspective on these issues. As the statements of the advocates for changing the current legal treatment of the nonprofit sector periodically recognize, the nonprofit sector fulfills many important missions in our society. To substantially damage their capacity to perform these missions would be a disservice to everyone—including the owners of competing small businesses. This means the for-profit sector needs to develop a better understanding of the diversity and complexity of nonprofit organizations and to look at the effect the implementation of its proposals may have on service delivery. If service delivery is diminished, is this sector prepared for the impact this may have on the span of government activity? If the income supporting the charitable, service, and community activities of nonprofits is diminished due to the implementation of its proposals, is the for-profit community prepared for the potential tax increases that may be required?

Among the attributes of the nonprofit sector is its promotion of volunteerism and pluralistic structures in our society. These factors play important roles in limiting the scope of government activity and in proving models for good citizenship. How might they be affected by the implementation of the proposals put forth by the Business Coalition for Fair Competition and the Small Business Administration?

The for-profit community must be certain that those now speaking on its behalf on this issue truly represent this entire segment of the economy. Clearly the Business Coalition for Fair Competition and its active supporters speak for a variety of small businesses that are in some level of competition with specific elements of the nonprofit sector. But do they speak for the many small businesses that provide goods and services to the nonprofit sector or the small businesses whose existence depends on purchases made by persons employed in the nonprofit sector? It is my belief that these small businesses have not been heard from to date.

In our nation's current love affair with free-market economic theories, we must be careful not to damage elements that have historically been part of our very fiber. During the past few years, our nation's major newspapers have editorialized on these issues. In an editorial titled "Charity and Profit" (July 9, 1988), the *Washington Post* came to this conclusion: "Non-profits have surely abused their privileges in some cases, but even the most narrow regulations cannot cover all situations. In some instances the best that can be hoped for is some earnest self-policing by non-profits and continued vigilance by those businesses that can make a case they are being unfairly undercut."

As Congress considers potential changes in federal statutes and state legislatures attempt to respond to partisan recommendations, we must all look to the effect these actions may have in the immediate future, as well as in the coming century. Most futurists see an expanded role for nonprofit organizations and assume the granting of tax advantages and other government benefits.

In analyzing Toffler's *The Third Wave,* Hopkins (1988) finds an expanded role for the nonprofit organizations. It is Toffler's view that society will only become more diverse. As an example, he discusses the expansion of religious organizations and forms. In addition to existing religions, Toffler sees the development of new religions and the growth of "new-old" religions, which refers to the continued growth of fundamentalist and neoorthodox religious groups. It is Toffler's view "that 'the new society is likely to be built around a network rather than a hierarchy of new institutions'" (Hopkins, 1988, p. 869). Hopkins notes that the essence of Toffler's projections is also found in the works of other futurists like John Naisbitt. Although this does not resolve what changes may be needed in the laws affecting nonprofit organizations, it does underscore the need for a long-term perspective.

Society also needs to be sure that, in an attempt to right a perceived wrong done to a particular set of small businesses, it does not do greater total harm. For those directly involved in these issues, it is a very emotional setting. People's livelihoods and philosophical beliefs are being challenged. Experience has shown that the way an issue is posed can play on these factors and gain a response that, on later reflection, is regretted.

A major area of volunteerism for me is working with youth athletics, which brings me into contact with a large number of other volunteers who represent a cross-section of society. Many of my co-volunteers are either owners or employees of small businesses. Sometimes, in explaining my field to them, I pose a series of questions on unfair competition, on the potential taxation of the property owned by these volunteer groups and income they generate through concessions, raffles, door-to-door candy sales, and the like.

As we discuss these questions, both their interest in my work and their uncertainty as to their answers increase.

As a general rule their responses initially tend to be quite supportive of the positions taken by advocates for small businesses. This is particularly true if the theoretically competing nonprofit is a large organization and has significant visible assets. As we discuss how the current laws actually operate, and how changes might affect the income of nonprofit organizations they are involved with, these responses tend to move in the direction advocated by the non-profit community. This change in position and uncertainty about what the best overall course of action seen in these responses is indicates the complexity of the issues and outcomes involved in the taxation of nonprofit organizations and the unfair competition debate.

As an immediate survival mechanism, nonprofit organizations need to upgrade their image and lobbying strength in the Congress and state legislatures. The leadership of nonprofit organizations should not believe that their critics are going to fade away. With the time brought by counterpolitical advocacy, the nonprofit community must then engage in the type of self-regulation and research that has previously been discussed. As the parties in the Carrier Dome political debacle in Syracuse learned, actions based on brinkmanship and political muscle are found over time to be terribly costly to everyone. There is no question that the antagonists on these issues can continue to do battle in the legislatures, the courts, and the media. Each party will win some victories and lose others, but if this course of action is followed, the nation will continue to lack a coherent approach toward the nonprofit sector. Additionally, both sectors will suffer economically. If, on the other hand, the parties can find the means to engage in meaningful dialogue and can construct a methodology to gather and analyze information, they can empower elected officials with the basis to make quality decisions.

Unrelated Business Income Tax Cases

Note: The cases that follow are a sampling of important federal court decisions on issues relating to the unrelated business income tax code sections.

American Bar Endowment v. United States, 761 F.2d 1573 (Fed. Cir. 1985) rev'd 477 U.S. 105, 106 S.Ct. 2426 (1986). The threat of unfair competition is a key factor in UBI. The Supreme Court found the income received by the exempt organization to be active. The organization provided its mailing list and additional services to a nonexempt organization to sell insurance. The Court also stated that this sales effort generated such large profits to the exempt organization that it was conducted in a commercial fashion.

American College of Physicians v. United States, 530 F.2d 930 (Ct. Cl. 1967). The net income from advertising was found not to be UBI. This led to the passage of I.R.C. Section 513(c) in the Tax Reform Act of 1969. Advertising income is UBI unless in and of itself it is exempt.

221

American College of Physicians v. United States, 106 S.Ct. 1591
(1986). The Supreme Court endorsed the "fragmentation test."
The Court also ruled that net advertising income, per se, is not
UBI. The test that the Court created will, in most circumstances,
make advertising income UBI. The Supreme Court stated that in
determining if advertising is related the standard is whether the
conduct of the organization in selling and publishing the advertising demonstrates a related function, not whether the advertising standing alone is educational. An item that courts should
look at is whether the advertising "provide(s) its readers a comprehensive or systematic presentation of any aspect of the good
or services. . . ." The Court also stated that a tax-exempt organization can "control its publication of advertising in such a way
as to reflect an intention to contribute importantly to its . . .
(exempt) function . . . [by] coordinating the content of the advertisements with the editorial content of the issue, or by publishing
only advertisements reflecting news developments."
American Institute for Economic Research v. United States, 302
    F.2d 934 (Ct. Cl. 1981). Because the plaintiff's primary purpose
    was commercial, tax-exempt status was denied.
American Society of Travel Agents v. Blumenthall, 46 U.S.L.W.
    2195 (U.S. Court of Appeals for the District of Columbia, 1977).
    Plaintiff wanted the travel service income from tax-exempt or-
    ganizations to be found to be UBI. The case was dismissed for
    lack of standing.
American Society of Travel Agents v. Simon, 36 A.F.T.R.2d 75-5142
    (D.D.C., May 23, 1975) aff'd 566 F.2d 145 (D.C. Cir. 1977). The
    court found that it is the purpose, not the size, of the program
    that determines substantial relationship. The plaintiff wanted
    income from the international student travel program sponsored
    by the University of Wisconsin to be found to be UBI.
Birmingham Business College, Inc. v. Commissioner, 276 F.2d 476
    (5th Cir. 1960). If income goes to "insiders" for private use, tax-
    exempt status will be denied.
Bob Jones University v. United States, 461 U.S. 574 (1983). This case
    defined a charitable organization. An entity operating in contra-
    venance of public policy, per se, cannot be charitable.

Carle Foundation v. United States, 611 F.2d 192 (8th Cir. 1979). A hospital's sale of pharmaceuticals to nonpatients is UBI.

Carolina Farm and Power Equipment Dealers Association, Inc. v. United States, 699 F.2d 167 (4th Cir. 1983). This defined trade or business and held that the fee that the plaintiff received for endorsing the sale of insurance was UBI.

Christian Stewardship Assistance v. Commissioner, 70 T.C. 1037 (1978). The court denied tax-exempt status where a substantial purpose was to give advice on tax avoidance.

Clarence La Belle Post No. 217 v. U.S., 46 U.S.C.L.W.2684 (8th Cir., June 12, 1978). This found UBI even though there was no competition with a for-profit entity (bingo games). There is no technical requirement of unfair competition for UBI to occur.

Cleveland Athletic Club, Inc. v. United States, 588 F.Supp. 1305 (N.D. Ohio 1984) rev'd 779 F.2d 1160 (6th Cir. 1985). This case developed a five-part test to determine whether there is a profit motive. The key factor is if there is a good-faith expectation, not a reasonable expectation, of profit.

Cleveland Creative Arts Guild v. Commissioner, 50 T.C.M. 272 (1985). Since the sale of artwork is a means of increasing public awareness, it is substantially related and no UBI.

Commissioner v. Groetzinger, 107 S.Ct. 980 (1987). The Supreme Court endorsed the "facts and circumstances test" in determining what is a trade or business.

Continental Trading, Inc. v. Commissioner, 265 F.2d 40, 43 (9th Cir. 1959) cert. den. 361 U.S. 827 (1959). The management of investments does not amount to a trade or business in this fact situation.

Cooper Tire and Rubber Company Employee's Retirement Fund v. Commissioner, 306 F.2d 20 (6th Cir. 1962). A single transaction, if large enough, can be a trade or business.

CORE Special Purpose Fund v. Commissioner, 49 T.C.M. 626 (1985). This denied allocation for expenses against unrelated business income because there was a lack of adequate records and accounting practices.

Disabled American Veterans v. United States, 650 F.2d 1179 (Ct. Cl. 1981). This set the test for determining when a solicitation with a premium is a trade or business.

Disabled American Veterans v. United States, 704 F.2d 1570 (Fed. Cir. 1983). The court allowed an allocation between taxable and nontaxable portions of the solicitation.

Eastern Kentucky Welfare Rights Organization v. Simon, 506 F.2d 1278 (D.C. Cir. 1974). The court found that the promotion of health per se is a tax-exempt purpose, if an appropriate class is served and the program is operated for public, not private, benefit. The source of payments for medical services is not determinative.

Edward Horton, Jr., 56 T.C. 147 (1971), nonacq. 1972-3 C.B. 4. Where an activity so furthers the exempt purpose of an organization, its size and extent are not relevant.

Elliot Knitwear Profit Sharing Plan v. Commissioner, 71 T.C. 765 (1979) aff'd 614 F.2d 347 (3rd Cir. 1980). Income from securities purchased on margin is debt financed and UBI.

est of Hawaii v. Commissioner, 71 T.C. 1067 (1979) aff'd 302 F.2d 934 (9th Cir. 1981). While the plaintiff's program is educational, it is part of a franchise system operated for private gain. Thus there is a substantial commercial purpose and tax-exempt status is denied.

Florida Trucking Association, Inc. v. Commissioner, 87 T.C. No. 66 (1986). The only case that has applied the Supreme Court's advertising standard enunciated in American College of Physicians. The advertising was not substantially related to an exempt purpose and there was "no systematic effort made to advertise products that relate to the editorial content of the magazine, no effort . . . made . . . to limit the advertising to new products."

Founding Church of Christian Scientology v. U.S., 412 F.2d 1197 (Ct. Cl. 1969) cert. den. 397 U.S. 1009 (1970). Because the income went to "insiders" for private inurement, tax-exempt status was denied.

Fraternal Order of Police, Illinois State Trooper Lodge No. 41 v. Commissioner, 833 F.2d 717 (7th Cir. 1987). If an exempt organization retains control over the enterprise that it has licensed, the income is not passive income.

Green v. Connally, 330 F.Supp. 1150, 1162 (D.D.C. 1971) aff'd sub. nom., *Coit v. Green,* 404 U.S. 997 (1971). One rationale for tax-exempt status is the fostering of volunteerism and pluralism.

Hi-Plains Hospital v. United States, 670 F.2d 528 (5th Cir. 1982). Based on the setting, the court found that serving the doctor's private patients did not generate UBI because this activity assisted with keeping doctors on the staff. This is substantially related to the hospital's primary purpose of providing medical services.

Hope School v. United States, 612 F.2d 298 (7th Cir. 1980). This circuit considers the threat of unfair competition a key factor in determining UBI.

Illinois Association of Professional Insurance Agents, Inc. v. Commissioner, 86-2 U.S.T.C. 9702 (7th Cir. 1986). The association's activity in developing an insurance program is active. All income derived therefrom is UBI.

The Incorporated Trustees of the Gospel Workers Society, Inc. v. United States, 510 F.Supp. 374 (D.D.C. 1981) aff'd 672 F.2d 894 (D.C. Cir. 1981) cert. den. 456 U.S. 944 (1982). The corporation loses its tax-exempt status because it used good management and business practices. Although the rationale is questionable, the outcome is reasonable since the corporation's income-producing activities had become so large that making money had become its primary purpose.

Industrial Aid for the Blind v. Commissioner, 73 T.C. 96 (1979). Plaintiff maintains its tax-exempt status because its primary purpose is the employment of the blind. The fact that it bought materials made by the blind and sold materials made by the blind was incidental.

Iowa State University of Science and Technology v. United States, 500 F.2d 508 (1974). Because this station is commercially licensed, generates the majority of its income from commercial sources, and competes with commercial stations, its income is UBI.

ITT Research Institute v. United States, 85-2 U.S.T.C. par. 9734 (Ct. Cl. 1985). The test used by this court to determine if research activity is exempt is the problem-solving nature of the activity. If the focus is problem solving, the activity is exempt; if it is a testing activity, it is taxable.

Michigan Earlychildhood Center, Inc. v. Commissioner, 37 T.C.M. 808 (1978). Because the primary purpose of this organization is education, tax-exempt status is granted. If the primary purpose were found to be custodial care, tax-exempt status would be denied.

Midwest Research Institute v. United States, 554 F.Supp. 1379 (W.D. Mo. 1983) aff'd 744 F.2d 638 (7th Cir. 1984). This court defined scientific research as experimentation to validate a scientific hypothesis.

Mobile Arts and Sports Association v. United States, 148 F.Supp. 31 (D. Ala. 1957). The court found the Senior Bowl (a college all-star football game) to be substantially related to the plaintiff's charitable purpose.

Mose and Garrison Siskin Memorial Foundation, Inc. v. United States, 603 F.Supp. 91 (E.D. Tenn. 1985) aff'd 790 F.2d 480 (6th Cir. 1986). Reinvesting the accumulated cash value of life insurance owned by a tax-exempt entity in income-paying investments is acquisition indebtedness and generates UBI.

National Association of American Churches v. Commissioner, 82 T.C. 18 (1978). Tax-exempt status is denied where the substantial purpose of the organization is to give advice on tax avoidance.

NCAA v. Commissioner of Internal Revenue Service, 90-2 U.S.T.C., par. 50,513 (10th Cir. 1990). The court held that the NCAA's share of net income from program advertising at its annual "Final four" basketball games is not UBI. Key to this ruling was the determination that the sales activity was not regularly carried on because it did not occur on a year-round basis. This conclusion was based on the court's determination that only the time period in which the programs were being distributed, and not the period over which the advertising was actually sold, was the period to be used to determine if the activity was regularly carried on. The NCAA did employ professionals to sell the advertising.

National Water Well Association, Inc., 92 T.C. No. 7 (1989). In this mailing list use case, the court found the income received by the exempt organization to be UBI. It must be noted that to receive the fee the exempt organization provided services in addition to making its mailing list available.

North Ridge Country Club, 89 T.C. 563 (1987) overruled U.S. Court of Appeals, 9th Cir. (1989). The court agreed with the IRS holding that a Section 501(c)(7) organization cannot offset losses from the sale of food and beverages to nonmembers against its investment income unless the organization can prove that it operates with a profit motive.

Oklahoma Cattleman's Association v. United States, 310 F.Supp. 320 (W.D. Okla. 1969). This is an example of a case where the court found that the plaintiff's income from the use of its mailing lists to sell insurance is passive and there is no UBI.

Orange County Builders' Association v. United States, 65-2 U.S. Tax Cas. 9679 (D. Cal. 1965). The annual sponsoring of a trade show is not a trade or business.

Parkland Residential School, Inc. v. Commissioner, 45 T.C.M. (CCH) 988 (1983). This advertising effort was found to be regularly carried on due to the extensive effort and planning. It was managed like a commercial venture.

Phi Delta Theta Fraternity v. Commissioner, 90 T.C.B. (May 16, 1988). The magazine focused on internal news about the fraternity and its members. This publication was found not to be substantially related to the organization's exempt purpose.

Plumstead Theater Society, 74 T.C. 1324 (1980) aff'd per curium, 675 F.2d 244 (9th Cir. 1982). The service fee income to the plaintiff was not passive and thus was considered UBI. But the plaintiff was allowed to maintain its exempt status even though it was a general partner. The court noted the requirements for an exempt organization to be a general partner and not endanger its exemption.

Portland Golf Club v. Commissioner, 110 S.Ct. 2780, 2785 (1990). This Supreme Court decision overturned a Tax Court ruling and agreed with the position of the IRS that Section 501(c)(7) organizations must be able to prove a profit motive in order to offset sales of food and beverages to nonmembers against investment income.

Presbyterian and Reformed Publishing Company v. Commissioner, 79 T.C. 1070 (1983). The Tax Court, as well as the United States district court for the District of Columbia, believes that if an organization is operated like a business, it is a business, and they will deny exempt status.

Professional Insurance Agents of Washington v. Commissioner, T.C.M. 1987-68 (Feb. 3, 1987). Fees received by a business league for promoting malpractice insurance are UBI. The plaintiff had a profit motive and the benefit was to the individual members, rather than the common business interest (not substantially related).

Regan v. Taxation with Representation of Washington, 461 U.S. 540 (1983). It is permissible for Congress to restrict the lobbying efforts of tax-exempt organizations. The creation of tax-exempt status legislation is a grant or subsidy that Congress modifies.

Rensselaer Polytechnic Institute v. Commissioner, 732 F.2d 1058 (2nd Cir. 1984). The court agreed with the plaintiff's allocation of expenses for a dual use facility. The court allowed the allocation to be based on the amount of time of actual use. The IRS advocated using the total amount of time available for use, which greatly increases the amount of deductible expenses.

St. Luke's Hospital v. United States, Dkt. No. 77-0679-CV-W-5 (W.D. Mo. 1980). There is no UBI on pathology tests conducted by teaching and research hospitals for nonpatients. It is substantially related to teaching, done for the convenience of staff and relatively small (therefore not commercial).

San Francisco Infant School, Inc. v. Commissioner, 69 T.C. 957 (1978). Because the school's purpose is education and not custodial care, it is tax exempt.

Service Bolt and Nut Company Profit-Sharing Trust, 78 T.C. 812 (1982) aff'd 724 F.2d 519 (6th Cir. 1984). The plaintiff is a limited partner. Although the interest income is passive and not subject to tax, the service fee income is UBI.

Shiloh Youth Revival Centers, 85 T.C. 565 (1987). The plaintiff stated that its exempt purpose was to rehabilitate young people. The court found that the goal of the organization was financial survival and not rehabilitation and rejected tax-exempt status.

Suffolk County Patrolmen's Benevolent Association, Inc., 77 T.C. 134 (1981). An annual event is not regularly carried on, even though there is extensive planning and the organization hires professional performers.

Trinidad v. Sagrada Orden de Predicadores, 263 U.S. 578 (1924). In this early case the court applied the destination of income test.

United States v. Properties of Social Law Library (1st Cir. 1939). This defined "charitable" as a generic term encompassing concepts such as "scientific," "educational," and other like purposes.

University of Massachusetts Medical School Group Practice, 74
   T.C. 1299 (1980). The court found that the collection and distribution of fees to member physicians was not impermissible "private inurement" because it assisted in providing clinical training
   for medical students.
Veterans of Foreign Wars, 89 T.C. 7 (1987). If a premium (gift) is
   included in a solicitation and the amount of the donation is close
   to the value of the gift, it is UBI.
West Virginia State Medical Association v. Commissioner, T.C.
   No. 41 (Sept. 20, 1988). This case found that the association
   lacked a profit motive in its journal advertising. Thus it was not
   a "trade or business" and there was no UBI.
Whipple v. Commissioner, 373 U.S. 215 (1963). Investing is not a
   trade or business.

Unfair Competition Cases

Note: The cases that follow are some of the major unfair competition actions.

First Street Books v. Marin Community College District, 256 Cal.Rppt. 833, review granted and opinion superceded by 775 P.2d 507, 260 Cal. Rppt. 182 (1989). Based on a then-existing California statute, which specified what a community-college-controlled bookstore could sell, the district was enjoined from selling trade books not required for a course. The fact that this bookstore was leased had no bearing. The controlling statute has since been amended while the case was on appeal. The case is now moot.

Jansen v. Atiyeh, 749 P.2d 1230 (1988). The Oregon Supreme Court allowed the board of higher education to define what is educational. Based on the board's action, most of the activities of Southern Oregon State College that were challenged in this unfair competition suit were allowed to continue. The plaintiff had challenged various housing, transportation, and other related services for nonstudents.

Travel Companies of Minnesota v. International Student Travel Association, File #448502 (Dist. Ct. 2nd Dist. Minn. Aug. 4, 1983). The plaintiff denied standing to challenge the defendant's exempt status in this unfair competition suit based on state law. The defendant is associated with the University of Minnesota.

Structure Probe, Inc. v. Franklin Institute, 450 F.Supp. 1272 (E.D. Pa. 1978). This is an unfair competition suit based on state law. The plaintiff contended that it was inappropriate for a nonprofit to enter into research competing with a for-profit. The court found that this was not barred by state law.

Property Tax
and Related Cases

Note: This resource contains a broad sampling of property tax cases. Please be aware that many of the cases discussed in Part Four are not included in this listing.

Adult Student Housing v. State Department of Revenue, 705 P.2d 793 (Wash. Ct. App. 1985). Because the plaintiff was found not to be a "school" under state law, no property tax exemption was granted. The plaintiff is a nonprofit organized to build and manage housing for students and faculty.

Alford v. Emory University, 216 Ga. 391, 116 S.E.2d 596 (1966). This granted property tax exemption for Greek housing.

Alpha Rho Zeta of Lambda Chi Alpha, Inc. v. Inhabitants of City of Waterville (Me. 1984) 477 A.2d 1131. This case granted property tax exemption for Greek housing; the property is owned by the college and is part of the housing program. The court found social and recreational activities incidental.

Appeal of the University of Pittsburgh, 407 Pa. 516, 180 A.2d 760 (1962). Based on the use of the home, the president's home is granted a property tax exemption.

Blair Academy v. Blairsstone, 95 N.J. Sup. Ct. 583, 232 A.2d 178 (1967). Even though food service was contracted, its primary purpose was to service the school. Therefore, property tax exemption was granted.

Board of Trustees of Ohio State University v. Kinney (Ohio 1983) 449 N.E.2d 1282. Property used to generate support for general university operating expenses is exempt from property tax even when leased to an entity not associated with the university.

Board of Trustees of the Leland Stanford Junior University v. County of Santa Clara, No. 337067 [Sup. Ct. Santa Clara Cty. (1978)]. This case upheld plaintiff's property tax exemption on its golf course. The course was used 49 percent by students, 46 percent by alumni, and 5 percent by the general public.

Butler University v. State Board of Tax Commissioners, 408 N.E.2d 1286 (Ind. App. 1980). The plaintiff's charter from the state exempted its rental property from taxation and was found to be controlling over recent state law.

Campus Lighthouse Ministries v. Buffalo County Board of Education, 404 N.W.2d 46 (Neb. 1987). Once a property tax exemption was administratively denied, the taxpayer could not pay the taxes and then choose to litigate to gain an exemption.

Cedars of Lebanon Hospital v. Los Angeles County, 35 Cal.2d 729, 221 P.2d 31, 34 (1950). The court held that property tax exemption statutes would be strictly construed.

Christian Manner International, Inc. v. Commissioner, 71 T.C. 661 (1979). The case held that there is no property tax exemption where the primary purpose is to generate a profit.

City of Ann Arbor v. University Cellar, 401 Mich. 270, 258 N.W.2d 1 (1977). Since the property did not belong to the state, a property tax exemption was denied. This state's property tax exemption statute covered "property belonging to the state." The court strictly interpreted the statute and found that affiliation with a state agency had no bearing.

City of Morgantown v. West Virginia Board of Regents, 359 S.E.2d 616 (W.Va. 1987). The court held that the city could not require the university to collect the town's 2 percent tax from all entertainment and athletic ticket sales, because these events were not held for private gain.

Pittsburgh v. Board of Property Tax Assessment, Court of Appeals
No. 3067 C.D. (Pa. 1989). There was a challenge to property tax
exemption for two YMCA facilities. Based on the laws of the
commonwealth of Pennsylvania, the court was not concerned
that the exempt organization generates most of its income from
fees or that it serves a predominantly middle- and upper-class
clientele. The case was remanded to determine the extent to
which excess income from fees was utilized and therefrom the
extent to which these facilities were exempt. The court endorsed
the concept that each YMCA facility will be examined separately.

City of Nashville v. State Board of Equalization (Tenn. App.) 363
S.W.2d 520 (1962). In this state the court determined that who is
the beneficial owner of the property, not who has legal title, is
the controlling issue in determining a property tax exemption.
Because the state benefits, the property is exempt.

City of Waterville v. Colby College (Me. 1986) 512 A.2d 1039. A
fraternity had successfully litigated to gain a property tax exemption on the basis of its relation to the college. The court ruled
that the tax refund belonged to the college.

Cleveland State University v. Perk, 26 Ohio St.2d 1, 268 N.E.2d 577
(1971). Property tax exemption is determined by the tenant's use
of the property, not by the landlord's.

*Commonwealth v. Progressive Community Club of Washington
County,* 215 Va. 732 (1975). No property tax exemption was
granted for a head-start school. State law grants exemptions only
to colleges and other similar institutions of learning.

Cook County Collector v. National College of Education, 41 Ill.
App. 633, 345 N.E.2d 507 (1976). This state uses a strict standard
in interpreting property tax exemption statutes. The court found
that the president's home was only incidentally related to the
college and denied tax exemption.

Cornell v. Board of Assessors, 24 A.D. 526, 260 N.Y.S.2d 197 (1965).
This denied property tax exemption.

DePaul University, Inc. v. Rosewell, 531 N.W.2d 884 (Ill. Ct. App.
1988). Because the university leased its tennis courts and club
house to a private church to use at designated times, there is no
property tax exemption.

District of Columbia v. Catholic Education Press, 199 F.2d 176

(1952) cert. den. 344 U.S. 986 (1952). The press was viewed as the church's alter ego and therefore its property tax exemption was granted.

District of Columbia v. Trustees of Amherst College (D.C. App. 1986) 515 A.2d 1115. Property used as short-term housing for persons visiting the college library is tax exempt even though a fee is charged. A vacant lot is not exempt because it is not being put to an educational use.

Emerson College v. City of Boston (Mass. 1984) 462 N.E.2d 1098. The court ruled that the city could not charge a private college a user fee for fire services. This is really a property tax in violation of state law.

Follet's Illinois Book and Supply Store, Inc. v. Issaacs, 27 Ill. 600, 190 N.E.2d 324 (1963). Because the sales by this leased store came from prices comparable to a competing retail store, the sales are subject to the state sales tax.

Gamma Phi Chapter of Sigma Chi Building Fund Corporation v. Dade County, 199 S.2d 717 (Fla. 1967). Some states have specified specific organizations that are exempt from taxes.

Indiana University Foundation v. Tax Commissioners, 527 N.E.2d 1166 (Ind. Tax. 1988). The plaintiff is granted a property tax exemption in proportion to its ownership of an apartment complex that it partially owns and uses to house students, faculty, and staff.

In re Albright College, 213 Pa. Sup. Ct. 479, 249 A.2d 835 (1965). The president emeritus's home was denied a property tax exemption.

In re Board of County Commissioners, 225 Kans. 517, 592 P.2d 875 (1979). Because the landlord charged greater than a nominal rent, the property was used for a commercial purpose and there was no property tax exemption.

In re Middlebury College Sales and Use Tax, 137 Vt. 28 (1979). The college ski area was used most by the general public and students from other schools. The court therefore denied property tax exemption.

Iowa Lakes Foundation v. Board of Revenue of Emmet County (Iowa App. 1986) 387 N.W.2d 377. A property tax exemption was denied to this foundation, which provided housing for community college students. The court based its decision on the fact that there was a fixed level of fees (no reduction for low-income students), the state had no legal obligation to provide student housing, and the foundation was a separate legal entity, not merged with the college. The court was not influenced by the fact that the college managed the housing facility.

Johnson v. South Greek Housing Corporation, 307 S.E.2d 491 (Ga. 1983). A property tax exemption was granted to this Greek housing facility.

Matter of the University of North Carolina (N.C. 1980) 260 S.E.2d 472. The state constitution states that all property owned by the state and its subdivisions is tax exempt. Regardless of the purpose to which the property is put and a recent statute to the contrary, this property will not be taxed.

Metropolitan Dade County v. Miami-Dade County Community College Foundation (District Court of Appeals of Florida, 3rd District, 1989) 545 S.2d 324 (1989). The facility was bought and was being renovated for the college. There was no property tax exemption at that time because it was not currently being used for a tax-exempt purpose.

National Collegiate Realty Corp. v. Board of County Commissioners of Johnson County (Kans. 1984) 690 P.2d 1366. NCAA headquarters was found to be used exclusively for educational purposes. The court granted a property tax exemption and found that the size of the operation is not relevant under Kansas law.

President and Fellows of Middlebury College v. Town of Hancock (Vt. 1986) 514 A.2d 1061. The fact that the college is the trustee is not relevant in determining a property tax exemption. Because the land is used primarily for recreation, it is not tax exempt.

Princeton University Press v. Borough of Princeton, 35 N.J. 209, 172 A.2d 420 (1961). No tax exemption was allowed because this entity was publishing works produced by others for a profit. Thus property was not being used exclusively for an exempt purpose.

Regents of the University of New Mexico v. Bureau of Revenue, 62 N.M. 76 (1957). State law exempted all sales and services by nonprofits from tax. The court held that the plaintiff's golf course, pro shop, and snack bar were exempt from taxation.

Southern Illinois University Foundation v. Booker, 425 N.E.2d 465

(Ct. App. Ill. 1981). Using the equitable interest theory, the court granted a property tax exemption.

State ex. rel. Wisconsin Building Corporation v. Baries, 257 Wis. 497, 44 N.W.2d 259 (1950). The court must determine who has beneficial ownership, not legal ownership. Because the state received the benefit, the property was tax exempt.

Stevens v. Rosewell (Ill. App., May 2, 1988). The court found that the land leased by a college to a McDonald's was not tax exempt.

Syracuse University v. City of Syracuse (N.Y. App. Div. 1983) 459 N.Y.S.2d 645. The plaintiff was denied summary judgment where the property was not used exclusively for an educational purpose. The court looks at the portion of income and usage from unrelated activities.

Trustees of Boston University v. Board of Assessors of Brookline (Mass. App. 1981) 416 N.E.2d 510. The fact that the president's house is not contiguous to the campus grounds is not a reason in and of itself to deny property tax exemption.

Trustees of Columbia University v. Town of Orangetown, Supreme Court of New York, County of Rockland, Index #5515/76, November 17, 1976. The Court found that a research facility is encompassed in "education" and granted a property tax exemption.

Trustees of Rutgers University v. Piscataway Township, 134 N.J.C. 85, 46 A.2d 56 (1946). The court denied property tax exemption for a 20,000 seat stadium where the campus had a student body of 1,700.

Trustees of Smith College v. Board of Assessors of Whatley (Mass. 1982) 434 N.E.2d 182. The complainant lacked standing to challenge the school's tax-exempt status under the state constitution.

Tusculum College v. State Board of Equalization (Tenn. App. 1980) 600 S.W.2d 739. No property tax exemption was granted for property leased to employees because there was available housing in the area. The president's house will be 50 percent tax exempt because that is the portion of the time that it is used for an exempt purpose.

University Auxiliary Services at Albany, Inc. v. Smith (N.Y. App. Div. 1980) 433 N.Y.S.2d 270. A nonprofit corporation providing services to a state university was granted a property tax exemption.

University of Hartford v. the City of Hartford (Conn. App. 1984) 477

A.2d 1023. No property tax exemption was allowed because the university's leasehold did not constitute ownership.

Utah County v. Intermountain Health Care, Inc., 13 Utah Adv. Rept. 14 (Sup.Ct. Utah) 709 P.2d 265 (Utah 1985). The court denied property tax exemption to two nonprofit hospitals and found that they did not provide sufficient charitable services but ran a "commercial" hospital.

Washington University Board of Regents v. Seattle, 741 P.2d 11 (Wash. 1987). The city could charge the university a street user fee and require the removal of a sky bridge.

Wheaton College v. Department of Revenue, 508 N.E.2d 1136 (Ill. App. Ct. 1987). The college leased a building and used it for student housing. Because the college did not own the building, there was no property tax exemption.

Worthington Dormitory, Inc. v. Commissioner of Revenue, 292 N.W.2d 276 (Minn. 1980). In this state, the court looked past the identification of the property owner to the purpose for which the property was used. It granted tax exemption to a nonprofit organized to own and operate housing for community college students.

Internal Revenue Service Materials

Note: The subject list that follows is solely intended to assist the reader in locating opinions of the Internal Revenue Service in a specific area. Please note the use of the following abbreviations:

GCM: General Counsel Memorandum
PLR: Private Letter Ruling
RR: Revenue Ruling
TAM: Technical Advisory Memorandum

Advertising

TAM 8418002, PLR 8539089, PLR 8538003, RR 73-424, 1973-2 C.B. 190, RR 82-139, and 1982-29 I.R.B. 6

Affinity Cards

PLR 8747066 and PLR 8823109

Allocation of Income

TAM 8406008

Alumni Association

PLR 8424001, RR 78-43, 1978-1 C.B. 164, RR 63-200, 1963-2 C.B. 208, and TAM 8115025

Athletic Camps

RR 76-402, 1976-2 C.B. 177, RR 80-297, 1980-2 C.B. 196, and PLR 8151005

Auxiliary Organization

RR 81-19 and 1981-1 C.B. 353

Bookstore

RR 81-62, 1981-8 I.R.B. 45, PLR 8004010, PLR 8605002, and PLR 8025222

Commercial-Type Insurance

PLR 8830603

Computer Sales

PLR 8025222

Credit Cards

PLR 8747066

Dual Use Facility

RR 80-298, 1980-2 C.B. 197, PLR 8034022, RR 78-98, 1987-1 C.B. 167, and RR 76-402, and 1976-2 C.B. 177

Financial Assistance Program (Student)

RR 69-257, 1967-1 C.B. 151, RR 66-103, 1966-1 C.B. 134, RR 67-291, 1967-2 C.B. 184, RR 64-264, 1964-2 C.B. 141, and PLR 8429102

Fragmentation Rule

RR 73-104, 1973-1 C.B. 263

Fraternities

PLR 8809087, PLR 8823088, and PLR 8832084

Government Function

PLR 8836003 and PLR 8419007

High School Interscholastic Athletics

RR 55-587, 1955-2 C.B. 261

Hospital

PLR 8809092, RR 85-110, 1985-2 C.B. 166, RR 69-268, 1969-1 C.B. 160, PLR 8230002, PLR 8016010, RR 68-375, 1968-2 C.B. 245, and RR 85-109, 1985-2 C.B. 165

Hotel (University)

PLR 8246014 and PLR 8537091: same as above

Incentive Compensation Plan

RR 69-383, 1969-2 C.B. 113, and PLR 8808070

International Student Center

RR 69-400, 1969-2 C.B. 114

Joint Venture

PLR 8432014 and RR 79-222, 1969-2 C.B. 236

Land Purchase/Sale (Debt-Financed Property)

PLR 8822057 and PLR 8017016

Law Review

RR 63-235, 1963-2 C.B. 210

Lawyer Referral Program

PLR 8542001 and RR 80-287, 1980-2 C.B. 186

Lease Agreements

PLR 8545070, PLR 8838047, RR 80-298, 1980-2 C.B. 197, RR 80-297, 1980-2 C.B. 196, PLR 8412007, and PLR 8403067

Life Insurance to Donors

PLR 8820061

Mailing Lists

PLR 8823109 (revokes PLR 8747066)

Management Services

PLR 8814004, PLR 8419085, PLR 7902019, and PLR 8015009

Museum

RR 73-105, 1973-1 C.B. 264, PLR 8814001, PLR 8432004, RR 73-15, 1973-1 C.B. 264, PLR 8605094, PLR 8034022, PLR 8303013, PLR 8328009, PLR 8326008, PLR 8605002, PLR 8032028, PLR 8814001,

RR 74-399, 1974-2 C.B. 172, RR 73-105, 1973-1 C.B. 204, and PLR 8432004: UBI

National Honor Society

RR 71-97, 1971-1 C.B. 150

Parking Garage

PLR 8545070

Political Activity

RR 86-43, 1986-2 C.B. 729, RR 72-512, 1972-2 C.B. 246, and PLR 8226144

Rental Housing

PLR 8801067 and RR 76-3, 1976-1 C.B. 169

Royalty Exception

RR 81-178, 1981 2 C.B. 135, PLR 8824018, PLR 8727066, PLR 8827017, RR 76-297, 1976-2 C.B. 178, PLR 88280117, and PLR 8511079

Sales to Nonmembers

RR 73-164, 1973-1 C.B. 233

Service to Members

RR 69-191, 1969-2 C.B. 146 and RR 78-51, 1978-1 C.B. 165

Social Clubs—Sales to Nonmembers

PLR 8551003

Substantially Related Test

PLR 8813067, RR 76-94, 1976-1 C.B. 171, RR 68-581, 1968-1 C.B. 263, RR 73-104, 1973-1 C.B. 198, PLR 8412030, PLR 8340102, PLR 8404045, and PLR 8351008

Testing

PLR 8417002, RR 68-373, 1968-2 C.B. 206, and RR 78-426, 1978-2 C.B. 175

Trade Association

PLR 8352090

Trade or Business

RR 69-574, 1969-2 C.B. 130, RR 60-86, 1960-1 C.B. 198, and RR 57-13, 1957-2 C.B. 316

University Athletic Events

RR 65-191, 1965-2 C.B. 157 and RR 80-296, 1980-2 C.B. 195

University Food Service

RR 58-194, 1958-1 C.B. 240

University Laundry Service

RR 81-18, 1981-3 C.B. 353

University Recreation Service

RR 79-98, 1979-1 C.B. 167

University Research

PLR 8409086, PLR 8409055, and PLR 8512054

University Residence Halls

RR 76-33, 1976-1 C.B. 169 and PLR 8138075

University Ski Facility

RR 78-98, 1978-1 C.B. 167

University Travel Service

RR 67-327, 1967-2 C.B. 187, RR 70-534, 1970-2 C.B. 113, and PLR 8115025

University Vending Program

RR 81-18, 1981-3 C.B. 353

University-Operated Radio

RR 55-676, 1955-2 C.B. 266

Utilities

PLR 7902019

Unrelated Business Income

PLR 8539091, PLR 8004010, PLR 7946003, PLR 8216009, PLR 8127019, PLR 8128004, RR 81-178, 1981-2 C.B. 135, RR 79-361, 1979-2 C.B. 237, PLR 8419085, PLR 8226019, and PLR 8226019

References

"ACE Response to Oversight Subcommittee Minority Report." *A.O.A Newsletter,* Feb. 1988, p. 6.

"Aggregation of a Church with Its Tax-Paying Subsidiaries Would Jeopardize the Church's Exemption (Part G, Oversight Committee Recommendations)." Unpublished address to the Honorable J. J. Pickle, chairman, Subcommittee on Oversight, from a multidenominational coalition of religious organizations. Washington, D.C.: Office of General Counsel of the United States Catholic Conference, Aug. 31, 1989.

Alexander, A., and Solomon, E. *College and University Law.* Charlottesville, Va.: Michie Company, 1972.

American Council on Education. "The Caffrey-Isaacs Model: Estimating the Impact of a College or University on the Local Economy." Washington, D.C.: American Council on Education, n.d.

American Council on Education. "Proposed UBIT Legislation Positions." Unpublished paper. Washington, D.C.: American Council on Education, 1989a.

American Council on Education. "Questions for Governors' Meeting." Unpublished paper. Washington, D.C.: American Council on Education, 1989b.

247

Arent, A., and others. Letter to Congressman Pickle on behalf of the National Association of College Stores, Washington, D.C., Aug. 1987.

Bennet, J. T., and DiLorenzo, T. J. *Unfair Competition: The Profit of Nonprofits.* Lanham, Md.: Hamilton Press, 1989.

Blumenstyk, G. "State Notes: Illinois Measure Would Bar City Tuition Taxes." *Chronicle of Higher Education,* Dec. 12, 1990, p. 21.

Boisture, R. "Revising the Tax Bite Debate." *World,* Summer 1989, p. 47.

Bookman, M. "ACUI—Action Statement on UBIT and Unfair Competition." Unpublished paper. Bloomington, Ind.: Association of College Unions-International, Mar. 1988a.

Bookman, M. "Legal Issues Affecting College Auxiliaries." Monograph 88-7, Institute of Higher Education Law and Governance, University of Houston, 1988b.

Bookman, M. *Contracting Collegiate Auxiliary Services.* Agoura Hills, Calif.: Education and Non-Profit Consulting, Inc., 1989.

Bookman, M. "Unrelated Business Income Tax (UBIT), Unfair Competition . . . What Does Our Future Hold?" 1989 ACUI Conference Proceedings. Bloomington, Inc.: Association of College Unions-International, 1990.

Bookman, M. "Colleges Must Report and Pay Taxes on Their Unrelated Business Income." *Chronicle of Higher Education,* Oct. 17, 1990, p. B1.

Burch, K., and Pattie, K. *Unfair Competition in the States.* Washington, D.C.: Business Coalition for Fair Competition, 1985.

Bureau of National Affairs. *Specialty Law Digest—Education.* Washington, D.C.: Bureau of National Affairs.

Business Coalition for Fair Competition. Press release. Washington, D.C., Aug. 28, 1990a.

Business Coalition for Fair Competition. "The Model Unfair Competition Bill Annotated." Washington, D.C.: Business Coalition for Fair Competition, 1990b.

"California Court Upholds an Injunction Barring Community Colleges from Selling Books That Aren't Specifically Required for Classes." *Chronicle of Higher Education,* Apr. 19, 1989, p. 29.

Catholic Health Association of the United States. *Preserving a Tradition of Service: Reflections on the Tax-Exempt Status of the*

Not-for-Profit Healthcare Institutions. With comments by J. Seay, T. Eckels, J. Fitzgerald, J. McGovern, and P. Fiduccia. St. Louis, Mo.: Catholic Health Association of the United States, 1989a.

Catholic Health Association of the United States. *Social Accountability Budget: A Process for Planning and Reporting Community Service in a Time of Fiscal Constraint.* St. Louis, Mo.: 1989b.

Cerney, M. "A Practitioner's View of Exempt Organizations in the 1990s." *Journal of Taxation of Tax Exempt Organizations, 1* (2), 5.

"Colleges Are Reviewing Their Community Activities as Business, States and IRS Step Up Scrutiny." *Chronicle of Higher Education,* Sept. 7, 1988, p. 25.

"Charity and Profit." *Washington Post,* July 9, 1988.

"Comments Regarding the Adverse Effects on Churches of the 'Discussion Options' for UBIT." Address to the Honorable J. J. Pickle, chairman, Subcommittee on Oversight, from a multidenominational coalition of religious organizations. Washington, D.C.: Office of General Counsel of the United States Catholic Conference, Aug. 31, 1989.

Copeland, J., and Rudney, G. "Business Income of Nonprofits and Competitive Advantages." *Tax Notes,* Nov. 24, 1986.

"Editorial Viewpoint on UBIT—Compounding a Crisis." *A.O.A. Newsletter,* June 1988, p. 5. Citing *Los Angeles Times,* May 11, 1988.

"Editorial View on UBIT—Creative Taxation 101." *A.O.A. Newsletter,* June 1988, p. 5. Citing *Orange County Register,* May 15, 1988.

"Editorial View on UBIT—Why the Rush to Tax Nonprofits." *A.O.A. Newsletter,* June 1988, p. 5. Citing *New York Times,* May 12, 1988.

"Egregious Cost of Compliance." *A.O.A. Newsletter,* July/August 1988, p. 8. Citing Nonprofit Organization Tax Letter, May 24, 1988.

Ellis, J. A. (ed.). *Specialty Law Digest.* Blain, Minn.: S.C.D. Publications, .

Fairweather, J. S. *Entrepreneurship and Higher Education: Lessons for Colleges, Universities and Industry.* ASHE-ERIC Higher Education Report no. 86, 1988.

Francis, J. A. Unpublished letter to Mary Jane Calais, Director of Government Affairs, National Association of College and University Business Officers, Apr. 1988.

"From Meeting and Athletic Camps to Language Institutes, Colleges Find Profitable Uses for Campuses in Summer." *Chronicle of Higher Education,* Aug. 18, 1989, p. 22.

Gaul, G. "Is It Time to Tax the Hospitals?" *Philadelphia Inquirer,* Nov. 2, 1989, p. 11E.

General Accounting Office. "Nonprofit Hospitals: Better Standards Needed for Tax Exemption." GAO/HRP-90-84. Washington, D.C.: General Accounting Office, 1990.

Gerard, N. "Presidential Perspective." *The Bulletin.* Bloomington, Ind.: Association of College Unions—International, 1988.

Goldstein, M. L. "Tax Exemptions: Fair or Foul." *World: The Magazine for Decision Makers,* Spring 1988, p. 1.

"Governors Ask Universities to Focus More Research on Community Needs." *Chronicle of Higher Education,* May 24, 1989, p. 25.

Gray, B. H. (ed.). *For-Profit Enterprises in Health Care.* Washington, D.C.: National Assembly Press, 1986.

Halloran, D. Unpublished letter to the Subcommittee on Oversight, House Ways and Means Committee, U.S. Congress, May 1988.

Halloran, D. Unpublished letter to the Subcommittee on Oversight, House Ways and Means Committee, U.S. Congress, Aug. 1989.

Hamm, K. "California AB 944 Task Force Report." Sacramento, Calif.: California Department of Commerce, Aug. 1989.

Hansmann, H. "The Role of Nonprofit Enterprise." *Yale Law Review,* 1980, p. 835.

Hill, F. "UBIT Would Undergo Wide-Ranging Revision Under Congressional Draft Report." *Journal of Tax Exempt Organizations,* Spring 1989, *1*(1), 35.

Hines, E. R. *Higher Education and State Government Renewed Partnership, Cooperation, or Competition.* Washington, D.C.: ERIC, Association for Study of Higher Education, 1988.

Holder, W. H. *The Not-for-Profit Reporting Entity.* New Milford, Conn.: Philanthropy Monthly Press, 1986.

Hopkins, B. *The Law and Tax Exempt Organizations.* (5th ed.) New York: Wiley, 1987.

Hopkins, B. R. (ed.). *The Nonprofit Counsel.* New York: Wiley, n.d.

Hopkins, T., Jr. "Foundations Supporting Public Universities: UBIT." Paper presented at the 28th annual conference of National Association of College and University Attorneys, Columbia, S.C., 1988.

"Illinois Legislature Limits Student Credit." *A.O.A. Newsletter,* Nov. 1989, p. 4.

INDEPENDENT SECTOR. *Government Relations Information and Action,* 9(6). Washington, D.C.: INDEPENDENT SECTOR, 1989a.

INDEPENDENT SECTOR. "INDEPENDENT SECTOR UBIT Working Group—Position Paper." Unpublished paper. Washington, D.C.: INDEPENDENT SECTOR, June 8, 1989b.

Internal Revenue Service. *Exempt Organizations Current Developments.* Servicewide edition 88-3, Document 660b, Rev. 4-89. Washington, D.C.: Department of the Treasury, 1989a.

Internal Revenue Service. *Internal Revenue Bulletin No. 1989-32,* p. 53. Washington, D.C.: Department of the Treasury, 1989b.

Internal Revenue Service. *Internal Revenue Bulletin No. 1989-45.* Announcement 89-138, p. 42. Washington, D.C.: Department of the Treasury, 1989c.

Jaschik, S. "Small Business Leaders Launch Campaign to Curb Campus Sales of Consumer Goods." *Chronicle of Higher Education,* Feb. 11, 1987.

Jaschik, S. "Three More States Adopt Measures to Restrict Campus-Run Businesses." *Chronicle of Higher Education,* Sept. 7, 1988, p. A1.

Kane, M., and Rosen, M. F. *Issues and Opportunities for University Communities: A Survey of Cities.* Washington, D.C.: National League of Cities, 1989.

Kaplan, W. *The Law of Higher Education.* (2nd ed.) San Francisco: Jossey-Bass, 1985.

Kay, D., Brown, W. A., and Allee, D. J. *University and Local Government Financial Relations.* Houston, Tex.: Institute for Higher Education Law and Governance Monograph 89-2, University of Houston, 1989.

Kinner, E. W., Fleischaker, M. L., and Aronsky, D. J. "Federal

Unrelated Business Income Tax ('UBIT'), White Paper." *College Store Journal*. Oberlin, Ohio: National Association of College Stores, 1987.

Kirby, D. J. "The Carrier Dome Controversy." *Change*, Mar./Apr. 1988, p. 44.

Kirschten, B. L., and Brown, W. F. "The IRS Narrows the UBIT Royalty Exclusion." *Journal of Taxation of Exempt Organizations*, 1989, *1*(2), p. 35.

Klinger, D. J. (ed.). "The Availability and Completeness of Returns of Tax-Exempt Organizations." *Business Officer*. Washington, D.C.: National Association of College and University Business Officers, 1988.

Klinger, D. J. (ed.). *Business Officer*. Washington, D.C.: National Association of College and University Business Officers, 1989.

"Knock Knock, It's the IRS." *A.O.A. Newsletter,* Jan. 1989, p. 7.

McGovern, J. "The Exemption Provision of Subchapter F." 29 Tax Lawyer 523, 1976.

"Marin Bookstore Case Resolved." *A.O.A. Newsletter,* Nov. 1989, p. 1.

Mathis, L. L. "The Non-Profit Difference." Outline for a slide presentation. Houston, Tex.: Methodist Hospital System, n.d.

Meyer, D. "Unfair." *University Times*. Pittsburgh, Penn.: University of Pittsburgh, 1987.

Mills, E. M. "Current Developments in UBIT." Conference proceedings of National Association of College and University Attorneys, Washington, D.C., 1988.

"The Model State Unfair Competition Bill Annotated." *Business Coalition for Fair Competition*, Aug. 28, 1990.

Moody, J. A. "Tax Policy: Some Issues for Higher Education." In J. C. Hoy and M. H. Bernstein (eds.), *Financing Higher Education: The Public Investment*. Dover, Mass.: Auborn House, 1982.

"NACS Fights California Bookstore Ruling." *A.O.A. Newsletter,* Feb. 1988, p. 7.

National Association of College Stores. *NACS Bulletin,* June 16, 1989.

National Association of College Stores. "Legislative Monitoring Report." Oberlin, Oh.: National Association of College Stores, June 19, 1991.

National Association of College and University Business Officers. "Policy Statement and Guidelines on Educational Business Activities of Colleges and Universities." *Special Action Report 87-6*. Washington, D.C.: National Association of College and University Business Officers, 1987.

National Association of College and University Business Officers. "Guidelines for Filing 1988 IRS Form 990 and 990T." Washington, D.C.: National Association of College and University Business Officers, 1989.

National Association of Retail Druggists. *Discriminatory Pricing*. Alexandria, Va.: National Association of Retail Druggists, 1989a.

National Association of Retail Druggists. *Drug Diversion*. Alexandria, Va.: National Association of Retail Druggists, 1989b.

National Association of Retail Druggists. *Mail Order Pharmacy*. Alexandria, Va.: National Association of Retail Druggists, 1989c.

National Association of Retail Druggists. *Non-Profit Competitors*. Alexandria, Va.: National Association of Retail Druggists, 1989d.

National Association of Retail Druggists. *Regulatory Flexibility Act: Impact on Small Business*. Presentation to the Committee on Small Business, United States Senate, Alexandria, Va., Oct. 17, 1989e.

National Association of Retail Druggists. *Require the Registration of Certain Non-Profit Hospitals—H.R. 273*. Alexandria, Va.: National Association of Retail Druggists, 1989f.

"New Threats to Commercial Nonprofits." *A.O.A. Newsletter*, June 1987, p. 4. Citing the *Chronicle of Higher Education*, Apr. 1, 1987.

Nichols, C. S., Naves, M. E., and Olswang, S. G. "Unrelated Business Tax and UC: Current Status of the Law." *Journal of College and University Law*, Winter, 1989, *15*(3) p. 249.

Nonprofit Advisory Group (in cooperation with Coopers & Lybrand USA). *Business Competition and Unrelated Business Income: A Sourcebook for Higher Education*. La Habra, Calif.: Nonprofit Advisory Group, 1988.

Nonprofit Times, Aug. 1988.

Swords, P. "A Bad Idea." *Philanthropy Monthly*, Oct. 1988, p. 9.

Pires, S. A. *Competition Between the Nonprofit and For-Profit Sec-*

tor. Washington, D.C.: National Assembly of National Voluntary Health and Social Welfare Organizations, 1985.

"Pressure Growing for Better Data on Nonprofit Organizations." *A.O.A. Newsletter,* July/Aug. 1988, p. 8.

Rapp, J. A. *Education Law.* Oakland, Calif.: Matthew Bender, 1989.

"Reconciliation Provisions." *A.O.A. Newsletter,* Nov. 1989, p. 2. Citing *Nonprofit Organization Tax Letter,* Oct. 11, 1989.

Rostenkowski, D. (chair, House Ways and Means Committee). Letter to the Honorable Lawrence G. Gibbs (commissioner, Internal Revenue Service), Oct. 14, 1988.

Rostenkowski, D. (Co-signed by chair of the Subcommittee on Oversight and the ranking minority member of both committees). Letter to Kenneth Gideon (assistant secretary for policy, IRS), Sept. 7, 1989.

"Salvation Army Unit Loses Tax Exemption." *A.O.A. Newsletter,* Nov. 1989, p. 7.

Schrage, M. "Entrepreneurial Gap at Local Universities." *Los Angeles Times,* Sept. 14, 1989, p. 1.

Schulze, D. (ranking minority member, Subcommittee on Oversight). Letter to Congressman J. J. Pickle and members of the Subcommittee on Oversight, Aug. 1989.

Seay, D., and Vladeck, B. *In Sickness and In Health.* New York: McGraw-Hill, 1988.

Seay, D., and others. "Holding Fast to the Good: The Future of the Voluntary Hospital." *Inquiry,* Blue Shield and Blue Cross Associations, Fall 1986, pp. 253–254.

Seitz, R. C. *National Organization of Legal Problems of Education Journal.*

Singer, B. *Nonprofit Organization—Operations Handbook for Directors and Administrators.* Deerfield, Ill.: Callaghan and Co., 1987.

Sloane, B. (assistant to the commissioner, legislative liaisons, IRS). Letter to Congressman Richard Schulze, 1988.

Small, J. A. *Non-Profit Organizations: Current Issues and Developments.* New York: Practicing Law Institute, 1984.

Stanion, T. *BCFC State-by-State Update.* Washington, D.C.: Business Coalition for Fair Competition, 1989a.

Stanion, T. *State Legislatures. Focus on Business Ventures of Nonprofits.* Washington, D.C.: Business Coalition for Fair Competition, 1989b.

Superintendent of Documents. *Regulator Program of the U.S. Government.* Washington, D.C: U.S. Government Printing Office, Apr. 1, 1988–Mar. 31, 1989.

Swain, F. S., and Mastromarco, D. R. "Measuring the Extent and Effect of Competition Between For-Profit and Tax-Exempt Entities." Paper prepared for the Conference on Commercial Activities of Nonprofits, New York University, Nov. 15 and 16, 1988.

"Tax on YMCA Upheld." *A.O.A. Newsletter,* June 1988, p. 6. Citing *NonProfit Times,* Apr. 1988.

Thomas, J. B. "States Join Unfair Competition Fight with Their Own Initiatives." *Business Office,* June 1988, p. 31.

"Town-Gown Battles Escalate as Beleaguered Cities Assail Tax Exemption." *Chronicle of Higher Education,* June 29, 1988, p. 18.

Treusch, P. E. "Daily Report for Executives." BNA, June 11, 1987, pp. J20-J27.

Treusch, P. E. *Tax-Exempt Charitable Organizations.* (3d ed.) Philadelphia: American Law Institute, 1988.

Trocchio, J., and Echols, T. "Being Accountable for Care of the Poor." Reprinted from *Health Progress,* Catholic Health Association of the United States, St. Louis, Mo., 1989.

"UBIT Preview." A.O.A. Newsletter, Oct. 1989, p. 5. Citing *The Nonprofit Counsel,* Sept. 1989.

Underwriters' Laboratories, Inc. "Statement of Underwriters' Laboratories, Inc." Unpublished statement, Jan. 1, 1988.

"Unfair Competition State Problems." *A.O.A. Newsletter,* Feb. 1988, p. 8.

United States Small Business Administration, Office for the Chief Counsel for Advocacy. *Unfair Competition by Nonprofit Organizations with Small Business: An Issue for the 1980s.* 3rd ed. Washington, D.C.: United States Small Business Administration, 1984.

United States Small Business Administration. "Issues Brief: Unfair Nonprofit Competition with Small Businesses." Paper prepared for the 8th national conference for State and Local Officials on Small Business, Washington, D.C., Nov. 1986.

United Way of America. "Position Paper—House Ways and Means Oversight Subcommittee Staff Recommendations on the Unrelated Business Income Tax." Unpublished paper. Washington, D.C.: United Way of America, June 9, 1989.

University of California. "University Business and Finance Bulletin, BUS 72: Establishment and Review of Auxiliary Enterprises." Berkeley: University of California. May 1, 1981.

University of California. "Memorandum of Understanding UCD LRP [Long Range Plan]." Agreement between the University and the city of Davis, California, June 22, 1989.

University of Michigan. "IRS Audit Unrelated Business Income— Listing IRS Audit Issues." Unpublished paper, Ann Arbor, Mich., 1986.

"University of Texas UBIT Audit." *A.O.A. Newsletter,* Jan. 1989, p. 7.

U.S. Congress. House. Rep. 1860, 75th Congress, 3rd Sess., 1939, p. 19.

U.S. Congress. House. Rep. 2319, 1950, pp. 36-37.

U.S. Congress. House. Subcommittee on Oversight of the Committee on Ways and Means. *Hearings Before Subcommittee on Oversight.* Parts 1–3, Serial 100-26, June 22, 25, 26, 29 and 30, 1987.

U.S. Congress. House. Subcommittee on Oversight of the Committee on Ways and Means. *Written Comments on Discussion Options Relating to the Unrelated Business Income Tax,* Apr. 21, 1988.

U.S. General Accounting Office. *Tax Policy: Competition Between Taxable Business and Tax-Exempt Organizations.* U.S. General Accounting Office report GAO/GGD-87-40BR. Washington, D.C.: Government Printing Office, 1988.

"Washington Unfair Competition Legislation." *A.O.A. Newsletter,* May 1988, p. 2.

Weisbold, B. A. *The Nonprofit Economy.* Cambridge, Mass.: Harvard University Press, 1988.

Wellford, W. H., and Gallagher, J. G. *Unfair Competition? The Challenge to Charitable Tax Exemption.* Washington, D.C.: National Assembly of National Voluntary Health and Social Welfare Organizations, 1988.

YMCA of the United States. "Reaffirming the YMCA Mission." Washington, D.C.: YMCA of the United States, 1987.

Index